BLACK AMERICA SERIES

MACON
GEORGIA

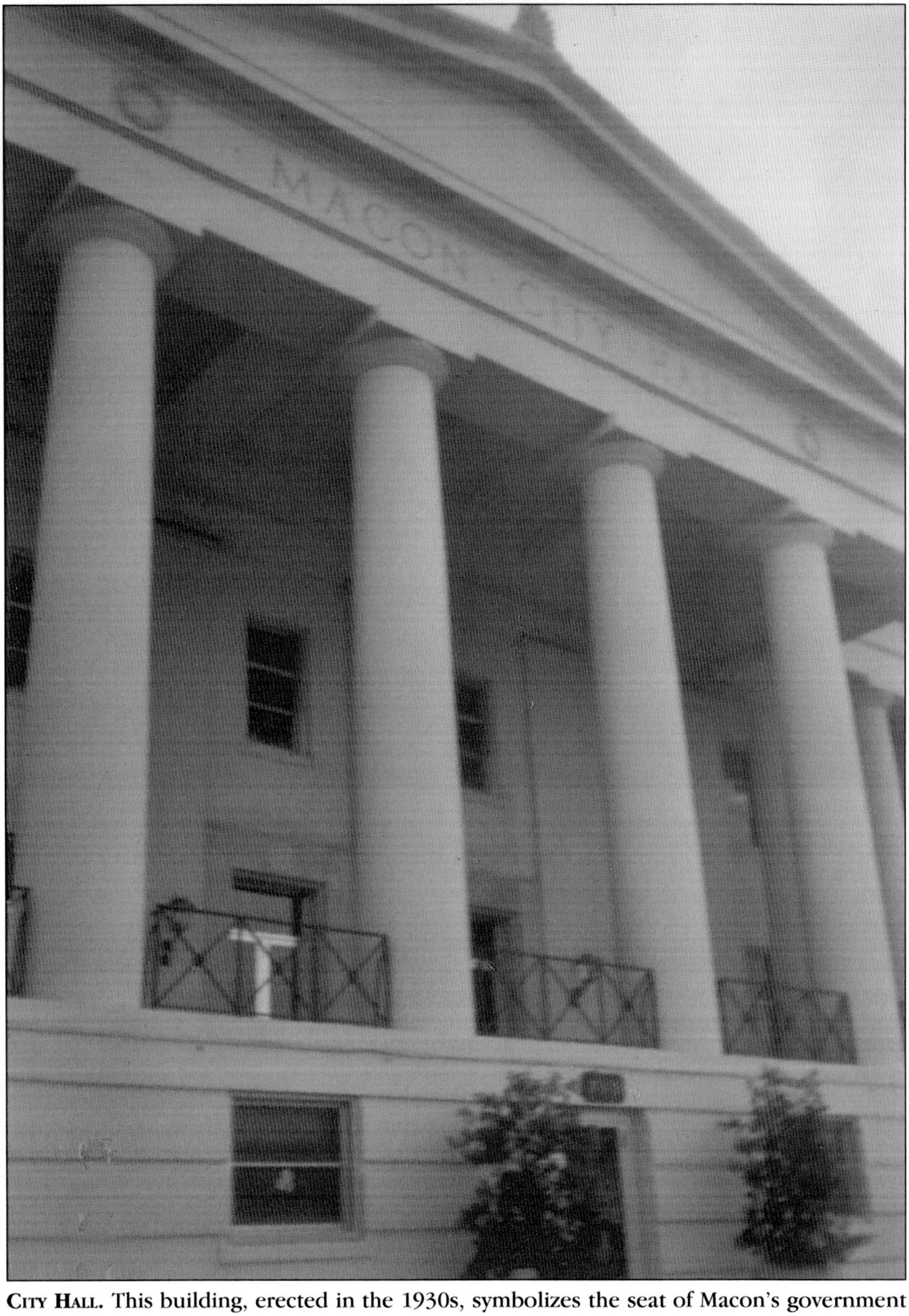

City Hall. This building, erected in the 1930s, symbolizes the seat of Macon's government and power. Many African-American craftsmen helped to complete this structure, working as diggers of the foundation, carpenters, plasterers, painters, brick masons, and roofers. The building is in the Greek Revival style that is so prevalent in the South.

BLACK AMERICA SERIES

MACON
GEORGIA

Jeanne Herring, Ed.S.

ARCADIA
PUBLISHING

ISBN 978-0-7385-0600-5

Published by Arcadia Publishing
Charleston, South Carolina

Printed in the United States of America

Library of Congress Catalog Card Number: 00-104882

For all general information contact Arcadia Publishing at:
Telephone 843-853-2070
Fax 843-853-0044
E-Mail sales@arcadiapublishing.com
For customer service and orders:
Toll-Free 1-888-313-2665

Visit us on the Internet at www.arcadiapublishing.com

This book is dedicated to the memory of my maternal great-grandfather, George Washington Howard, who I've never met but heard inspiring family stories about all of my life. He left a legacy of vision, sacrifice, hard work, and entrepreneurship for his descendants to emulate.

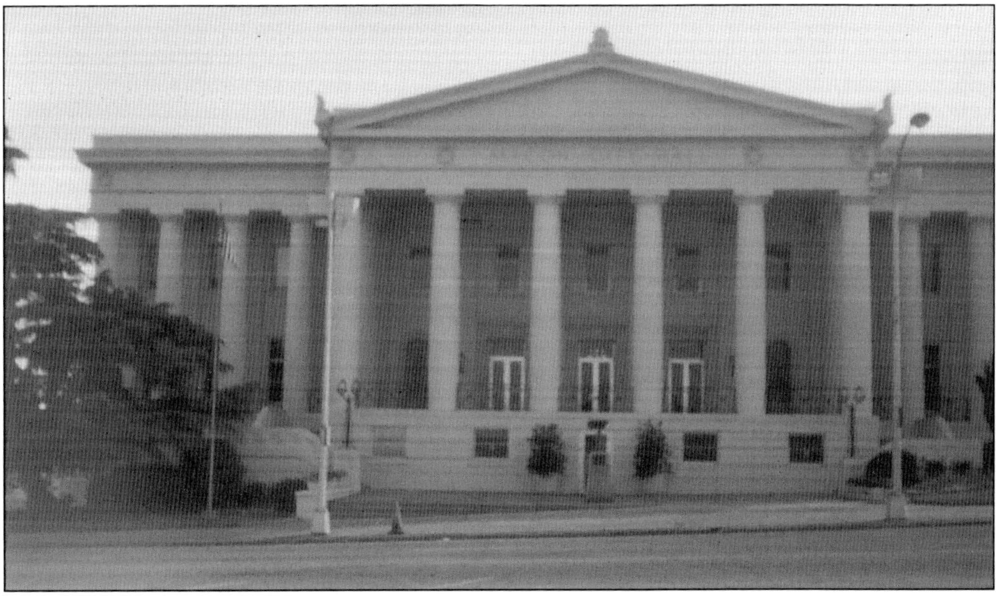

MACON CITY HALL. This picture shows a frontal view of city hall. Today, African-American leadership is headed by Mayor C. Jack Ellis. He was elected to office in 1999.

Contents

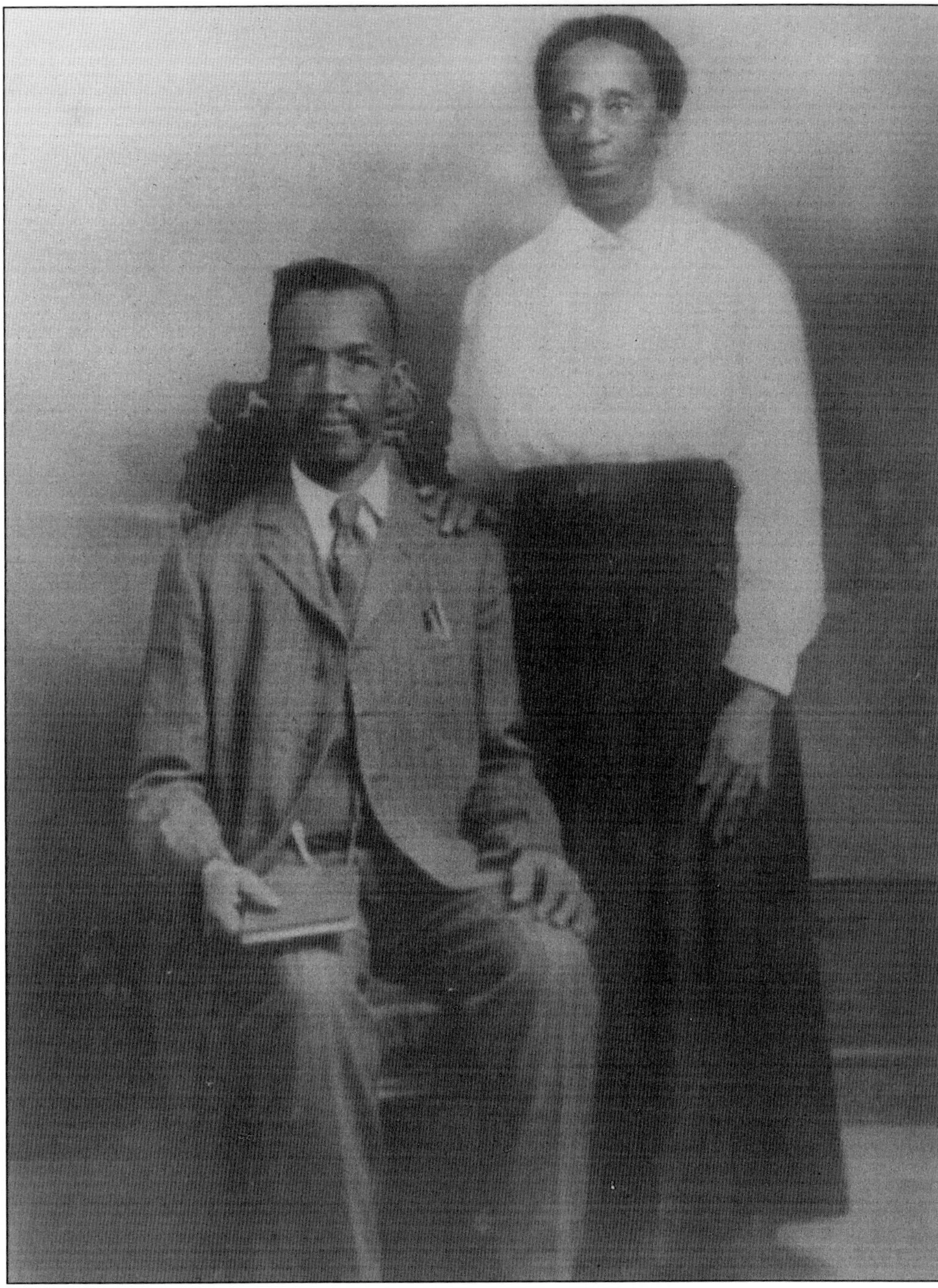

George Washington Howard. George Washington Howard was born at the end of the Civil War, in April of 1865. His father had been a slave on a plantation in Forsythe, GA. George and his brother Isaac made their way to Bibb County, where George became a farmer and landowner. He and his wife, Susie Styles Howard, were the parents of 12 children. He accumulated approximately 775 acres in what is now North Macon. He died at the age of 71 in 1936. (Courtesy of Lois H. Miller and Lorena H. Latham.)

INTRODUCTION

Several years ago my husband and I pulled up our Macon roots and moved approximately 100 miles away. We came to settle in a place called Columbus, GA, which is bordered to the extreme west by the Chattahoochee River. It is a city of some 200,000 citizens. Portions of the city have a military flavor as the Fort Benning Army Base is situated to the south of the city. The reason behind the move was that my husband had accepted a position to pastor a local church. I was a secondary school teacher at the time, and was confident that I would quickly secure a position in the local system. Our children were pretty good about the change; they took it in stride.

The idea of leaving my hometown, family, friends, and acquaintances was quite disturbing to me, even though I was far from being a kid. Nevertheless, that is how I felt, like a kid leaving home for the first time. It has been stated, "home is where the heart is." And the first few years in Columbus, my heart was most definitely in Macon. There are many words that come to mind when I think about the word "home"—foundation, roots, base, refuge, relaxing environment, safety zone, love, happiness, and family ties. When the term home is heard in a song, or read in a poem, or verbalized in an expression, for many of us, it conjures up scenes that have taken place in one's family life. Sometimes the scenarios are so vivid that one might even hear sounds and smell fragrances from the home place. For example, in Macon, if you drive down Cotton Avenue, you will smell the wonderful aroma of hot dogs, chili, and onions coming from the Nu Way Weiner Shop. They really make the best hot dogs in the world. If you are fortunate enough to receive an invitation to my mother's home for dinner, on any given Sunday, you might smell the aroma of baked hen and cornbread dressing radiating from the kitchen window. That is what saying the word Macon does for me. Home is Macon and Macon is home.

Located in central Georgia, Macon was a pleasant place to grow up, even during the age of segregation. I was born in the late 1940s and grew up in the 1950s and 1960s. In Macon, segregation was completely and totally enforced, and the lives of blacks and whites seldom crossed socially. Georgia is a state that historically embraced the philosophy of the Deep South, and the race relation message was immensely clear. But, for a little black girl like me, the ugliness of the system was not as profound until much later. There were separate schools, hospitals, recreation areas, grocery stores, beauty and barbershops, restaurants, churches, and neighborhoods. One of the largest and most completely segregated yet self-sufficient communities in Georgia at the time was the Pleasant Hill community. It really was a city within a city. In many ways, Pleasant Hill sheltered its residents from the outside world, commanded by whites. So, in reality, there were two Macons—black Macon and white Macon. There would be no blending of the races as each strove to exist in the Bibb County area. There was always a distinct line between both groups. Black communities like Summerfield, Stinsonville, and others tried to be the soothing medicine for blacks after experiencing daily stings of second-class citizenship. They grew and developed out of a need to protect their own from the outside world.

Many black men and women in Macon developed a work ethic that is still being carried on today. Most did not have a formal education, yet they were extraordinary. They emerged from the eras of slavery and Reconstruction with strong wills. They had a desire to be the very best that they could in an oppressive society. They also knew their choices were to swim or sink—no lifelines were thrown out to them. The majority never received accolades or praises of any kind. They just worked! Ditch diggers, blacksmiths, peach pickers, bakers, corn grinders, dairymen, cotton pickers, iron workers, farmers, cooks, carpenters, masons, housemaids, nannies, street layers, and countless other workers helped to build Macon.

George W. Howard, Andrew Tolliver, and Solomon Humphries were some of those early hard working contributors to Macon's society. They were landowners, and along with their families and others, they created a productive community and developed great citizens. Education was one of the main catalysts for success among blacks in Macon. Some of the finest scholars of African-American descent obtained their educational roots in Macon—my place of beginnings and for so many others, the nurturing spot, the foundation, the home! This material will show a segment of Macon's African-American experience. Let's take a look at how it all began.

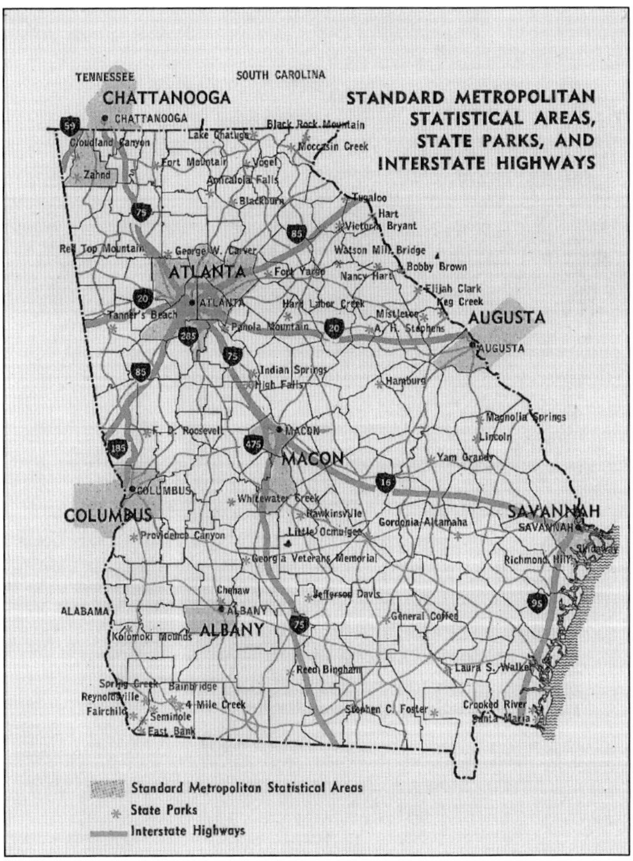

MACON AND THE SURROUNDING CITIES AND TOWNS.

Passages to Ponder

We are the children of those who chose to survive.
—Nana Poussaint in *Daughters of the Dust*

If you have ever doubted your ability to survive, look at your ancestors.
Don't limit yourself to parents and grandparents,
go all the way back to the root—to those who were born into a barren land
and built the pyramids. In the oasis of your mind is the consciousness
of those who character the stars, kept time by the sun,
and planted by the moon. In the center of your being
is the strength of those who planted the crops, toiled in the fields,
and banqueted on the others discarded.
In the light of your heart is the love of those who bore the children
who were sold away only to one day hang from a tree.
In the cells of your bloodstream is the memory of those who weathered the voyage,
stood on the blocks, found their way through the forest,
and took their case to the Supreme Court.
With all of that going for you, what are you worrying about?

God makes three requests of his children:
do the best you can, where you are, with what you have now.

There are no guarantees in life, but it is a sure thing
that you will get back what you give.
If you give 100 percent of your attention, energy, and time to something,
you will get exactly that back. Spending your time and attention
focused on what you cannot do and do not have assures that more of the same will come.
When you concentrate on lack, weakness, fault, and blame,
it is sure to become reality. Nobody has everything, but everybody has something.
Use it wisely, freely, with love.

Wherever you are, use your time, energy, and talents
to do the best you can right now. Give no thought to what is missing.
Spend no time wishing it were better. Make sure you give all that you have
to make sure you will get all that you need.

No man can serve two masters . . . or else he will hold to the one, and despise the other.

—Matthew 6:24

You cannot love while hating, progress while oppressing,
come together in disunity, build while tearing down,
join while separating, understand while not listening,
give while withholding, create while destroying, or overcome while in fear.
It is simply impossible!
People of color must make a choice—
either we accept what we believe others are doing to us,
or reject it and do something else.
If we love each other as a foundation for our own progress,
we do not have to worry about others hating us or hating them back.
If we work with everyone for human good,
giving what we can to create what we want,
we will not be disturbed by what anyone attempts to keep from us.
If we stand on the faith of our ability to survive,
it does not matter who is out to destroy us.
If we celebrate, support, and nurture ourselves,
we will not need anyone else to do it for us.

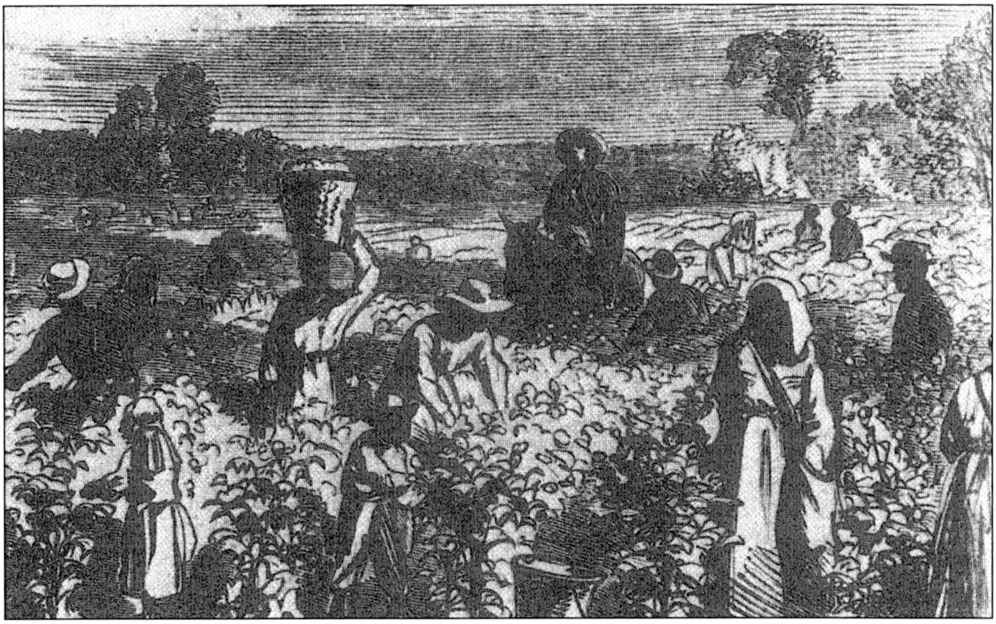

SLAVES IN THE COTTON FIELD. This was a typical scene for most blacks in the South—working on cotton plantations, day in and day out. Most slaves died in this hopeless state. Even after slavery, many African-Americans still worked in the cotton fields in order to survive. The share cropper system was almost as bad as slavery. The workers never could make headway or get ahead, and remained always in debt. If you talk to elderly blacks today who have worked in the cotton fields, a negative response is always given, such as "I don't ever want to see another cotton field as long as I live."

One

Founding a City

The city of Macon, also known as "the Heart of Georgia" and the "Queen Inland City of the South," is a special place that was thought out very carefully by its early leaders. Bibb County was named for an illustrious North Carolina statesman, William Wyatt Bibb. The area was planned and laid out in 1822–1823. The General Assembly alotted approximately 21,000 acres of land for the construction of Macon (the Creek Nation originally existed on this land, but they were forced to leave by 1827). Macon's design was similar to that of a square. Originally, the plan called for 60 city blocks, each covering about 4 acres. A public square was laid out with a courthouse and public buildings. The Ocmulgee River ran down the middle of the city, as shown on early maps. Many shade trees were planted along the square and broad streets were set out at a right angle. The plan also called for garden lots on the outskirts of the city and a "common," public land reserved for future growth patterns. On this land, the people had the freedom to cut timber and raise hogs, cows, and chickens. Macon eventually became a place where a great deal of commercial business was conducted. There was one crop that would make Macon prosperous and that crop was cotton. Slavery would be the "peculiar system" that would create tremendous wealth for some of Macon's white citizenry.

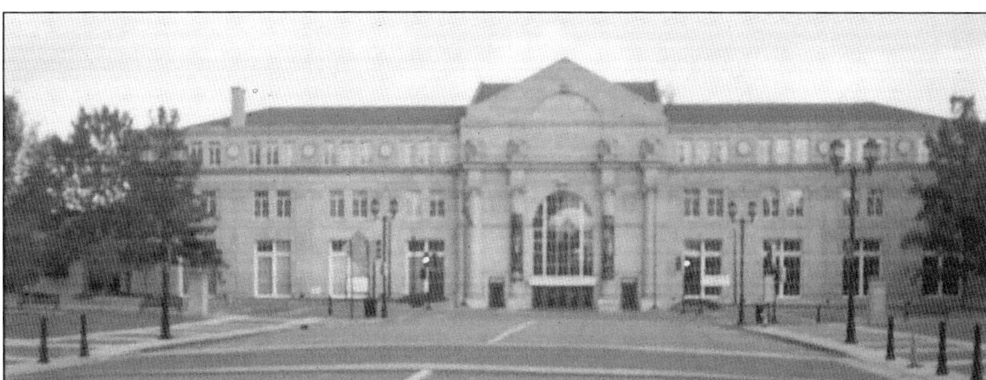

The Central City Terminal Station. This impressive building was once the busiest of places, and the Southeast's railroad center. People would assemble here to board trains that would take them through Georgia and to various places in the U.S. The station was built in 1916. Many African-American workers labored in various capacities to complete the building. A hundred trains a day would pass through this station, one being the "Nancy Hanks." I remember going to this station when I was four years old with my grandmother, Mrs. Anne Howard. We were visiting relatives "up north" in Detroit, MI. My grandmother prepared our lunch because the dining car was segregated, and we were not allowed to purchase any meals.

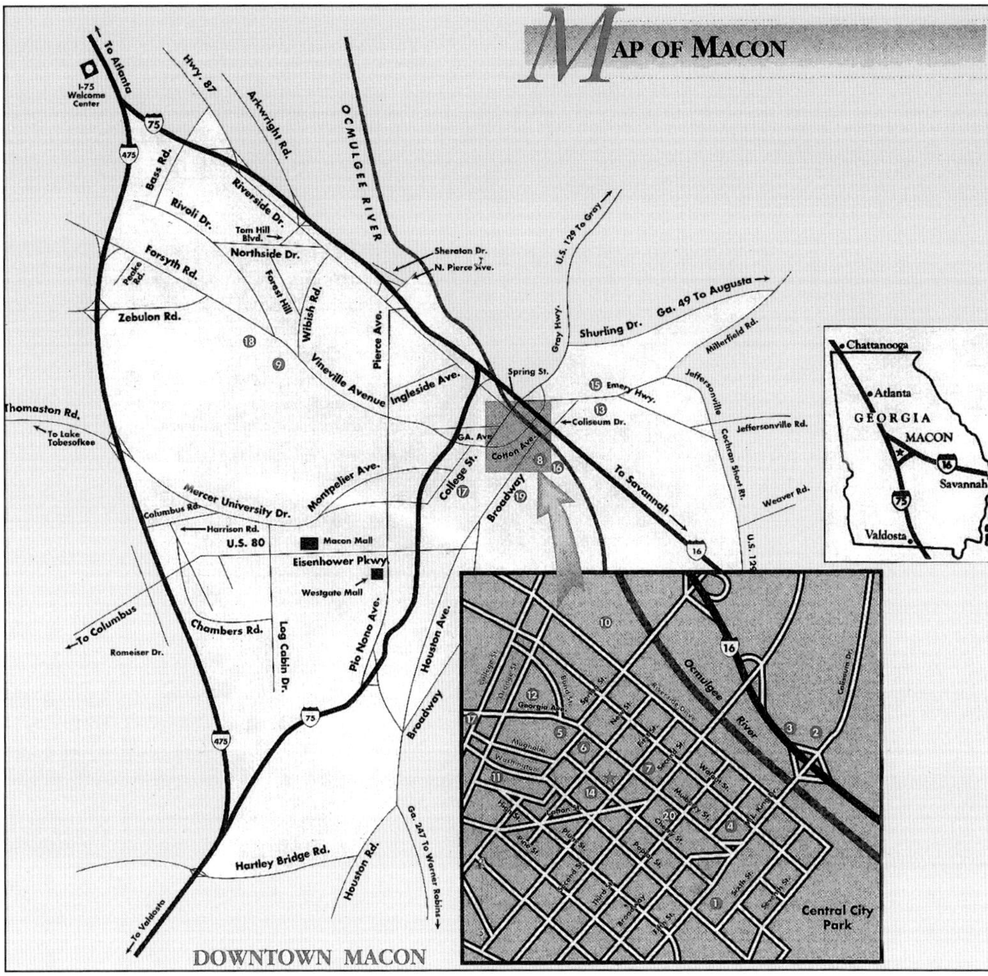

Downtown Macon. Commercialism was developing rapidly. Banks, retail stores, hotels, trading, and manufacturing companies were springing up and performing well. However, there was much more than business going on in Macon during these early years. Education was a high priority. Facilities such as the State Academy for the Blind, medical schools, and Georgia's first college for women were established. Presbyterian, Methodist, Episcopal, Baptist, and Roman Catholic churches were established. Wesleyan College, Mercer University, and Macon State College would add to Macon's fine examples of academic excellence. Because of the distinct line of separation known as segregation, most African Americans were excluded from participating in advancements made in the early history of Macon. Today, however, the city has progressed to a point of economical, political, educational, spiritual, and most of all multicultural acceptance that past generations (black and white) would never have envisioned. It is truly a city for the 21st century.

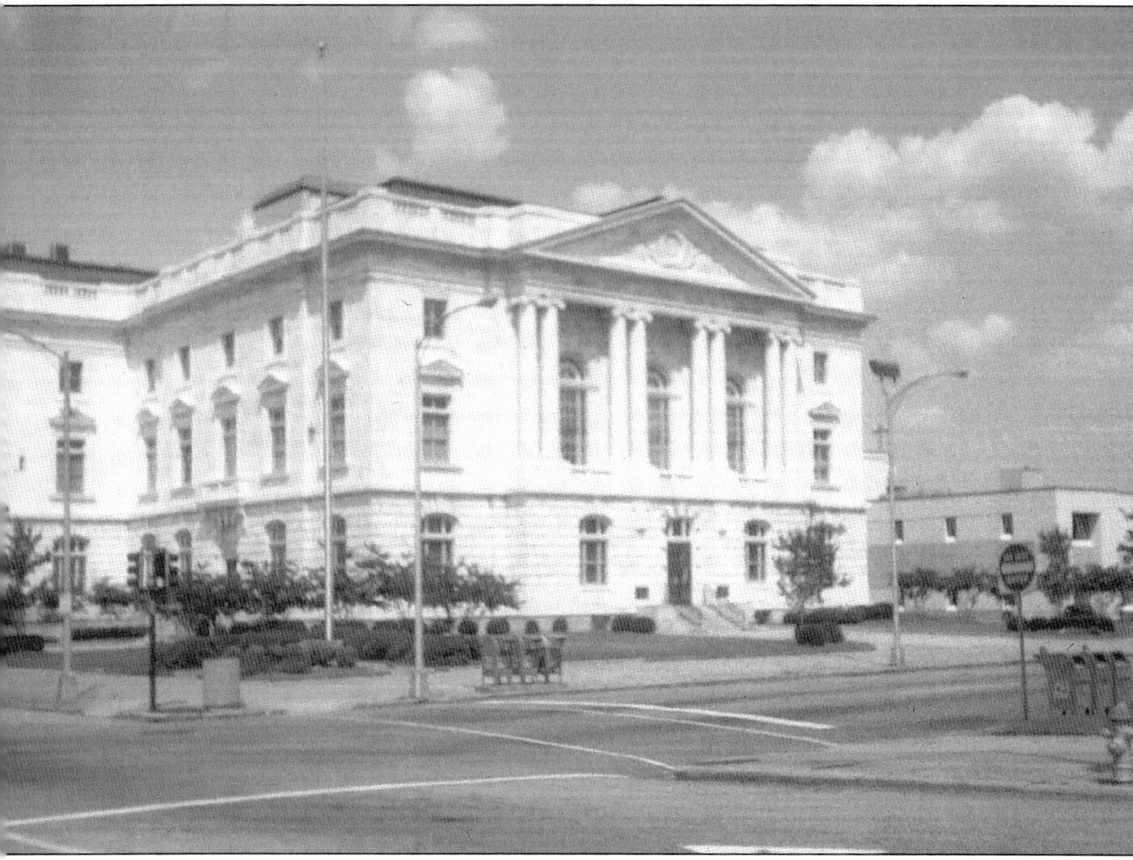

The Old Post Office. This building features the typical Greek Revival-style architecture that was common among builders in the South. The style has been a preference for public buildings in America, and Macon boasts many examples. There are Corinthian columns across the top front floor of this building, a beautiful representation of labor. According to oral history, African Americans helped to complete this structure. It is located in downtown Macon.

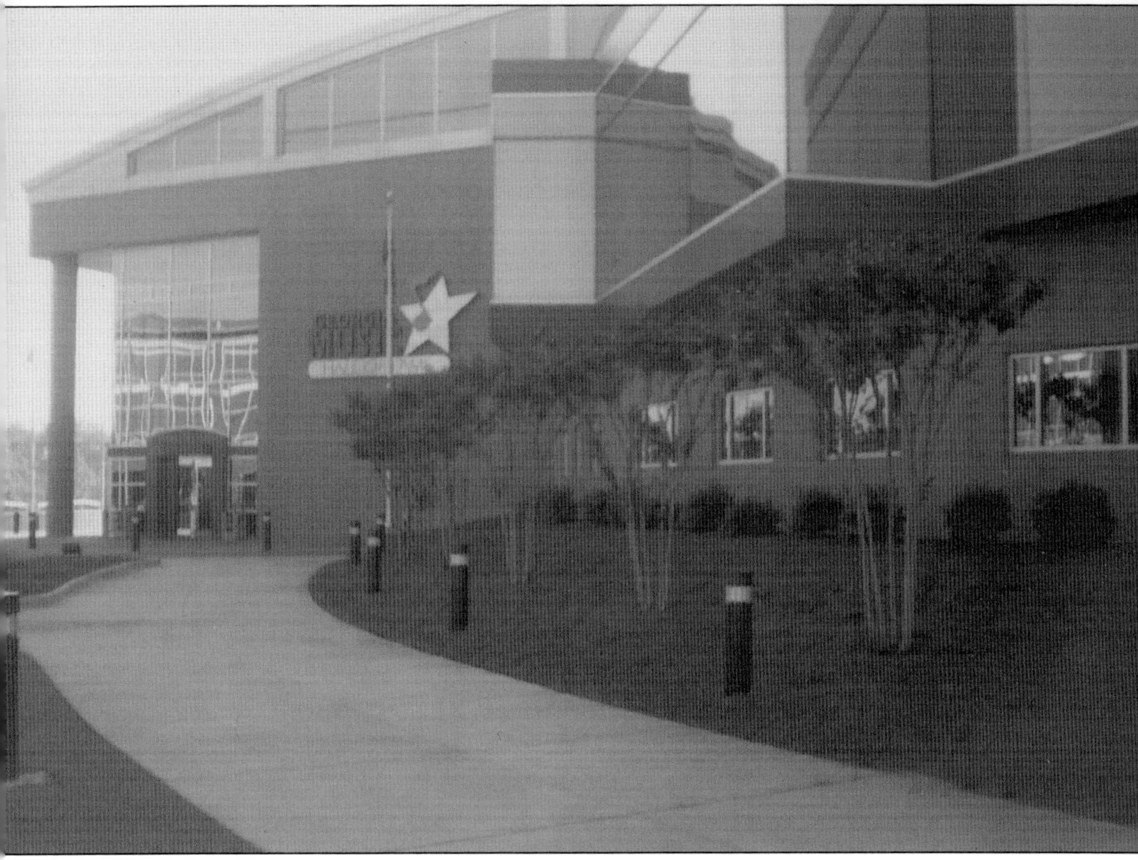

The Georgia Music Hall of Fame. Located on Martin Luther King Boulevard, this museum houses memorabilia and displays exhibits about famous musicians and singers from all over Georgia. Some of Macon's stars include Alan Evans, Richard Penniman, James Brown, Otis Redding, and Percy Welch. The city's diverse musical community has produced myriad artists, from world-traveled country legends like Trisha Yearwood to the internationally renowned rhythm and blues legend Ray Charles. Big band and Southern rock artists are also highlighted at the museum, which brings Georgia's rich musical heritage and worldwide impact to life.

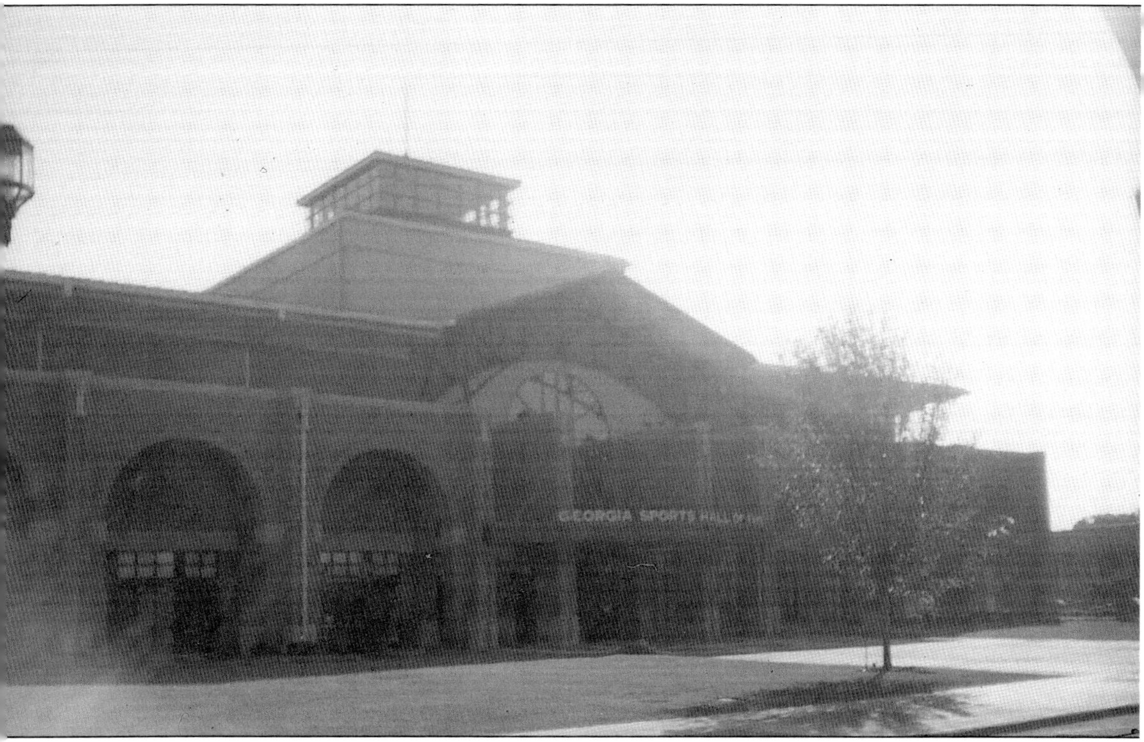

The Georgia Sports Hall of Fame. The Georgia Sports Hall of Fame is located on Cherry Street. This museum houses memorabilia from athletes from all over the state. Some of Macon's famous athletes are Johnny "Blue Moon" Odom, Miles Patrick, Jeff Malone, Tiger Flowers, Jim Parker, Tammy Hart, Elmore Smith, Julius Adams, James T. Thomas, Norman Nixon, Louis Linder, Terry Fair, Walter Daniels, Jessie Hubbard, Corey Williams, Larry Emory, Chris Robinson, Milton Cyler, Alice Coachman, and Brenda Cliette.

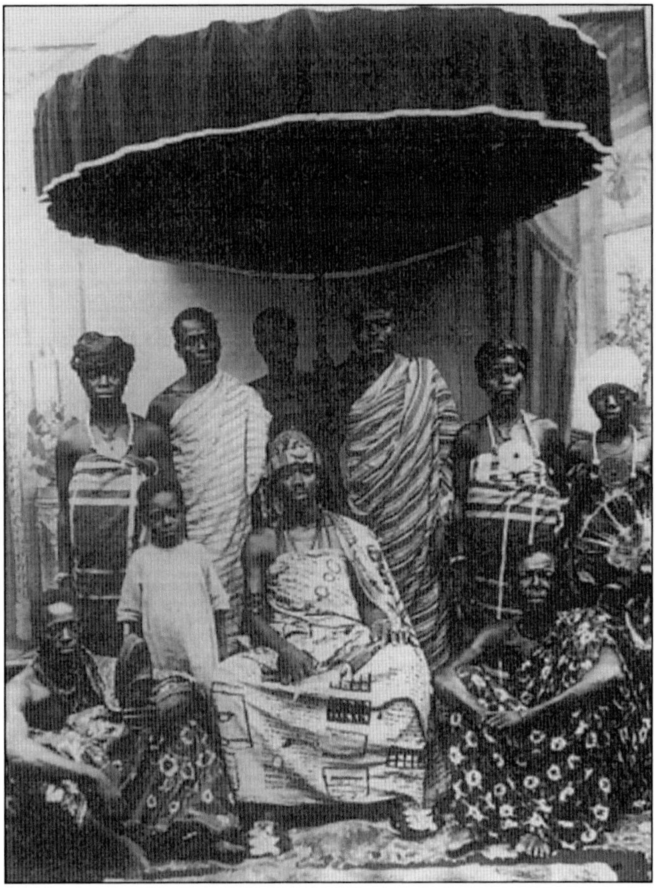

An African Royal Assembly. This is a picture of an African king and his court (Asante). He is sitting under a ceremonial umbrella that symbolizes his position. Some Macon slaves have been traced back to the Asante people. This picture shows a place of power before slavery in America.

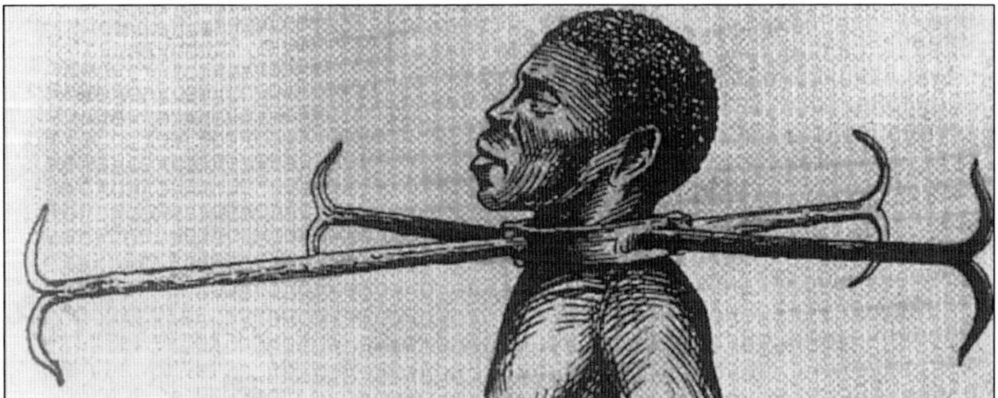

A Slave. This picture shows a captive African wearing a slave yoke to prevent him from running away. This method of control and abuse was also used to prevent enslaved people from lying down and sleeping.

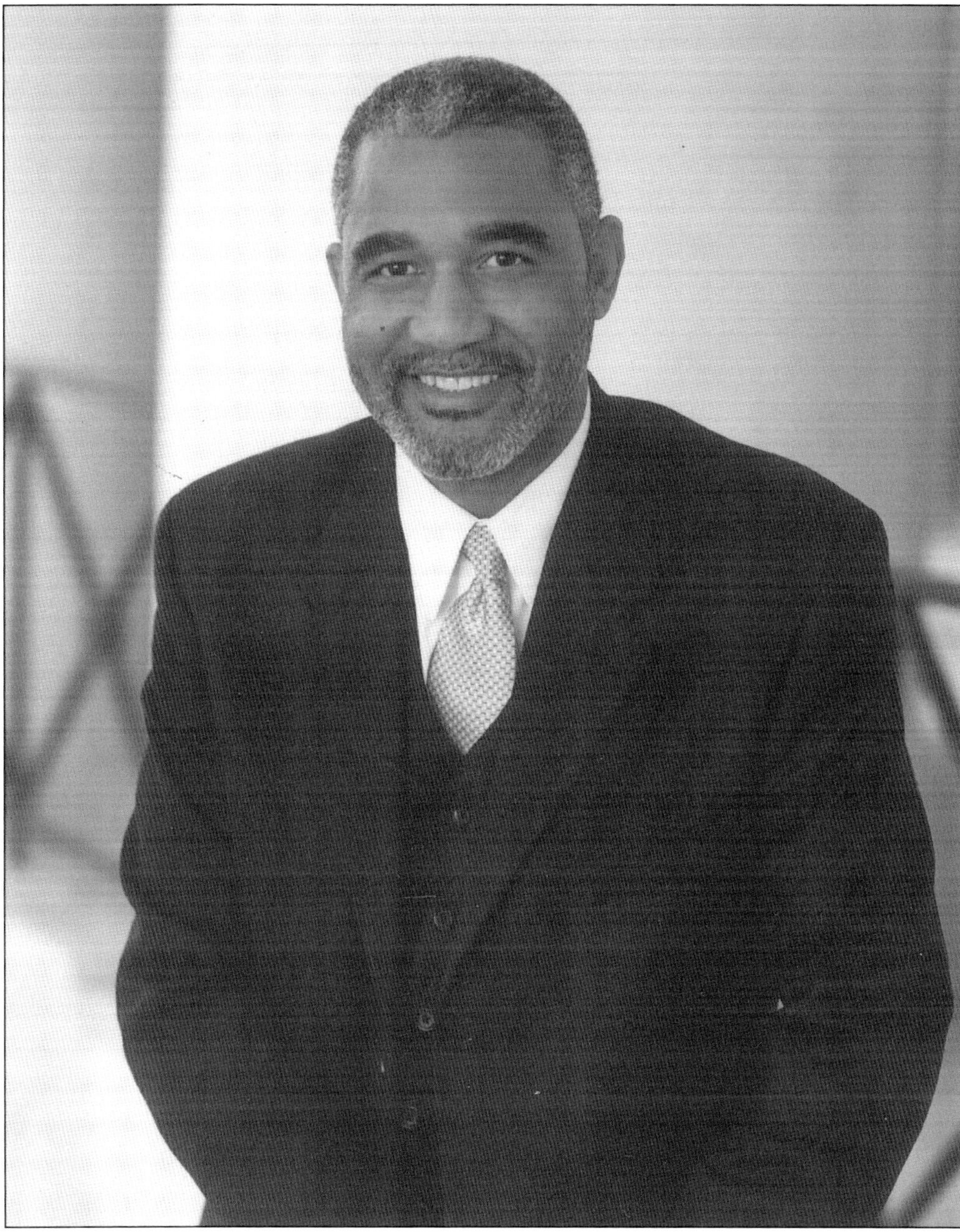

His Honor, C. Jack Ellis. Ellis is the first African-American mayor in Macon's 176-year history. Mr. Ellis was elected mayor in July 1999. He is a native of Macon, and a retired U.S. Army senior non-commissioned officer. He was awarded three bronze stars, the Army Commendation Medal for valor and heroism, and the Purple Heart for wounds received in combat. Ellis and his administration have focused on improving the quality of life for every family in Macon, enhancing the economic vitality of neighborhoods, reducing illiteracy and crime, and doing all within their power to properly guide the youth of Macon.

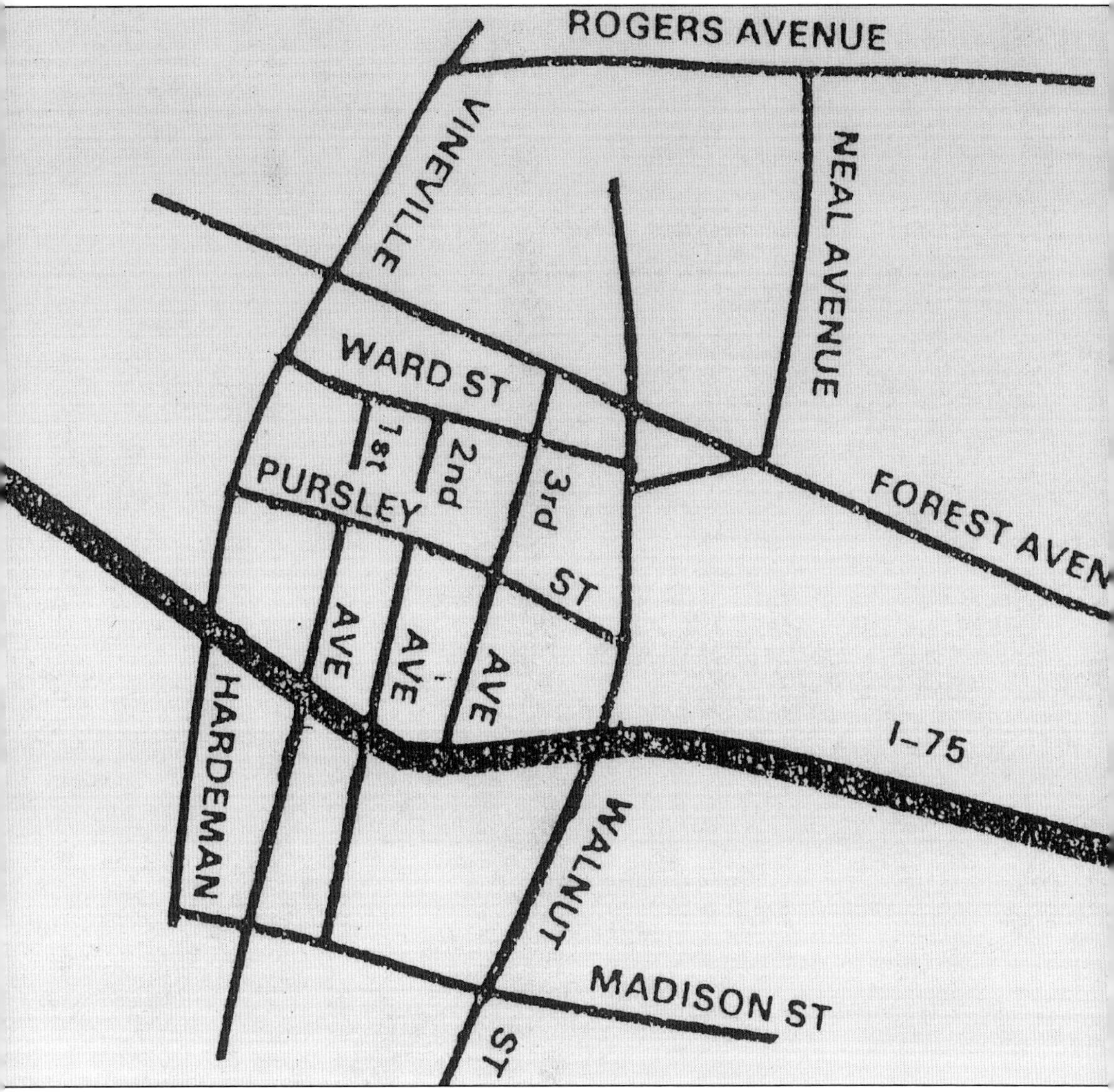

The Pleasant Hill Historic District.

Two

Pleasant Hill and Summerfield

Several black communities developed in Macon after the initial founding of the city in 1823. Pleasant Hill was one of those communities. It was organized in 1872, and considered a thriving community by 1879. Some other black communities in Macon were Unionville, Tybee, Stinsonville, Fort Hill, East Macon, and Summerfield. My mother was born in the Summerfield community and my father was born in Pleasant Hill.

Pleasant Hill's development goes back to perhaps 1870, when early black residents of the city settled Madison Street, Monroe Street, and Jefferson Street. Its expansion occurred as the Vineville community developed, and by the early 20th century, it was a thriving neighborhood of small businesses, doctors, educators, mail carriers, grocers, and countless other self-employed men and women. The name Pleasant Hill came about because the land was located in a wooded area where honeysuckles and other wild plants abounded. Quick running springs ran through lower Middle Street and lower Vineville Avenue to Forest Avenue. Blacks built homes there, ranging in style from shotgun to the more elaborate two-story Victorian cottages. Many blacks purchased enough land so that they could keep pigs, chickens, and even cows. Most families had kitchen gardens from which to feed their families. Occupations in the community ranged from carpenters to bankers. Outstanding citizens were produced such as Jefferson Long, a United States Congressman. Today, Pleasant Hill is on the National Register of Historic Places.

No one is exactly sure how the Summerfield community received its name. A Methodist church in the area at one time was named Summerfield, and the local school, established on Old Lundy Road (now named Forest Hill Road), was named Summerfield Cold School. The once-rural community, located in what is referred to now as North Macon, is an area of tremendous development. The "New Macon" is a beautiful, upscale community. There are expensive shops and boutiques, restaurants, bookstores, hotels, and large business complexes everywhere you look, and a contagious spirit of development invading those in the world of building. However, when my maternal great-grandfather, George Washington Howard Sr., began to purchase his several hundred acres of land (775 acres according to Bibb County Court House records), North Macon was a veritable forest with paths through the woods. There were several families living in the area. These families include the Halls, Montfords, Peytons, Popes, Williams, Dumas, Brooks, Bates, Jacksons, and Usserys. The two most prominent families in the areas were the Howards and Tollivers. In this community, family prevailed. Daily activities were centered on preparing meals, working the fields, quilt making, communal social gatherings, and church work. Pleasant Hill and Summerfield had a commonality. They served to protect their citizenry from the outside world and to make life worth living, despite segregation.

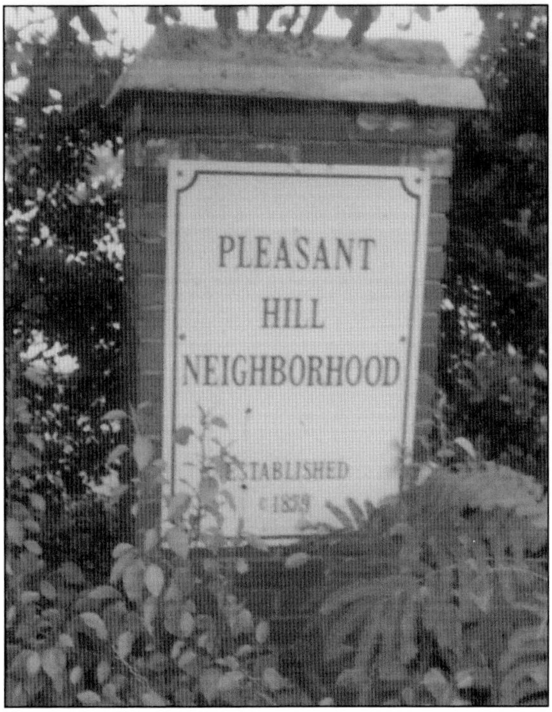

A PLEASANT HILL NEIGHBORHOOD MARKER. This is a picture of an entrance into the historic district of the African-American community. The marker is located on the corner of Walnut and Monroe Streets.

THE HOME OF AGNES MAY. This home is located on Davis Street in the Pleasant Hill area. Ms. May became the first Jeans School supervisor for Bibb County in 1942. As a Jeans teacher, Ms. May went about the countryside from one school to another overseeing the implementation of educational curriculum. According to oral history, she was very efficient in her duties.

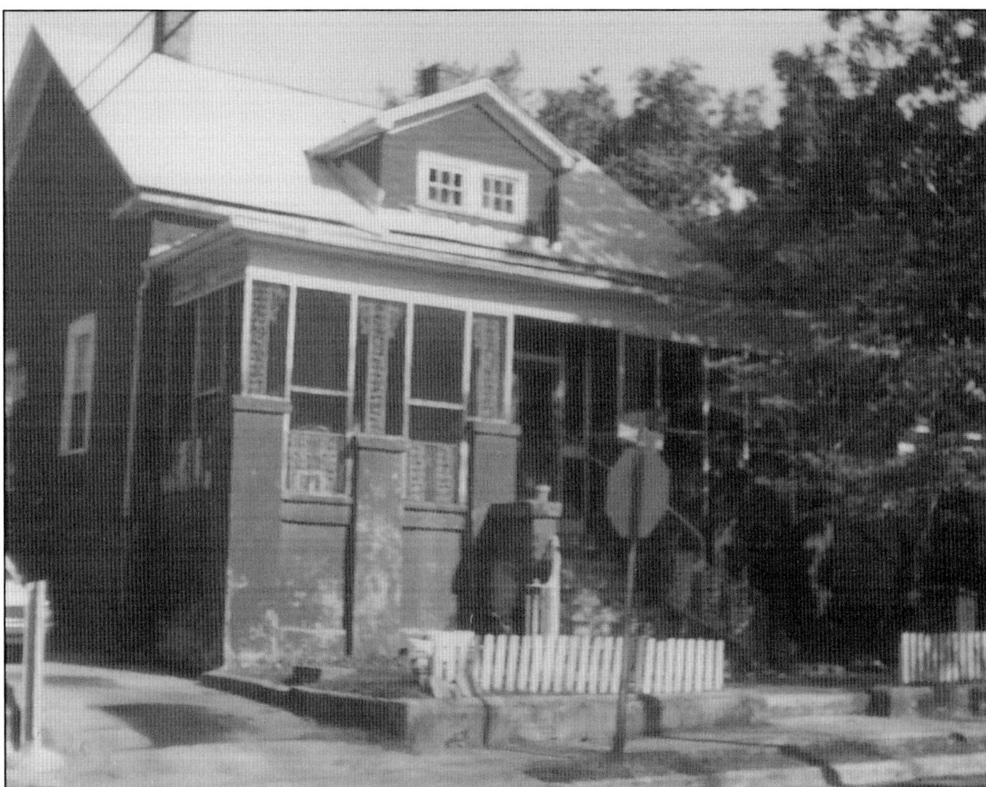

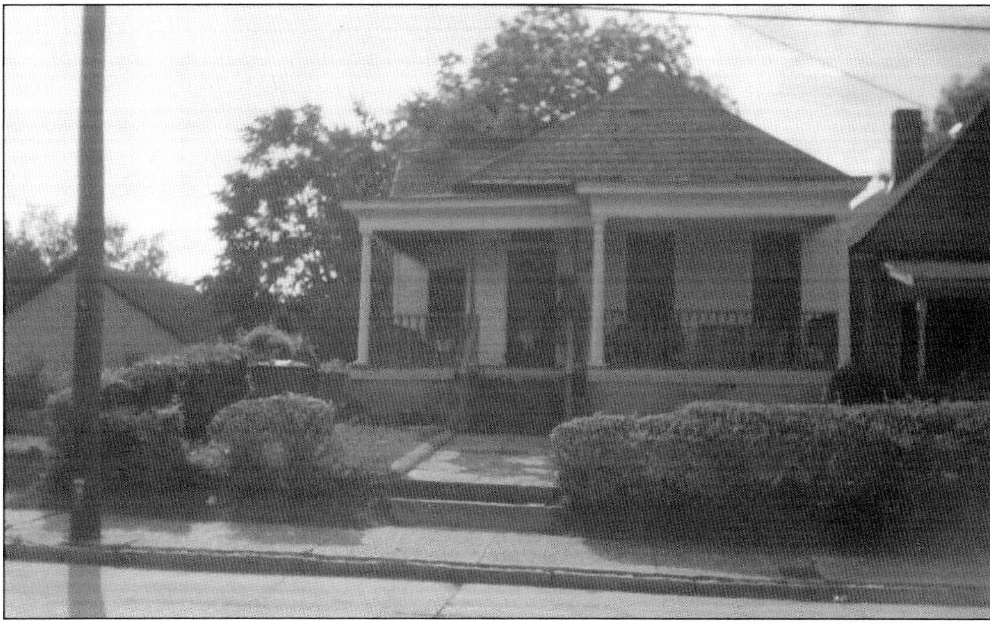

Homes. This home illustrates the style of homes found in the Pleasant Hill community. It is the residence of Mrs. Dorothy Holmes at 339 Monroe Street.

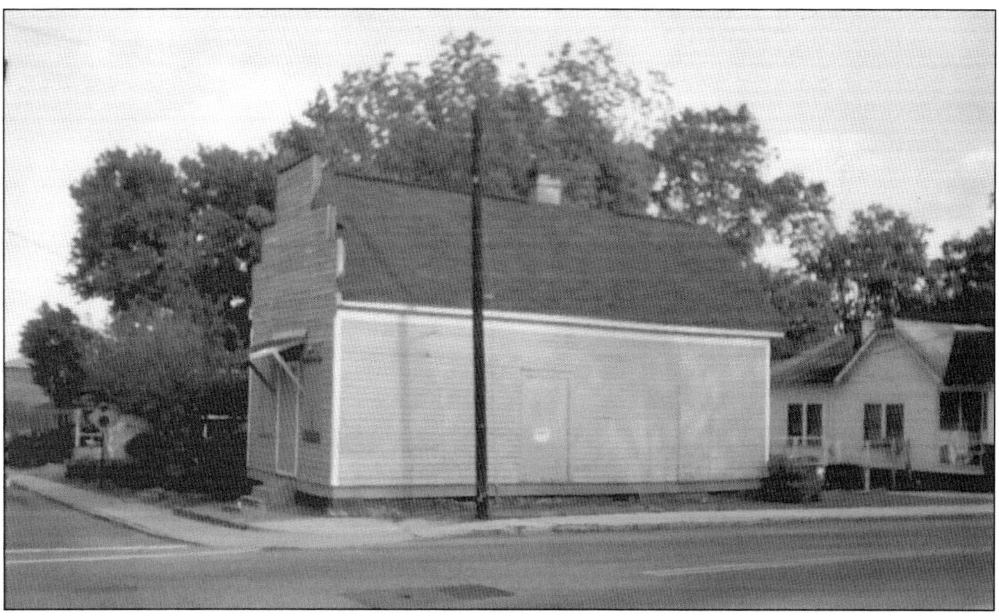

A Neighborhood Store. Once a neighborhood grocery, this store is no longer in business. It was built in the 1940s or 1950s in the Pleasant Hill area on the corner of Third and Forest Avenue. The Robinson family operated the establishment at one time. Some family members lived in the house next door.

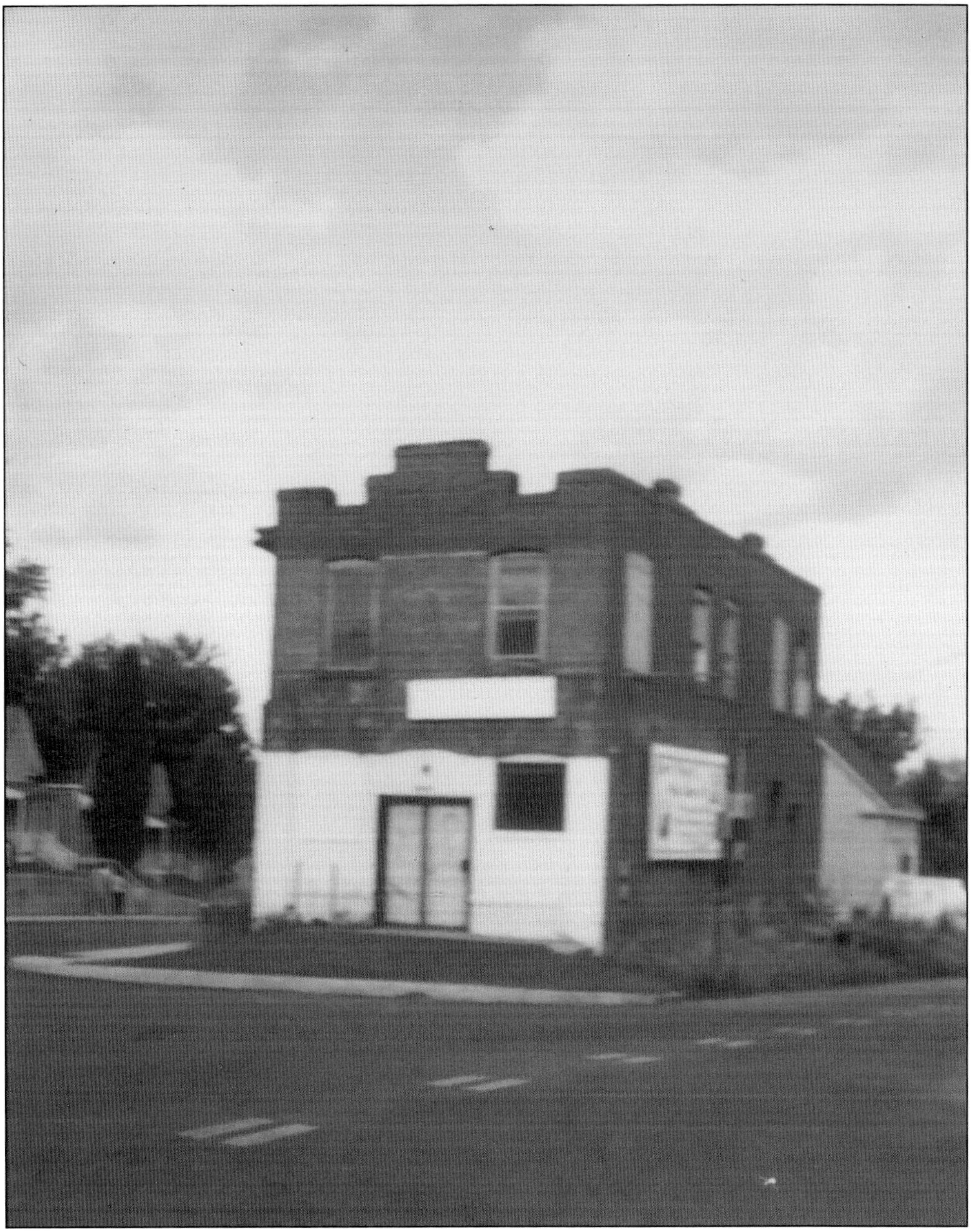

ANOTHER NEIGHBORHOOD STORE. Another neighborhood store in the Pleasant Hill community is pictured here at the Third Avenue cul-de-sac. It is no longer operating. Such businesses were established because African Americans felt that they were not welcome in the white-owned stores. Quite often they experienced humiliating situations dealing with whites. Consequently, many black businesses began to develop in Macon.

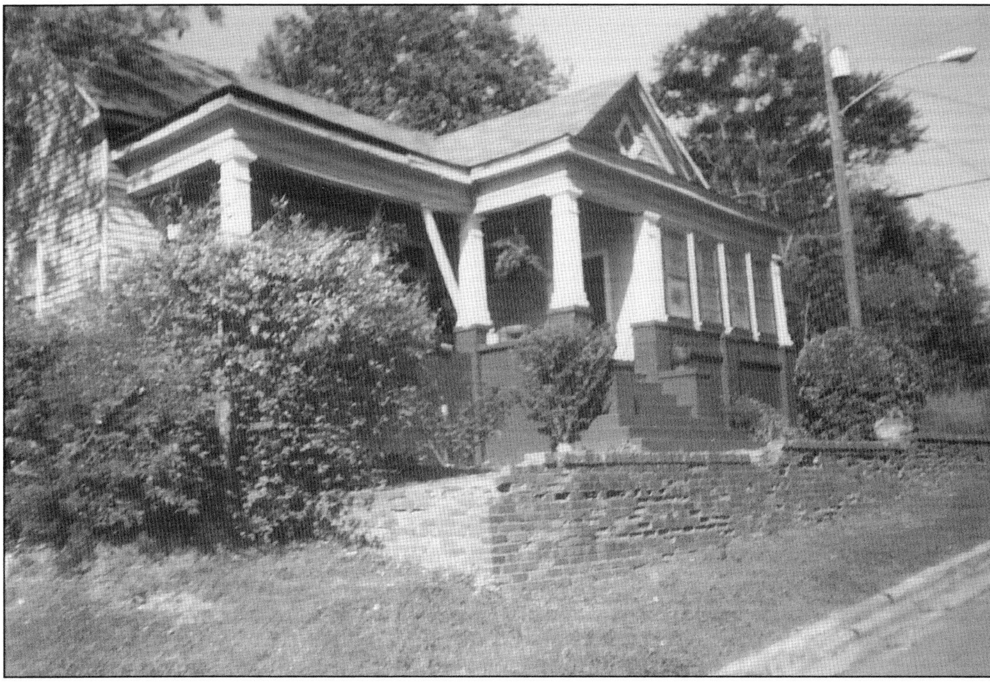

The Home of Mattie Jones. Ms. Jones was the Pleasant Hill Playground director for many years. Her home was located at the corner of Davis Street and Fifth Avenue.

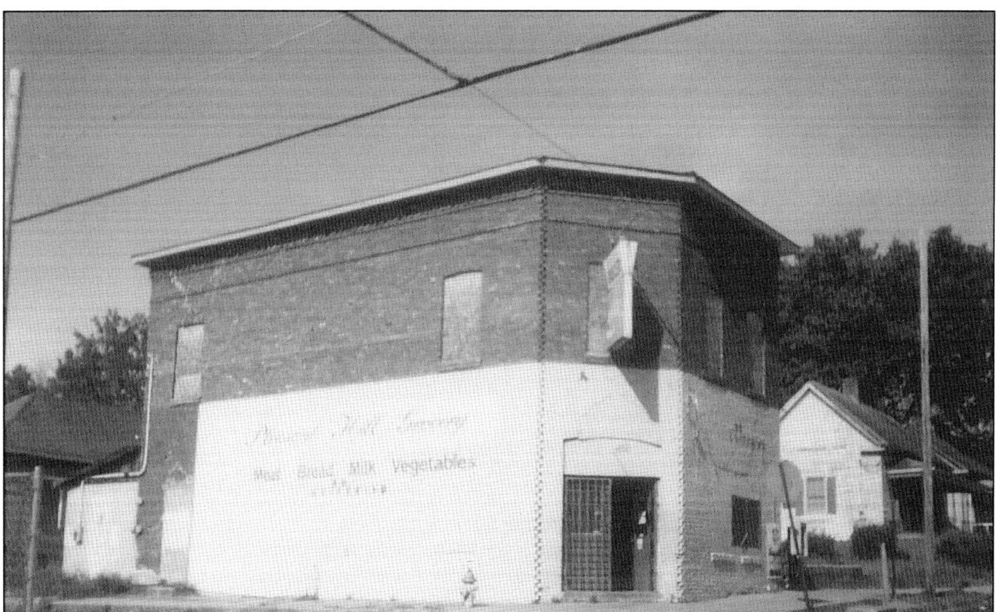

Pleasant Hill Grocery. This is another picture of a neighborhood grocery store. Listed underneath the name of the store are items for sale. The store is located on the corner of Third Avenue and Ward Street.

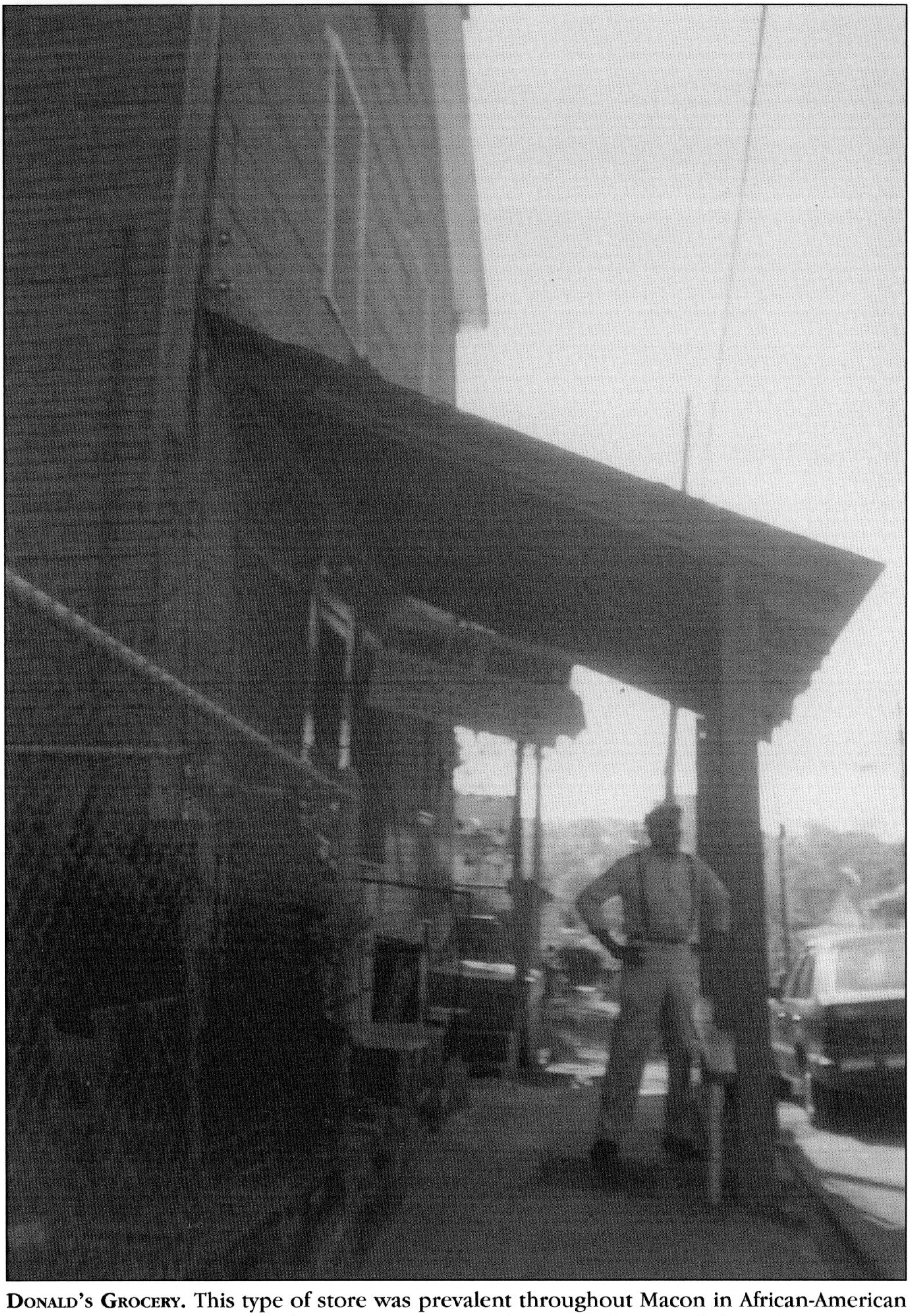

Donald's Grocery. This type of store was prevalent throughout Macon in African-American communities. Located on 1767 Fourth Avenue in Pleasant Hill, it is still doing business. Mr. Barrows posed for the picture. His nephew, Donald Barrow, owns the store today.

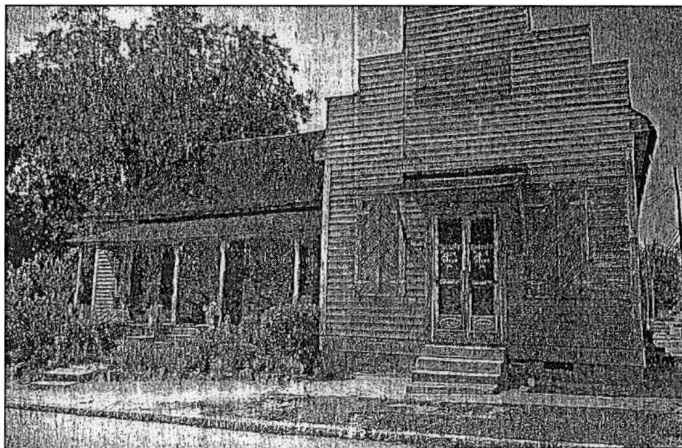

LOUISE GRIFFITH/Macon Telegraph and News

amily businesses, like this Third Avenue grocery store, were a hallmark of self-reliance

A new life

Pleasant Hill's listing on national historic register hailed as signal of rebirth

By Larry D. Wilder
Macon Telegraph and News

Mayme Wesley recalls the early development of the Pleasant Hill neighborhood, when property was first being purchased and homes were being built.

"When my father moved here, people weren't buying lots just for homes; they were buying by the acre," Wesley said Wednesday morning at her Third Avenue home. "We still own my father's two acres."

Her health wouldn't allow the 96-year-old to attend a ceremony Wednesday afternoon at Booker T. Washington Community Center, where Pleasant Hill's inclusion on the National Register of Historic Places was highlighted. But Wesley's contributions to the history of the area didn't go unnoticed.

A portrait of Wesley at her home was among the photographs on display during the brief ceremony held in the center's auditorium. And Maryel Battin, executive director of the Macon Heritage Foundation, called Wesley one of the key resource people assisting in recapturing the history of Pleasant Hill.

Elizabeth Lyon of the Atlanta Office of Historic Preservation told a group of about 75 people that Pleasant Hill is one of the most significant black historic district in the state.

(See HISTORIC, page 2B)

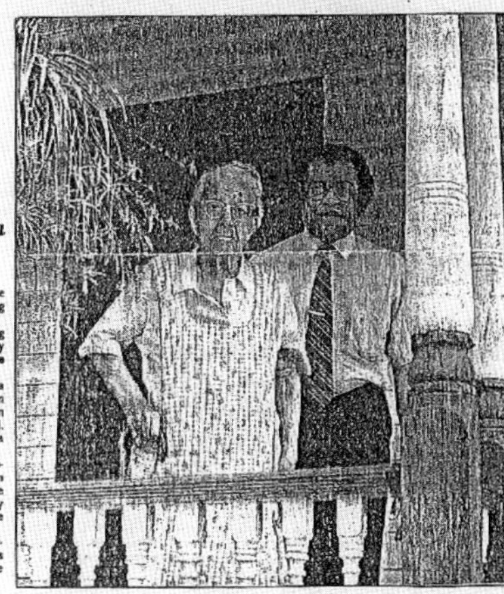

Robert Williams joins Mamye Wesley on the porch of her home

Historic From page 1B

"The benefits of being listed are tax credits for income-producing property and, when funding is available, eligibility for some grants," said Lyon. "The properties are important and have preservation value. The listing gives you a tool and a sense of value and pride."

Several elected officials attended the ceremony, including Mayor George M. Israel. Israel called the work being done in Pleasant Hill a "renaissance of a neighborhood."

A TOUR OF Pleasant Hill reveals a rich mixture of shotgun houses on the outskirts of the community and more ornate late Victorian and neoclassical homes in the center of the area — original structures still intact. Robert Williams and Albert Howard also played key roles in researching the community's history for its presentation as a historic district. Both men have spent all their lives in the community and are direct descendants of early founders. The declared historic district is roughly bounded by Madison Street, Rogers, Neal and Wise avenues.

"Community Development did some work in Pleasant Hill to try and revitalize pieces of property," Williams said in an interview before Wednesday's ceremony. "After all of the money was spent, the Macon Heritage Foundation tried to determine whether there was interest in Pleasant Hill becoming listed. It's one of the few black areas in the country, as I understand it, that has maintained the integrity of the neighborhood.

"Basically, with the exception of the expressway coming through, the community is the same. One thing that concerns people is, is there a means of revitalizing? If we could, it would be a great village-type situation. It would make it one of the special places where people would like to come and just go through."

THE DEVELOPMENT of Pleasant Hill started in the early 1870s, when wealthy white families built shotgun houses for black servants along Madison Street and Monroe Avenue. The area continued to develop through the 1930s. Education, it seems, was the glue that held the community together. Pleasant Hill was known as an education center for blacks, since public schools for blacks went no higher than sixth grade during the late 19th and early 20th centuries. Ballard Normal High School, St. Peter Claver, the Academy for the Blind, the North Macon Colored School and Beda-Etta College were all located in Pleasant Hill.

"It's true that we had a lot of schools coming in," Howard said. "The first was Lewis High School. We had two private schools taught in people's homes. There was no public education for blacks at the time."

"Stephen Ballard gave money to establish Ballard Normal School," Williams added. "The Regency Apartments on Forest Avenue is on the site where Ballard Normal was established. It closed in 1942 when it merged with the public school."

IF EDUCATION was a trademark of the community, so, too, was self-reliance. Many families operated various businesses within and outside the neighborhood.

"There were a number of entrepreneurs," said Williams. "People in the area took pride in establishing themselves as community leaders."

During the earlier days, streets weren't definitive enough to have names. Houses were scattered about, wherever people bought lots. As streets developed, most people settled them by occupation. For example, doctors lived on First Avenue, while mail carriers lived on Second Avenue and so on.

Some of the more prominent names to emerge from Pleasant Hill's earlier days include Lewis Williams, B.S. Ingram, Minnie L. Smith and Wesley — all important contributors to education. Albert B. Fitzpatrick was manager of the black-organized People's Health and Life Insurance Co.

Then there was L.J. Max, owner of Wages and Earners Bank and editor of the Negro section of *The Macon Telegraph*. Sara Bailey was noted for starting the first Girl Scout troop for blacks.

"One of the interesting things is when Pleasant Hill was established it had very much of a village atmosphere. It didn't have wide-open spaces," said Battin, who coordinated efforts to have the community placed on the Register. "It's really like going into a totally different town because of the scale and size. It's very much kept its original configuration. Our survey mentioned that it is one of the most intact black residential areas that was developed originally as a black residential area. It's not a situation where whites moved out and blacks moved in."

Williams said many of the residents now living in Pleasant Hill are direct descendants of the people who settled there before there were streets and lights.

"This cannot be the end of something but the commencement of the beginning of something big," Williams said.

A NEW LIFE, *C.* 1990S. These articles share information about the history of Pleasant Hill. They focus on how being placed on the National Register of Historic Places will help bring the community back to life. Robert Williams and another longtime resident stand in the image at right on her front porch discussing the matter. Development of the area was one of the main concerns—keeping the area alive for the next generation to experience. "Don't let the community die" was and is the sentiment about Pleasant Hill. (Courtesy of *Macon Telegraph and News*.)

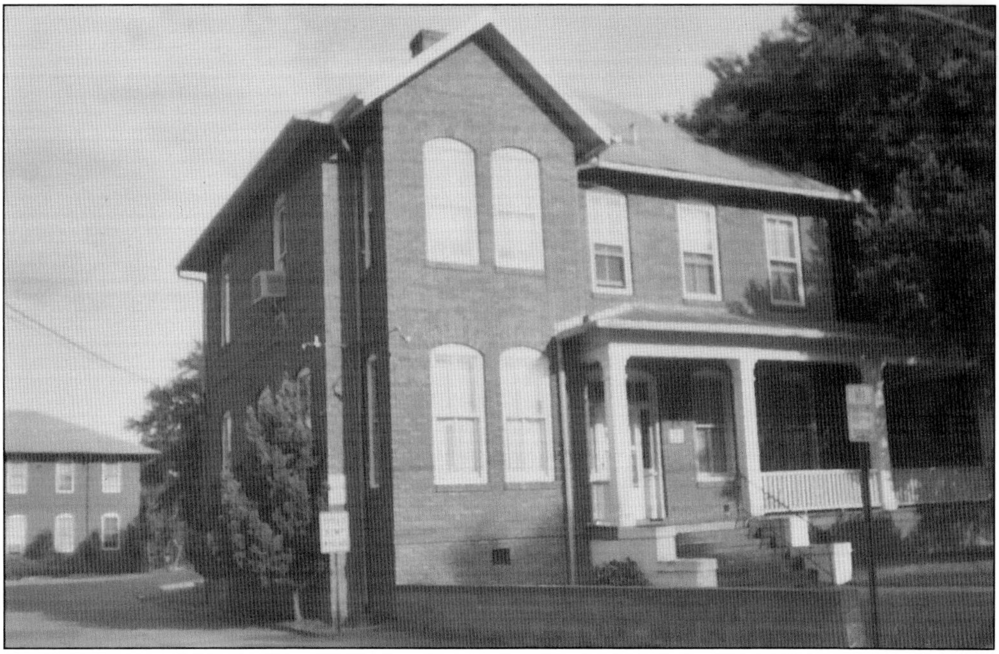

St. Peter Claver's Rectory. This building is a home for Catholic priests, and is a part of the parish. Four buildings make up the parish grounds. The school is in the background. The convent (shown on the facing page) is where the Sisters of the Blessed Sacrament lived. The parish was established in 1915.

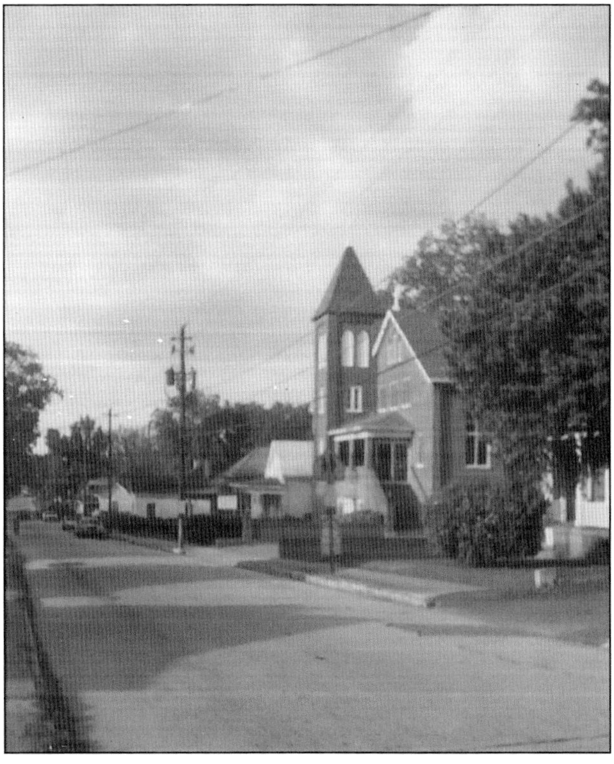

Ward Street. Many private homes lined this street on both sides. These are homes of the 1930s, '40s, and '50s. St. Peter Claver's steeple can be seen on the right in the distance.

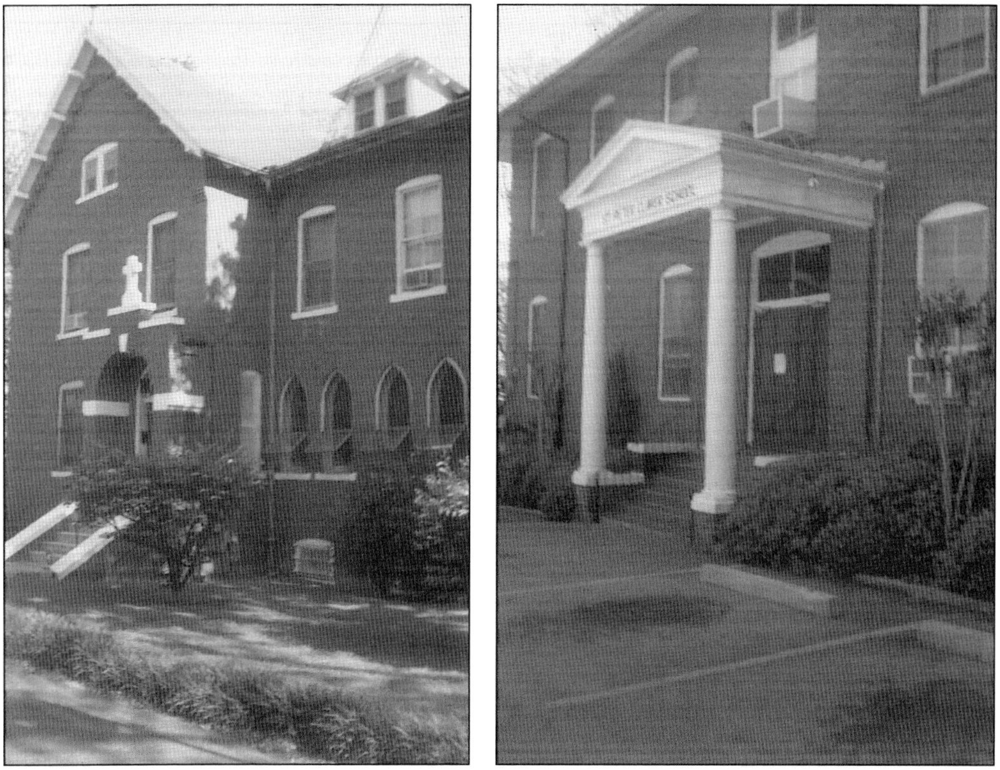

The St. Peter Claver Church, Pastor Rectory, Sisters Convent, and School. This parish was named for a Spanish Jesuit missionary who was known as "the Apostle of the Blacks." He ministered to West African slaves, then being imported in large numbers. Peter Claver was born in 1580, and died in 1654. He declared himself "the slave of the Negroes forever." The parish was established on Ward Street in 1915 by a tenacious priest from Belgium, Father Ignatius Lissner, and an heiress from Philadelphia, PA, Mother Katharine Drexel. She turned her back on her family's fortune and founded a religious order of women who are known as the Sister of the Blessed Sacrament.

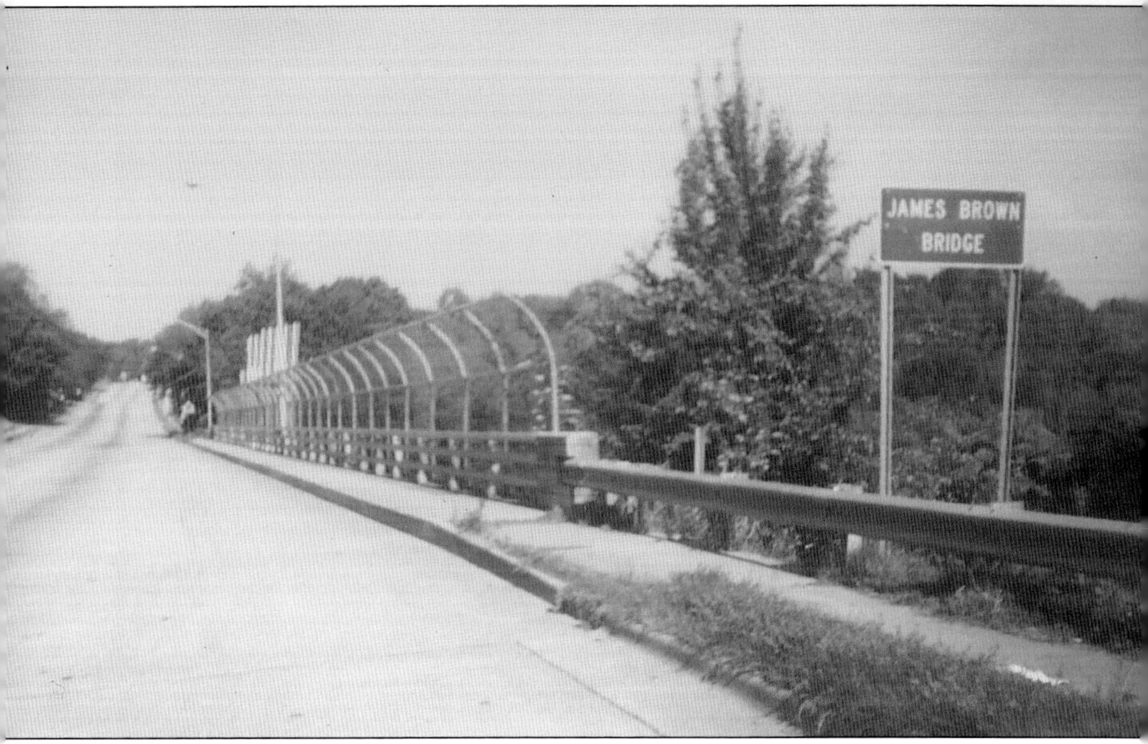

THE JAMES BROWN BRIDGE. This bridge, located on Walnut Street, was named for the "Godfather of Soul," James Brown, in 1967. Born in Augusta, he spent most of his early musical life in Macon, performing in theaters and nightclubs. Many of his earliest supporters came from Macon and helped to promote his career.

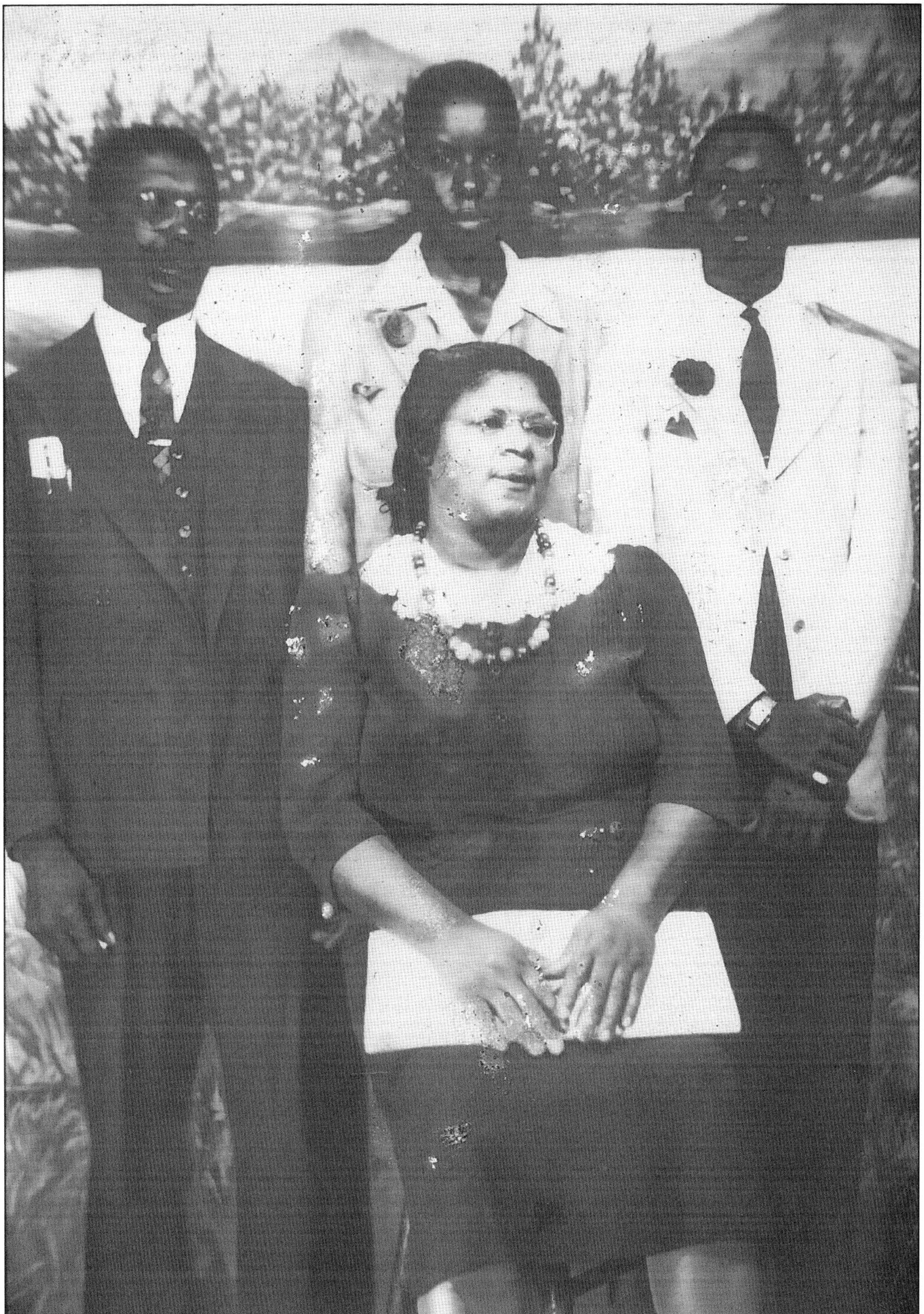

The Clowers Family. Seen from left to right *c.* 1934 are Ernest Clowers Sr., Leroy Clowers, Ernest Clowers Jr., and Elsie Mae Gray Clowers (seated). The Clowers family resided in Pleasant Hill. (Courtesy of Jeanne C. Herring.)

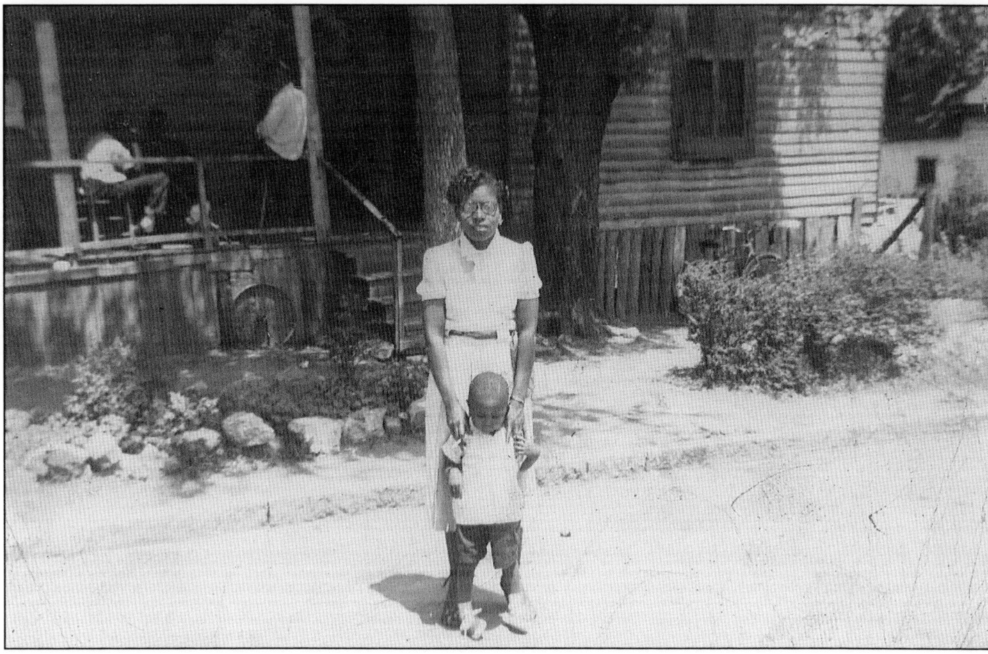

Lorena Howard Latham. Lorena is shown here *c.* 1949 with an unidentified child. The home is located on Fourth Avenue in Pleasant Hill. (Courtesy of Lorena H. Latham.)

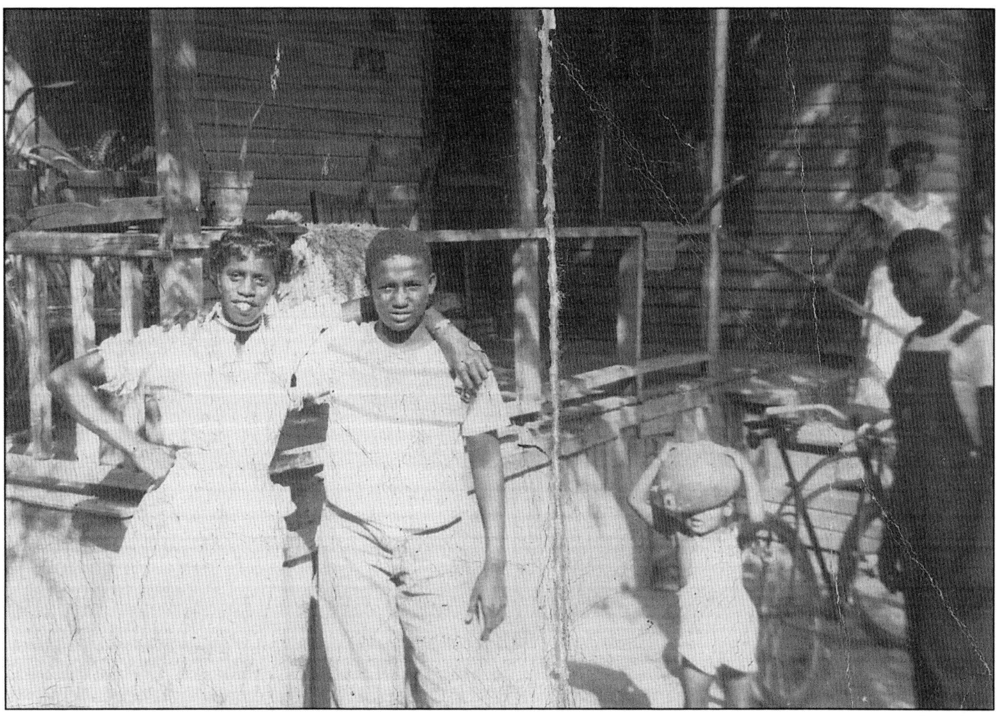

Connie Howard and "Honey Child" Latham. The two are pictured here from left to right at the home of Mr. and Mrs. Latham on Fourth Avenue in Pleasant Hill. This photograph was taken *c.* 1952. (Courtesy of Lorena H. Latham.)

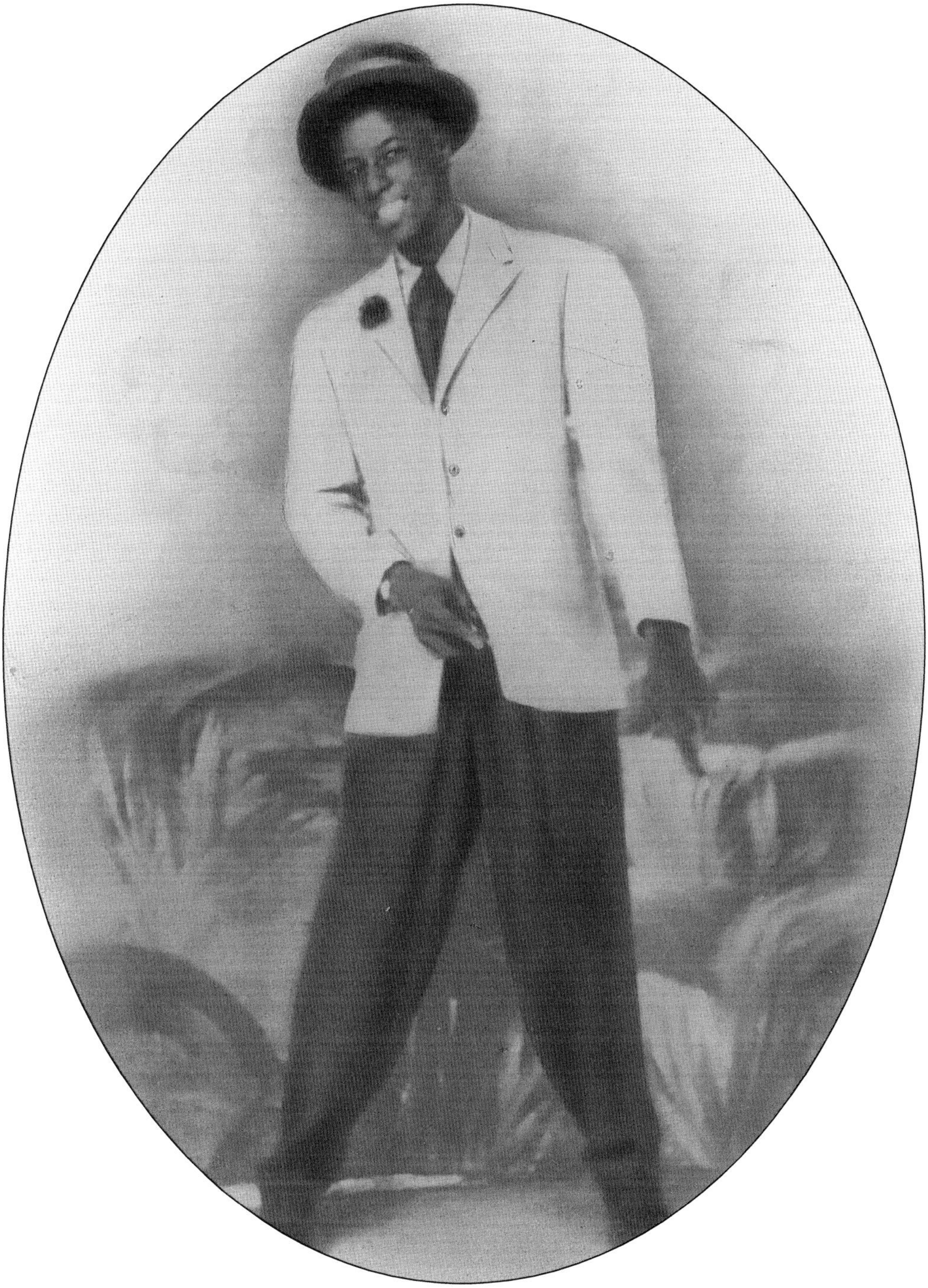

Leroy Clowers. Pictured here going out dancing is the father of the author, *c.* 1940s. (Courtesy of Jeanne C. Herring.)

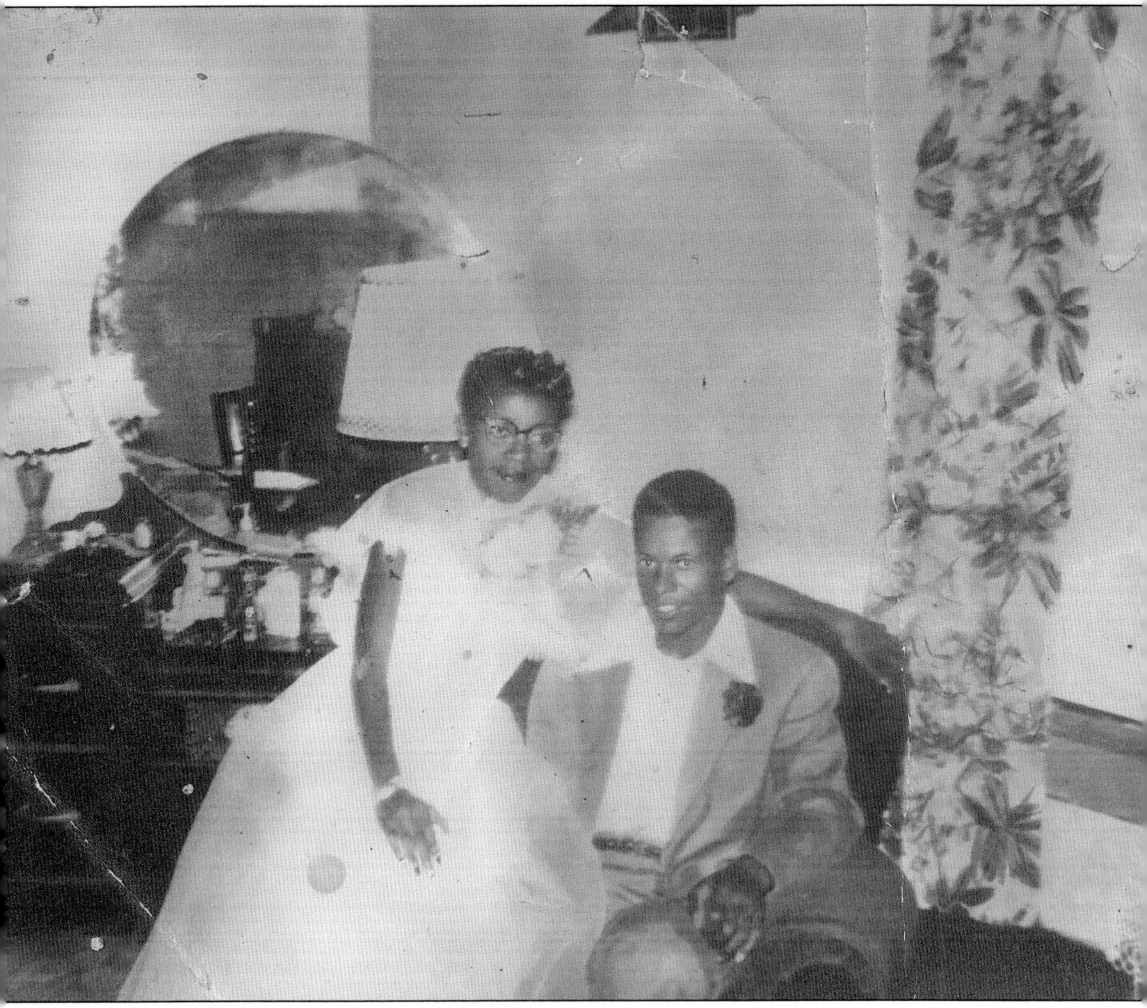

The Prom. Annie Ruth Howard and J.W. Lundy are pictured before leaving for their high school prom at Ballard-Hudson Senior High. The photograph was taken in the home of Mr. and Mrs. Latham in Pleasant Hill, *c.* 1953. (Courtesy of Lorena H. Latham.)

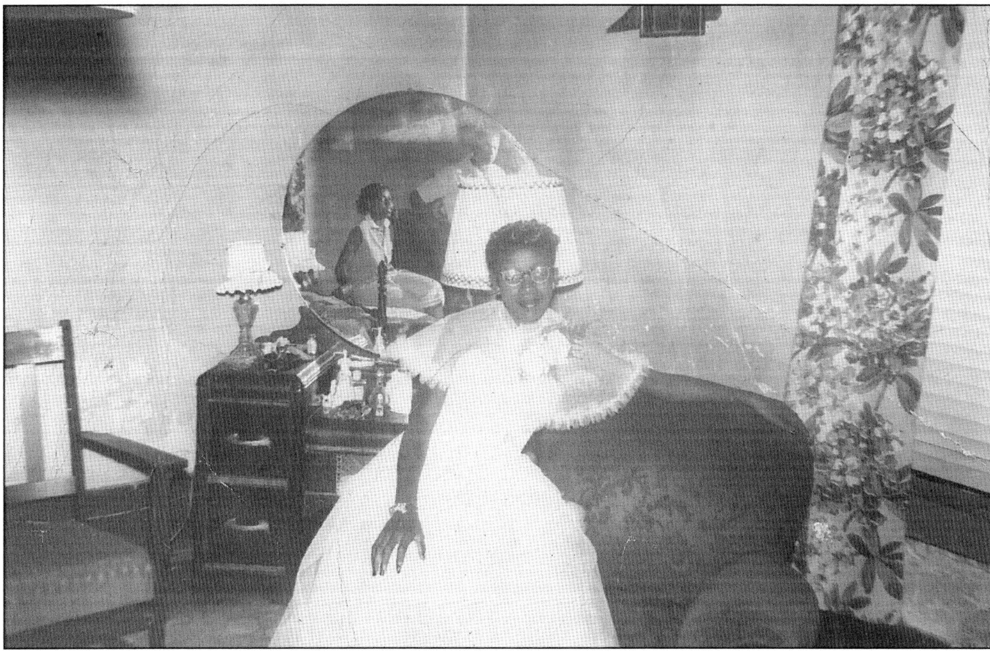

Annie Ruth Howard. Pictured here ready for the prom, Annie Ruth is getting advice from family and friends, two of which are visible in the mirror. This photograph was taken *c.* 1953. (Courtesy of Lorena H. Latham.)

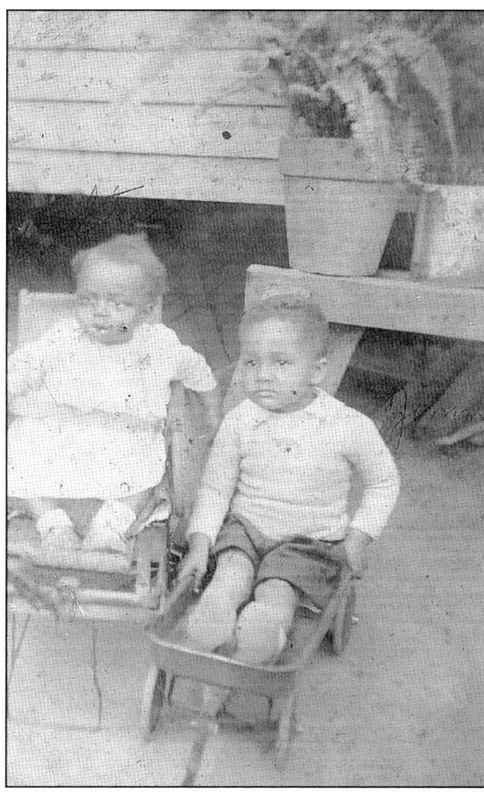

"I'm in the Wagon, Now Let's Go." Pictured from left to right are Walter Latham and his brother James. They were in the yard of their home in Pleasant Hill, *c.* 1930 (Courtesy of Lorena H. Latham.)

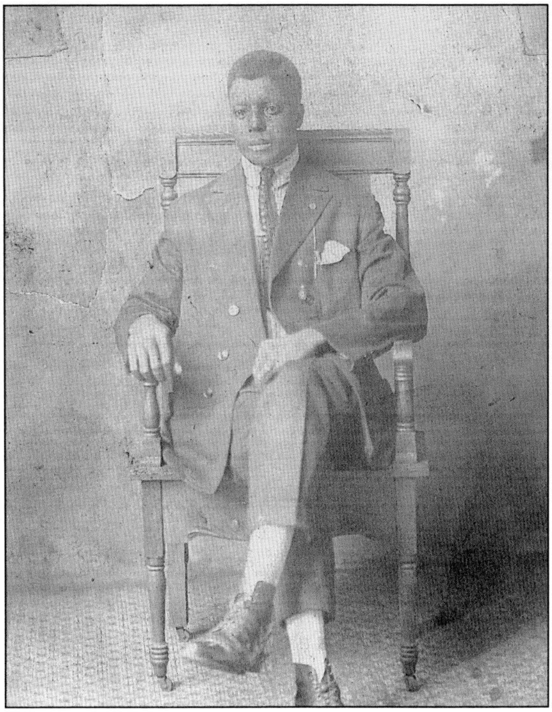

Ernest Clowers. Clowers was the paternal grandfather of the author. He was born January 18, 1900. This picture was taken when he was 22 years of age in Asheville, NC, *c.* 1922.

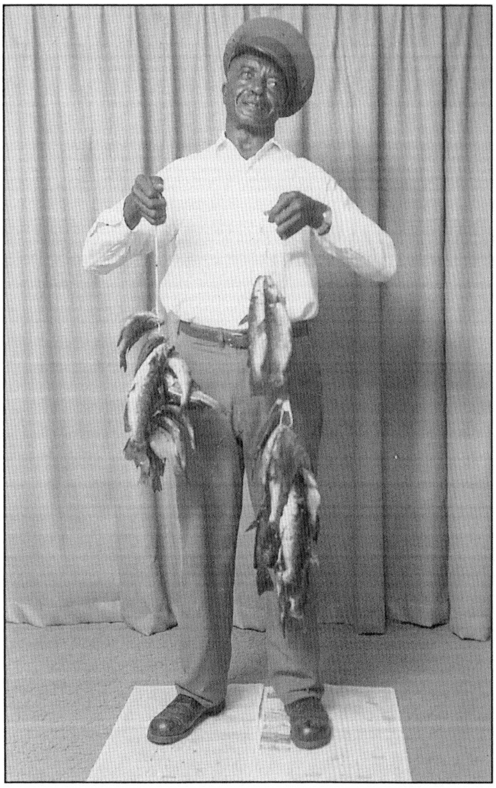

"These Did Not Get Away," Ernest Clowers Sr. A longtime resident of 1785 Fifth Avenue in Pleasant Hill, Ernest Clowers Sr. is shown here on a fishing trip in Fort Lauderdale, FL, January 1, 1968. (Courtesy of Jeanne C. Herring.)

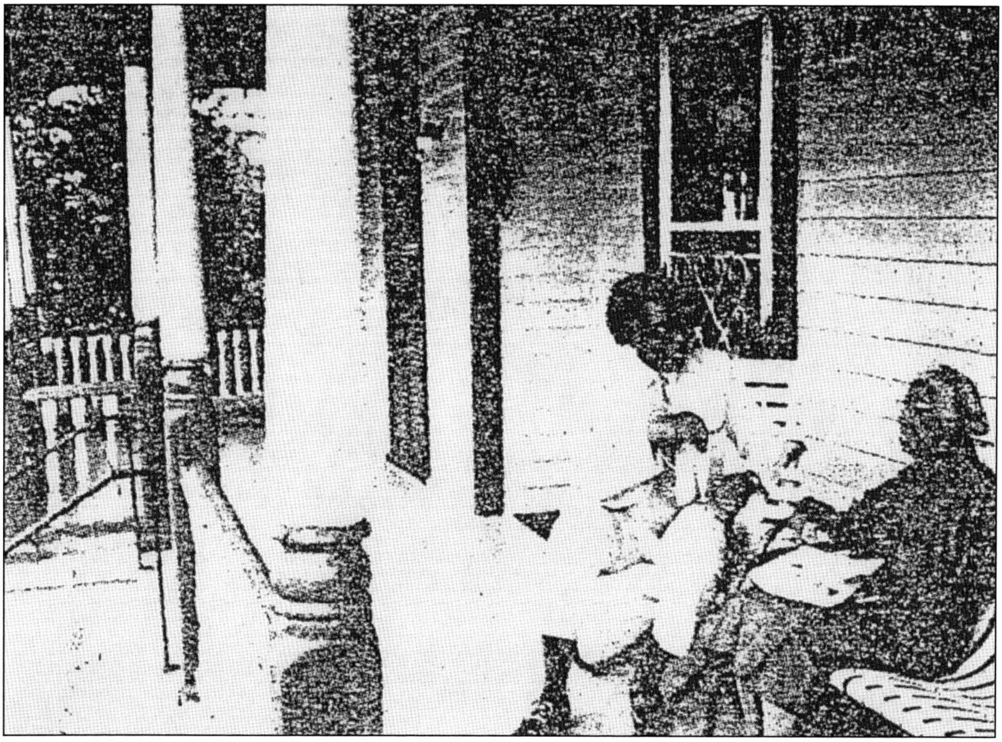

"PLEASANT HILL'S RICH HISTORY MAY BE RECOGNIZED," C. MID-1990S. This article came out in the *Macon Telegraph* before Pleasant Hill was designated as a National Historic District. The nomination was submitted by Mrs. Maryel Battin, Macon's Historic Foundation director. (Courtesy of *Macon Telegraph and News.*)

Pleasant Hill's rich history may be recognized

Susan Long
Macon Telegraph and News

Ninety-two-year-old Mayme Wesley put down her cane and settled back in a white metal chair on the front porch of her Pleasant Hill home to catch a cool breeze on a hot day.

She has lived most of her life in the yellow and green house on Third Avenue which her father built in 1895.

With an amazing recollection for details, the 1910 graduate of Payne College talks about the Pleasant Hill of her childhood.

Looking at the house across the street, she points to where the owner's barn and stables used to be and reminisces about the trolleys that used to go up and down Third Avenue.

With luck, those memories will soon be preserved for future generations.

THE MACON Heritage Foundation feels that the Pleasant Hill community should be a National Registered Historic District. The organization recently received a Historic Preservation Fund Grant to complete survey work it has already begun for the nomination.

The foundation is using the $1,400 grant to pay a consultant to compile the data collected by the foundation and volunteers from the Pleasant Hill District.

The nomination will be submitted by Sept. 30, according to MHF Director Maryel Battin.

If approved by the National Park Service, Pleasant Hill will be one of the few black residential areas in the country designated as a National Registered Historic District, Battin said.

"Not more than 10 percent of the 1,500 national register listings are black," she added.

In Georgia, the only other black national historic district is the area around the home of Martin Luther King Jr. in Atlanta. The black Victorian district in Savannah is a national historic district also, but it was not built as a black district, explained Battin.

"Almost all of Pleasant Hill was built by and for blacks, and it's integrity is still there," she said.

PLEASANT Hill's development goes back to around 1870 when Madison, Monroe and Jefferson streets were settled by early black residents of the city.

Its expansion occurred as the Vineville community developed, and by the early 20th century it was a thriving neighborhood of small businesses, doctors, dentists, educators, mail carriers, grocers, draymen and many other self-employed citizens.'

The district earmarked for the registry will extend from Madison Street about one mile to Rogers Avenue and from Hardeman Avenue to Neal Avenue. It will back up to the Intown Historic District on one side and the Vineville Historic District on the other side.

The principal arteries are Forest Avenue, Green-Walnut-Douglass Avenue, Pursely Street and Ward Avenue. Secondary streets are First, Sec-

Summerfield reunion aims to rekindle community spirit

Continued from 1B

SUMMERFIELD COMMUNITY REUNION

Saturday, Aug. 2, noon, at Lundy Chapel Baptist Church, 2081 Forest Hill Road.

Drumming demonstration is planned for 1 p.m. Other activities to include a maypole, horseshoes, marbles. Catherine Meeks of Mercer University, editor of "Macon's Black Heritage: The Untold Story," will sign copies of the book.

No charge to attend. Participants were asked to take a covered dish.

Call Barbara Tollver Rodgers, 477-2331.

"There was a little conflict there," she said.

But there also was a great sense of community. The farm women would put up their fruit and vegetables at a community canning house not far from the school, and in the fall, the menfolk would go around house to house to help chop wood for one another, while the women cooked a communal meal and boiled peanuts.

"I used to love the time of wood cutting," Rodgers said. "Everybody would have their supply of wood. That's the way the community worked."

"We did our own sewing. We had our own recipes that we cooked. We had crafts we would show at the

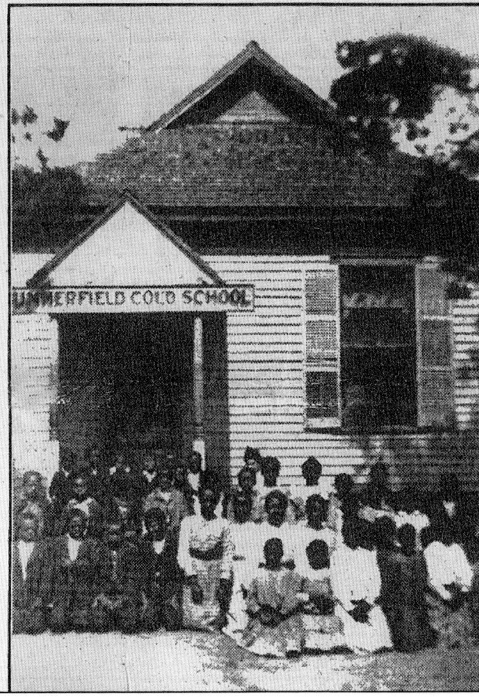

A Summerfield Reunion. Shown below on the grounds of the Lundy Chapel Church during a Summerfield reunion are, from left to right, Minnie T. Dumas, Barbara T. Rodgers, Alvesta M. Brown, and Isabella D. Jackson. More than 50 people from all over the U.S. participated in the reunion.

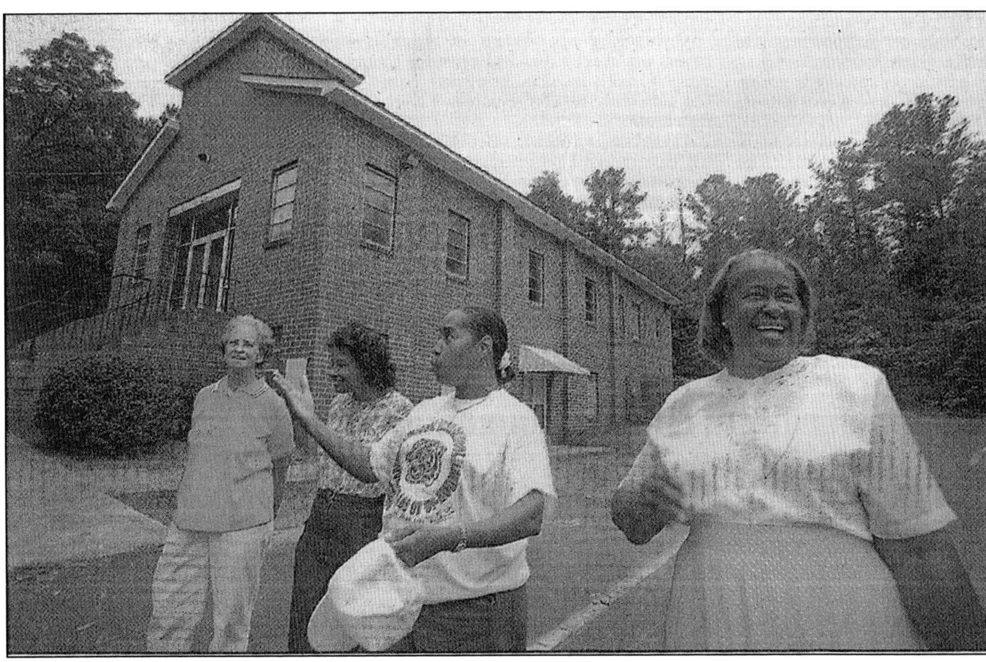

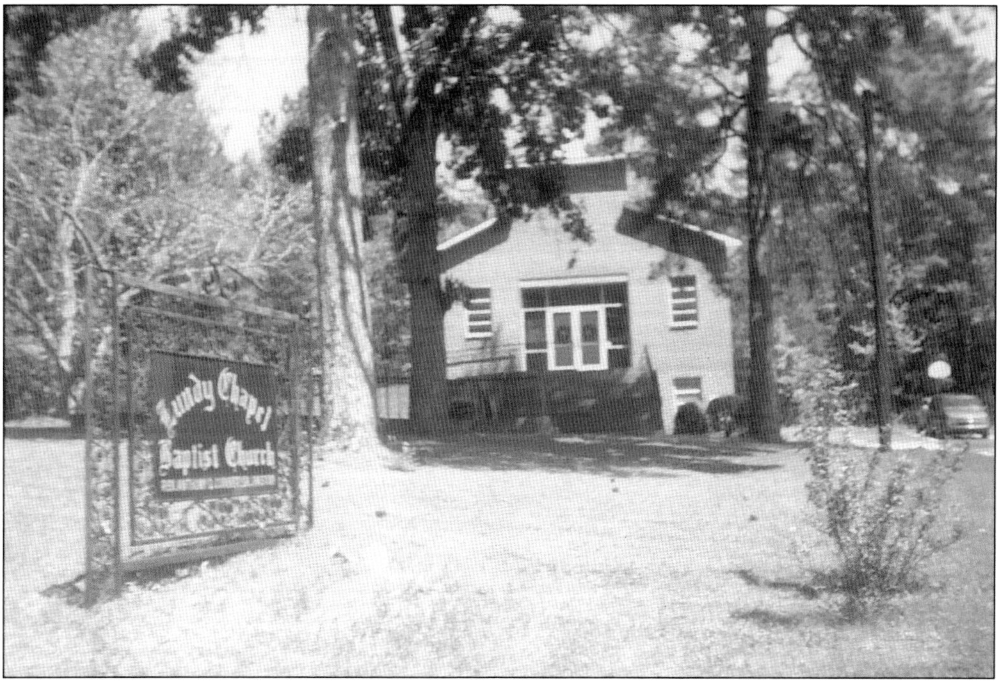

The Lundy Chapel Baptist Church. This church is one of the oldest African-American churches in Macon. It was established in 1868 on Old Lundy Road under the leadership of Rev. Dan Parsons, and started under a bush arbor, progressing to a log cabin, then to a wooden frame structure, and finally to a brick edifice (which took many years to complete). Charlie Bowman, George W. Howard, Isaac Howard, Andrew Tolliver, Allen Ward, Benjamin Hutchins, Peter Taylor, Reddick Lawson, Peter Lawson, and Oliver Griffin were religious leaders instrumental in bringing the church to fruition in the early years. Services are still held at the church today.

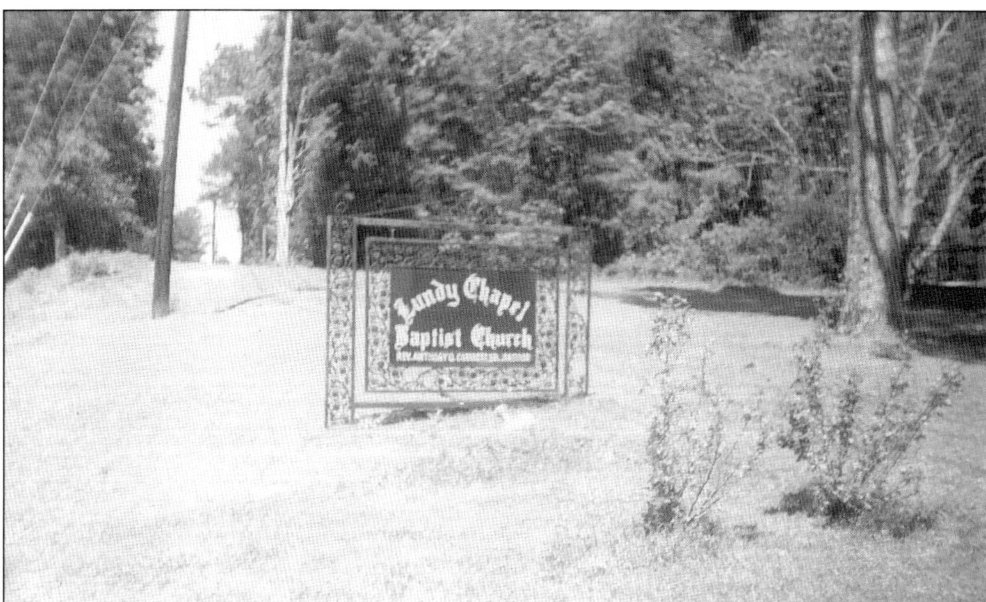

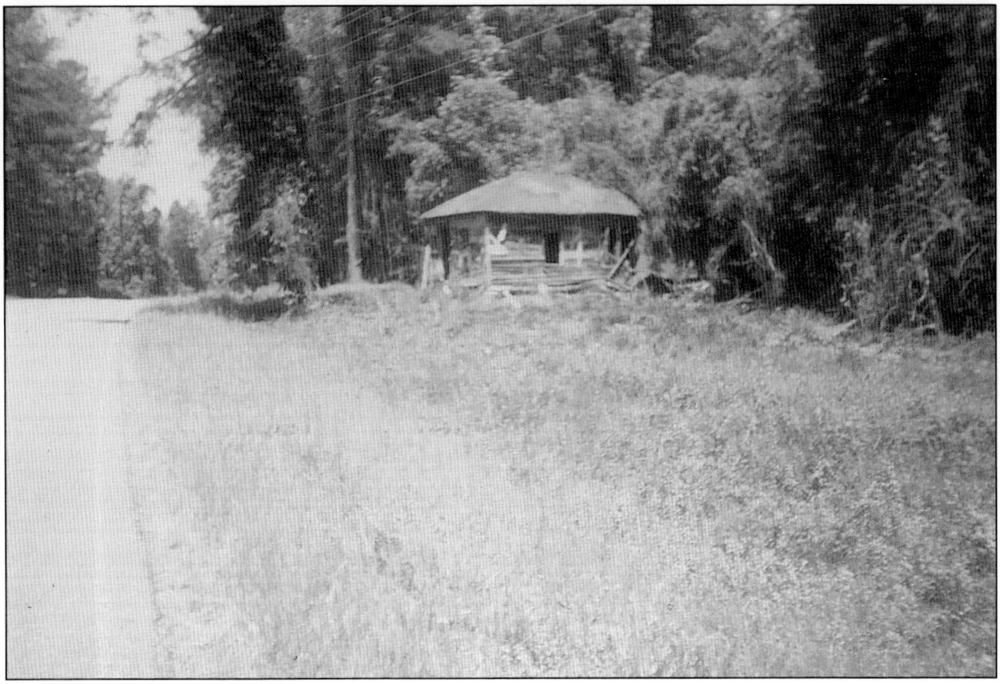

A Frame House. This home once belonged to Ms. Kate Ussery, and is located off Forest Hill Road. It is approximately 85 years old.

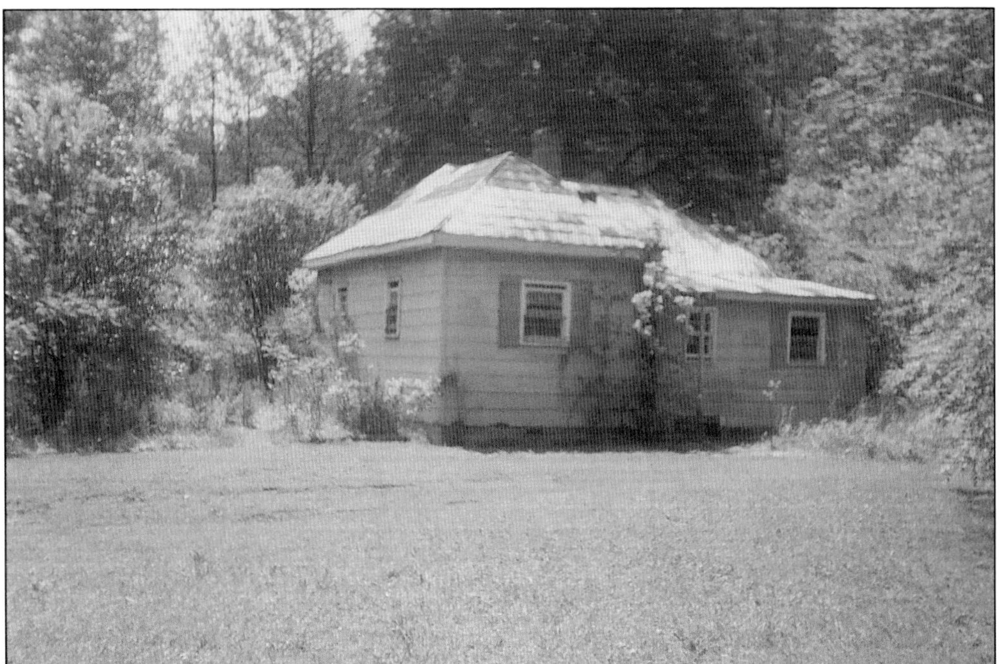

The Home of John and Carrie Howard Pope. This home is located in the old Summerfield community, now a part of North Macon.

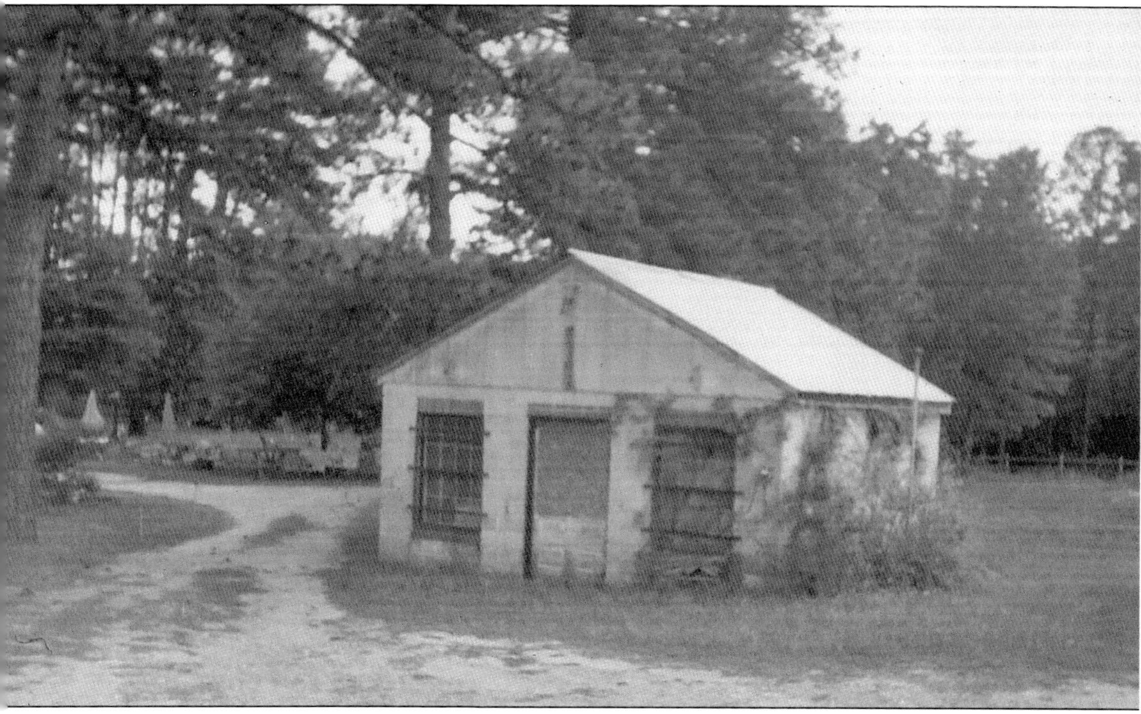

The Dumas Brothers Grocery Store. Serving members of the Summerfield community and African Americans who lived in the surrounding rural area, this building was established in the 1950s. The Dumas family was a very enterprising clan, and also operated a sawmill business. They participated in everything from neighborhood clubs and organizations and church work (performed by the women) to starting lucrative businesses (done by the men). Family members continue to live and work in the Summerfield area to this day, including Rev. Moses Dumas, Mrs. Willie Mae Dumas, Mrs. Isabelle Dumas Jackson, and Mr. John H. Dumas Jr.

The concept of community entreprenuership is not new. It was difficult to risk money in order to earn more, and investment always came hard in the African-American community. There was pressure to hold on to what little money that could be put away, and not risk it in financial ventures. The Dumas family and others started small, but progressed to better lives and financial situations in the 20th century. Their children will no doubt continue the tradition in the new century.

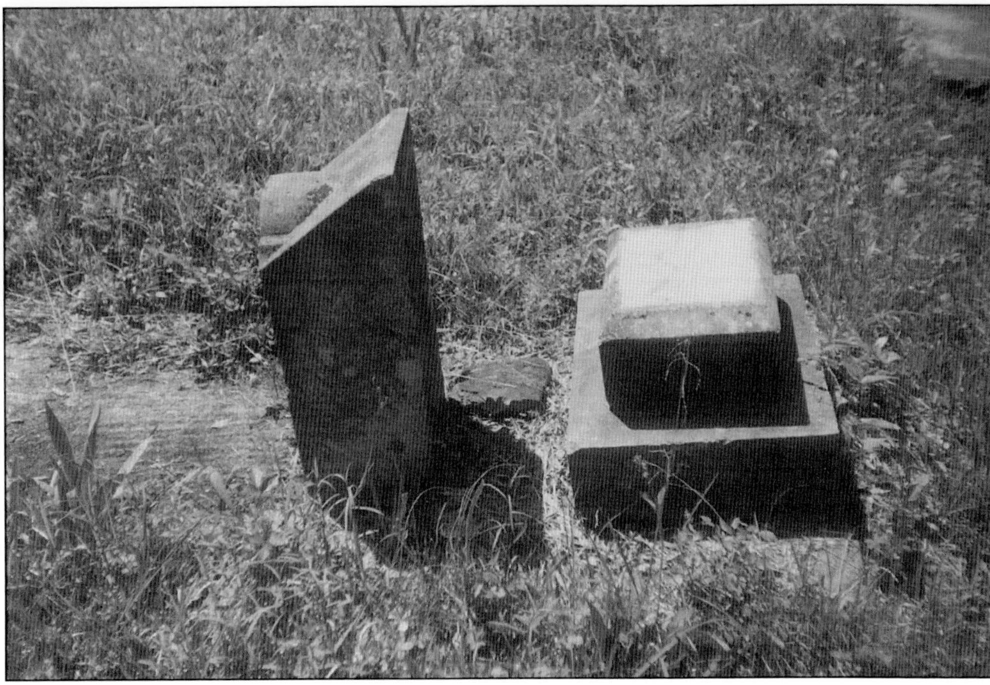

LUNDY CHAPEL CEMETERY SCENES. The Lundy Chapel Cemetery, established in 1868–1869, is one of the oldest African-American cemeteries in Macon. Family members take turns caring for the site. The land was originally donated by George W. Howard.

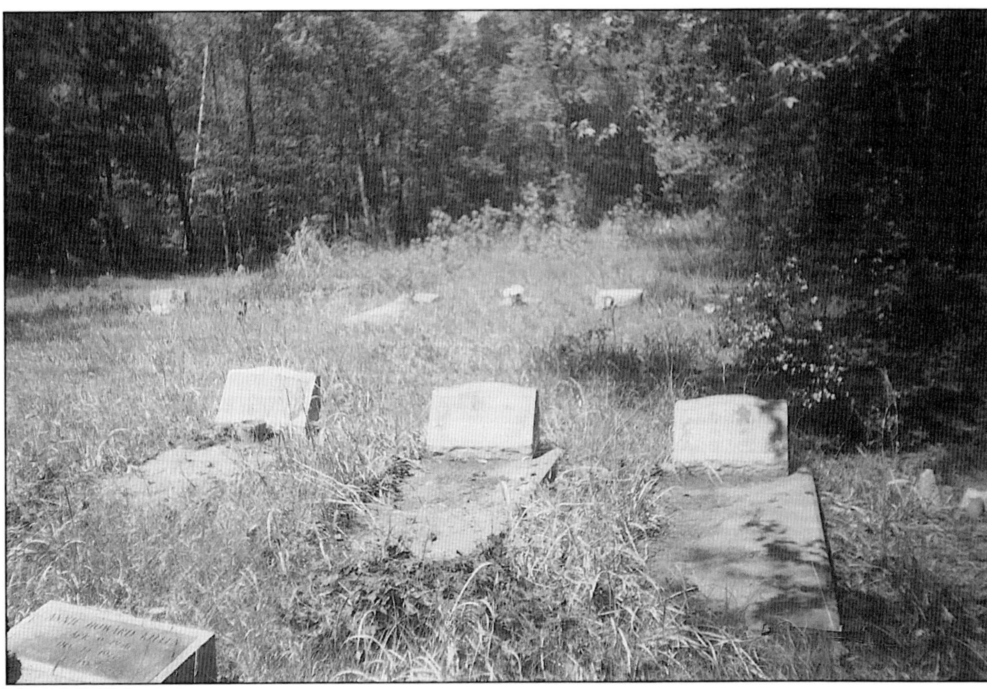

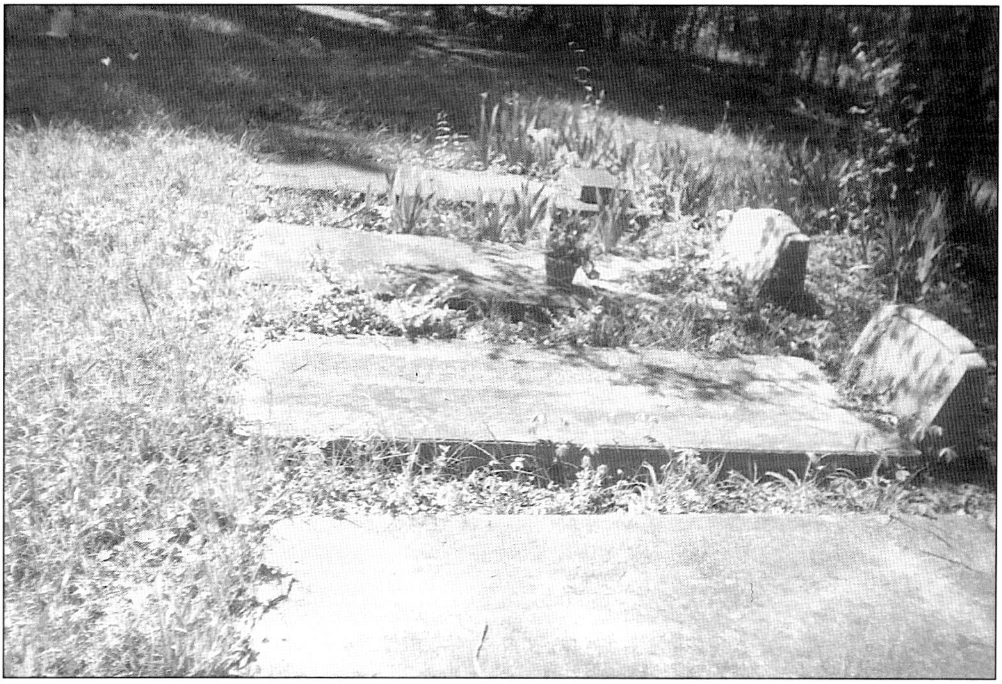

The Lundy Chapel Cemetery. The cemetery is located off Forest Hill Road behind the Lundy Chapel Church. George Washington Howard and many of his descendants are buried here. The Andrew Tolliver Family Cemetery is located in close proximity to this one. Mr. Tolliver was an outstanding pioneer and leader in the Summerfield community.

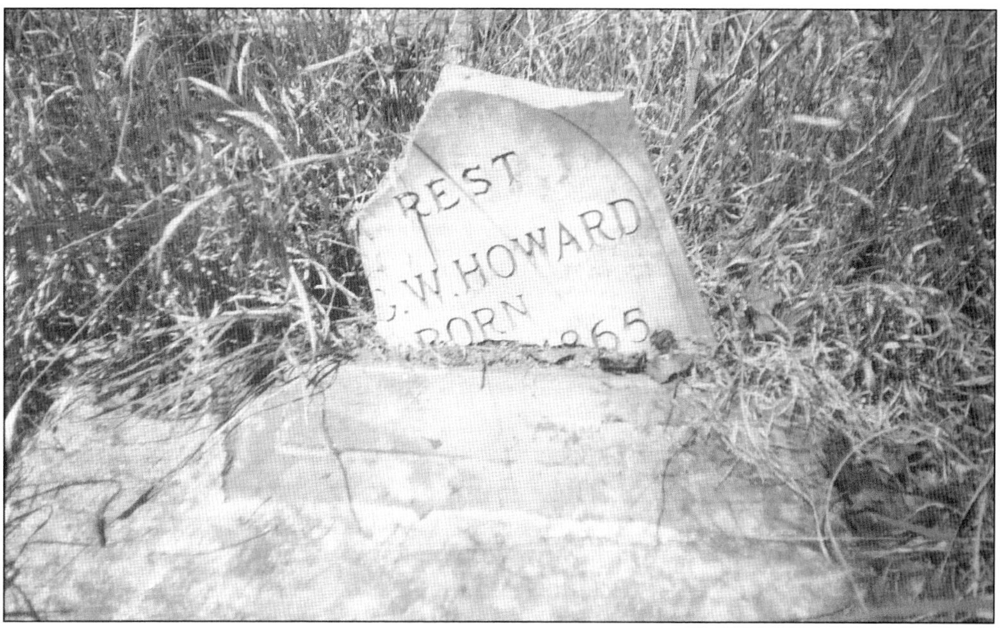

The Final Resting Place of George Washington Howard. Several years ago, this cemetery was vandalized and many old headstones and slabs were broken and destroyed. This is what remains of his once statuesque headstone. He was born in 1865 and died in 1936.

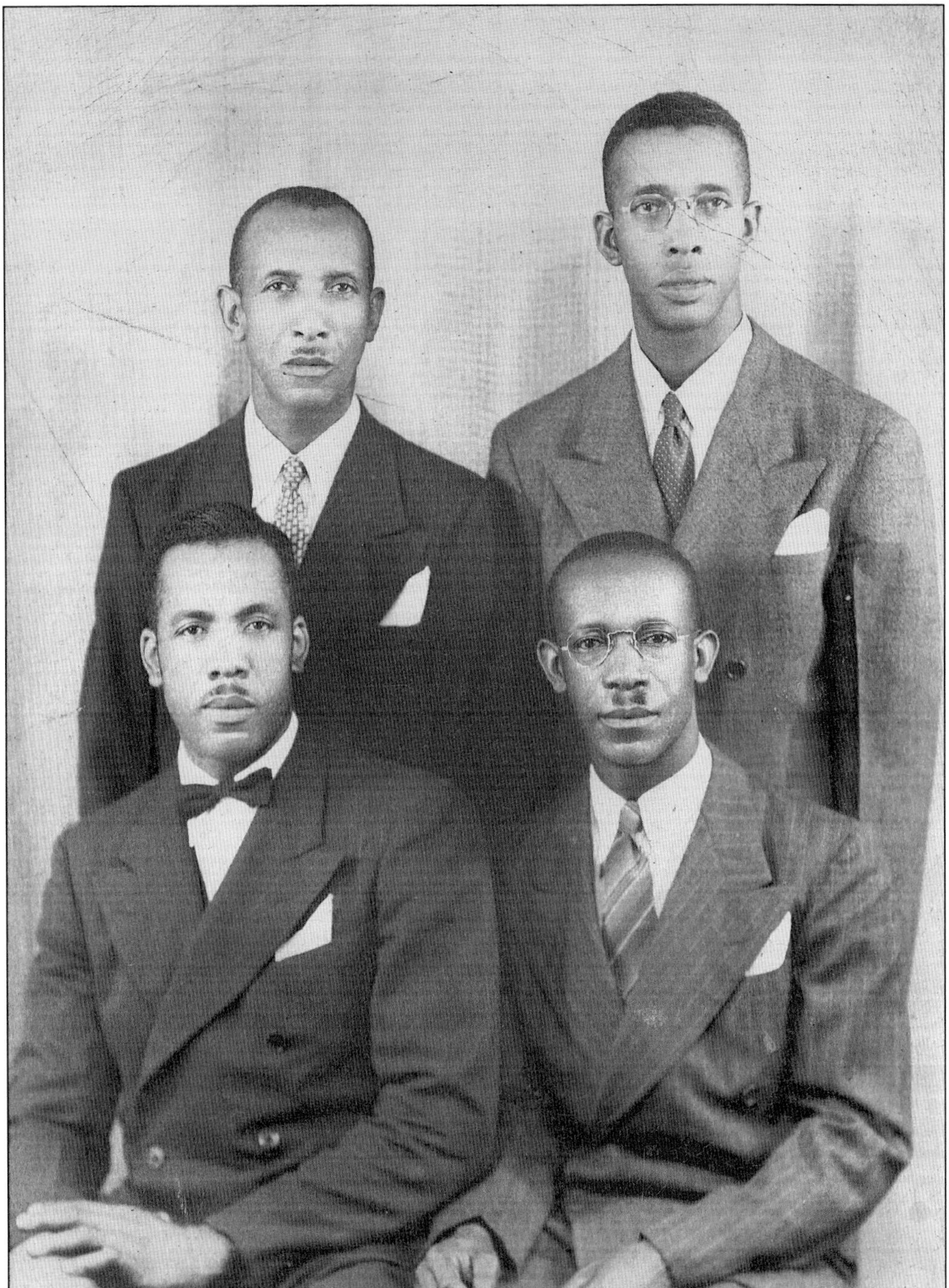

The Sons of George Washington Howard. After becoming adults, Isaac, Green, and George Jr. left Macon during the era of the great migration and moved to Detroit, MI. Emanuel also moved to Michigan but did not like the cold weather; he returned to Macon with his family shortly afterwards. This photograph was taken *c.* 1945 (Courtesy of Lois H. Miller and Lorena H. Latham.)

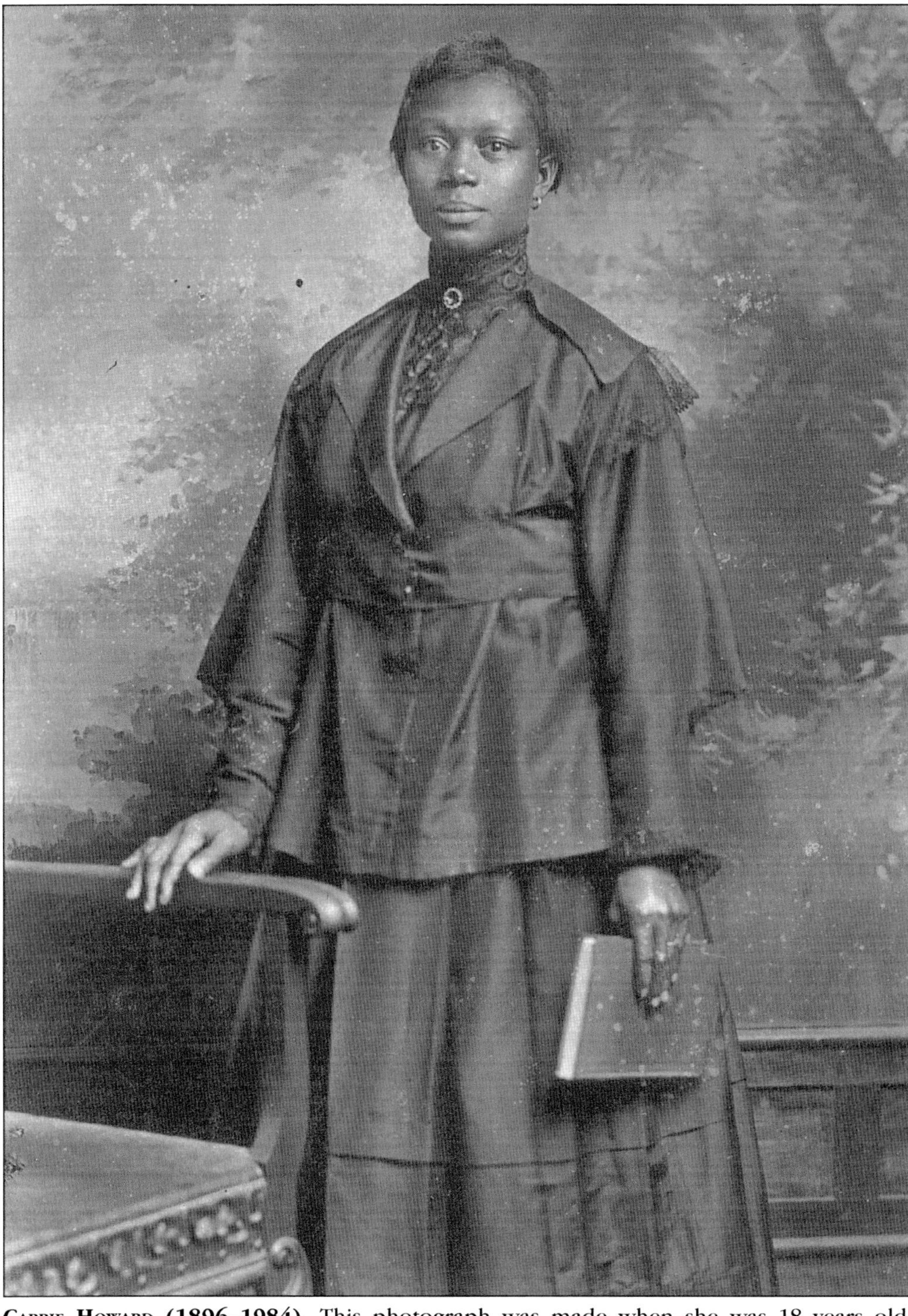

CARRIE HOWARD (1896–1984). This photograph was made when she was 18 years old, *c.* 1914. According to her daughter Susie, "Miss Carrie," as she was affectionately known, made the entire outfit herself. She was the sister of the four gentlemen on the preceding page. (Courtesy of Susie P. Ussery.)

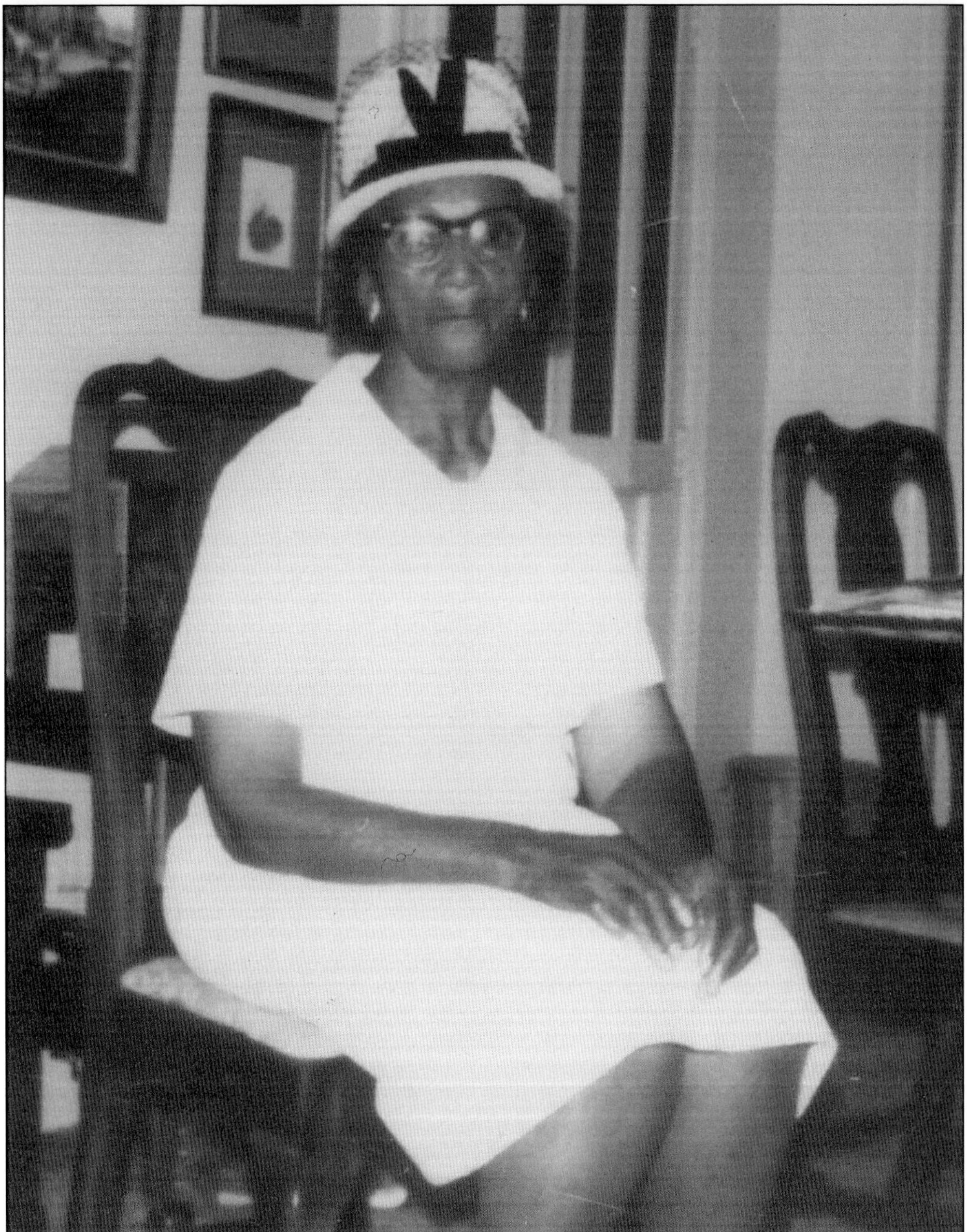

Carrie Howard-Pope. This photograph shows Miss Carrie at age 86. She was a wife, mother, grandmother, and great-grandmother at the time it was taken. She was known throughout the community for her poetry (dialogues), and was an orator who would speak at family gatherings and church meetings. Oral histories exemplify her virtue and willingness to share. One family story told by Mrs. Lois Miller is how Miss Carrie would never allow a visitor to leave her home without some type of gift. Sometimes the gift could be an egg, a slice of cake, a dime or quarter, or perhaps syrup and biscuits. This was Southern hospitality at its best! This photograph was taken *c.* 1983. (Courtesy of Susie P. Ussery.)

LEVI MILLER. Miller is pictured as a baby wearing a beautiful hand made christening gown, *c.* 1914 (Courtesy of Lois H. Miller.)

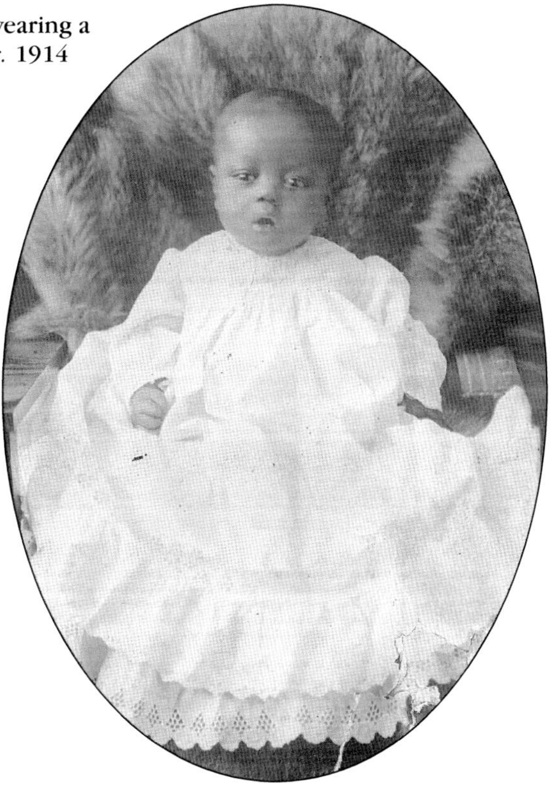

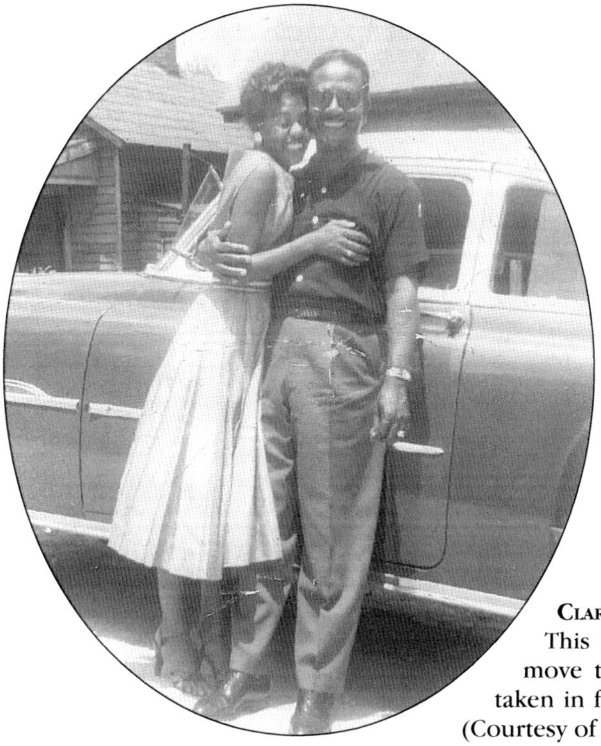

CLARA BELLE MILLER AND JOHN J.H. MILLER. This father and daughter left Macon to move to Cleveland, OH. The picture was taken in front of friend's home in the 1950s. (Courtesy of Lois H. Miller.)

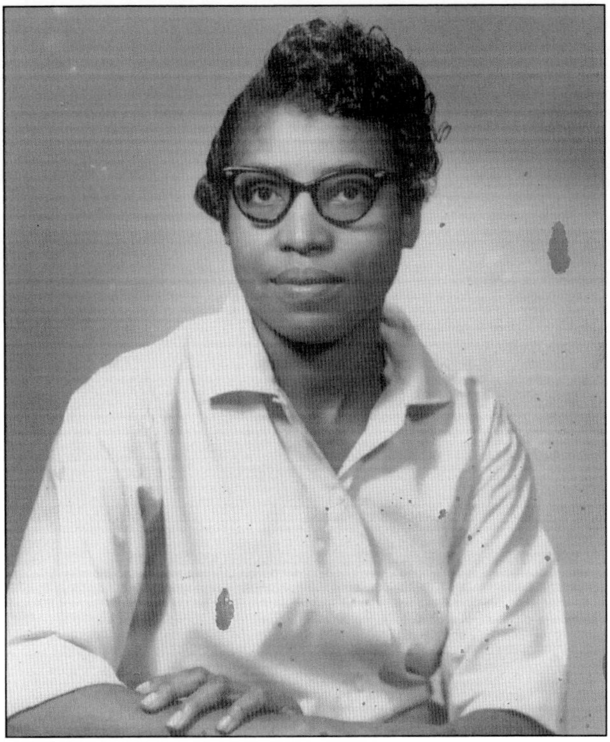

LORENA HOWARD. The daughter of Emanuel and Annie Howard Sr., Lorena is photographed here *c.* 1946. (Courtesy of Lorena H. Latham.)

LORENA AND WALTER LATHAM. This photo was taken *c.* 1958 on Riverside Drive on a Sunday afternoon. (Courtesy of Jeanne C. Herring.)

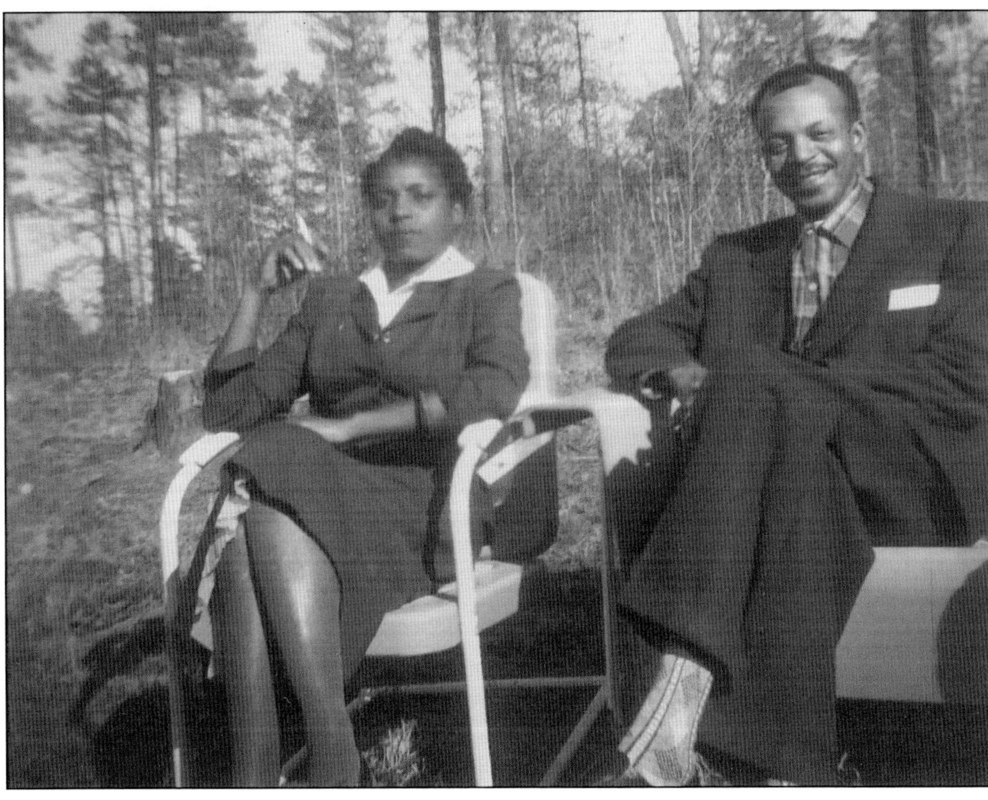

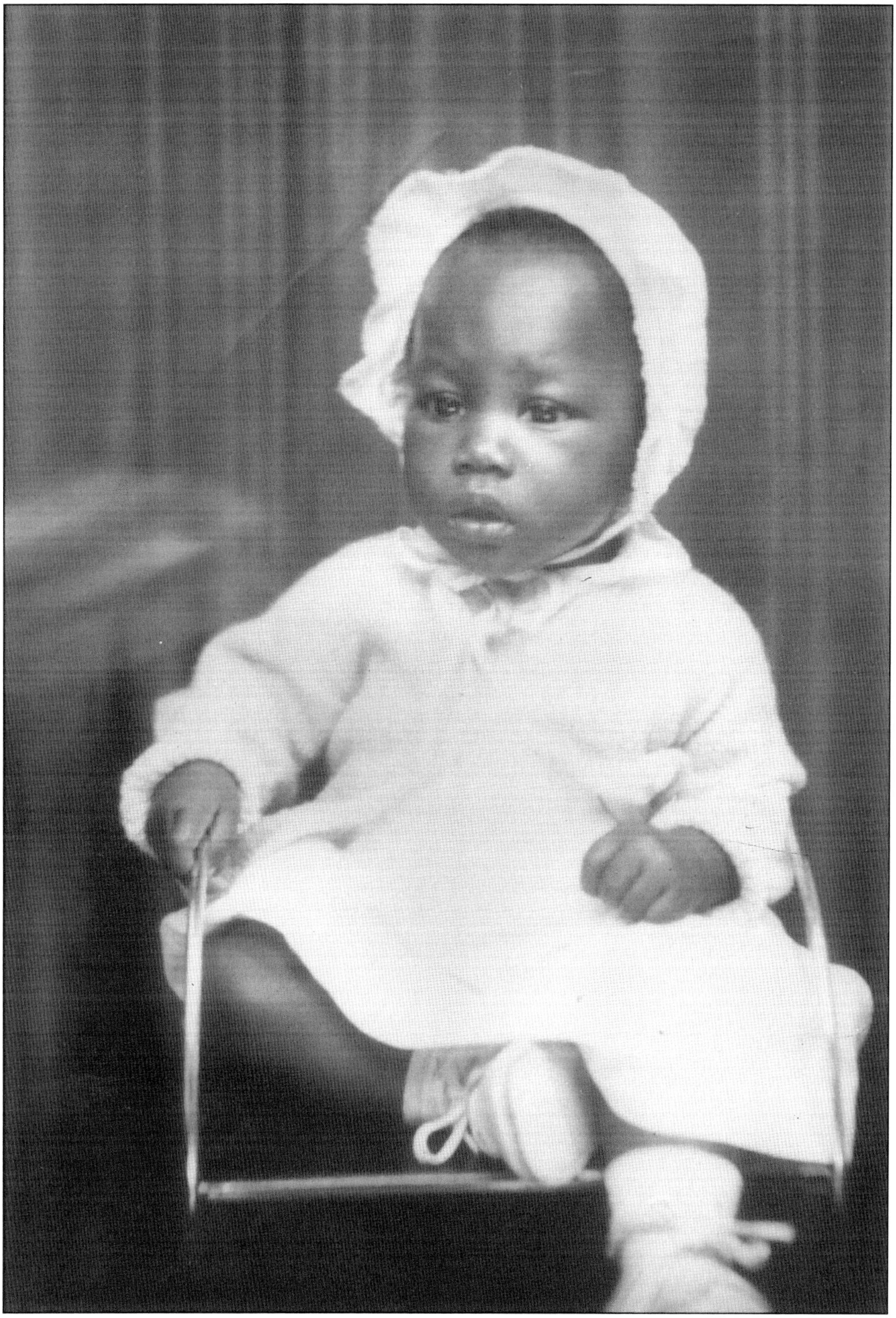

PATRICIA USSERY. Dressed up for the camera in a beautiful spring outfit *c.* 1953, Patricia is the daughter of Joseph and Susie P. Ussery. (Courtesy of Susie P. Ussery.)

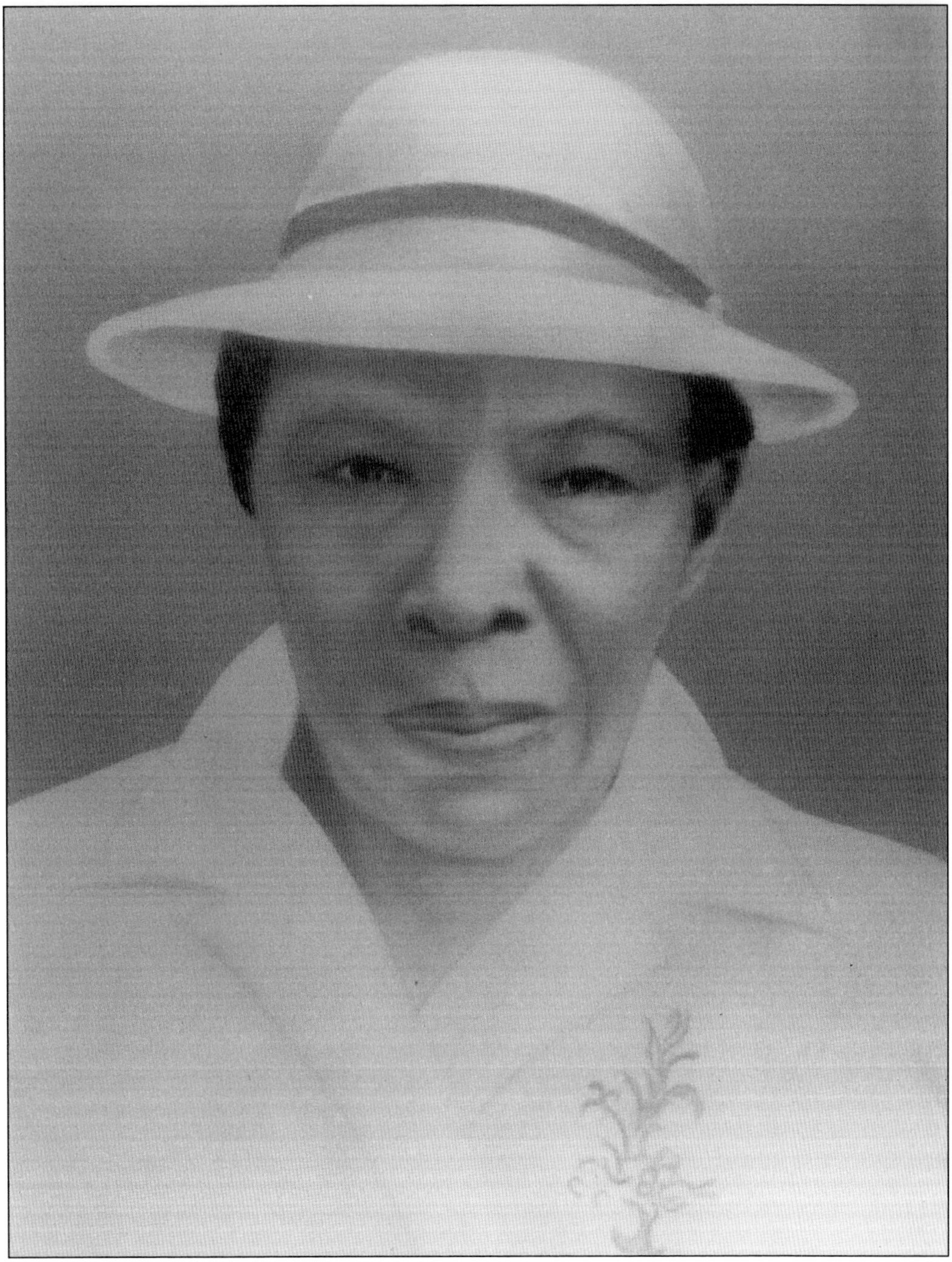

Kate Ussery. According to oral history, Mrs. Ussery held one of the most important positions in the Summerfield community—she was a mid-wife. Along with another lady, Mrs. Rena Simmons, Mrs. Ussery delivered babies throughout the community. This was during the time when medical care for African Americans was almost nonexistent. Living in the rural areas only made getting competent care more difficult, especially when faced with the obstacles of white supremacy and segregation. Mrs. Ussery and Mrs. Simmons fulfilled a much-needed service. This photo was taken *c.* 1935 (Courtesy of Susie P. Ussery.)

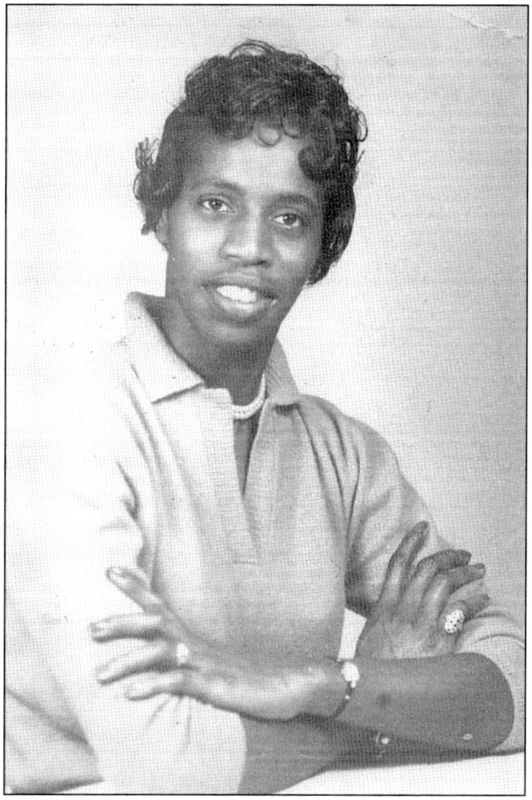

Carmen Virginia Howard. The daughter of Mr. and Mrs. Emanuel Howard, Carmen is pictured here *c.* 1960 (Courtesy of Lorena H. Latham.)

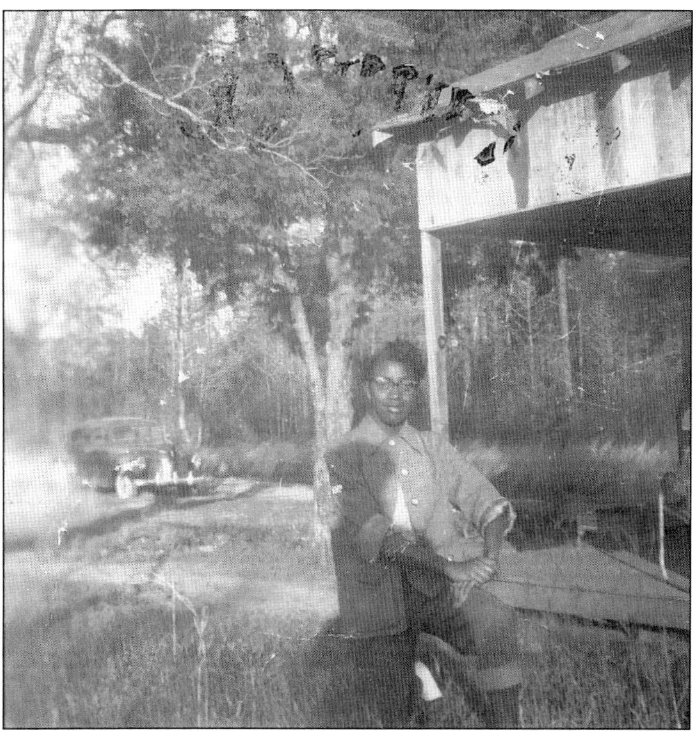

Annie Ruth Howard. Annie Ruth is pictured in the side yard of her parent's home at the age of 15, *c.* 1951. The child sitting on the porch is unidentified. This home was located Arkwright Road, and the property belonging to Mr. and Mrs. Emanuel Howard Sr. (Courtesy of Lorena H. Latham.)

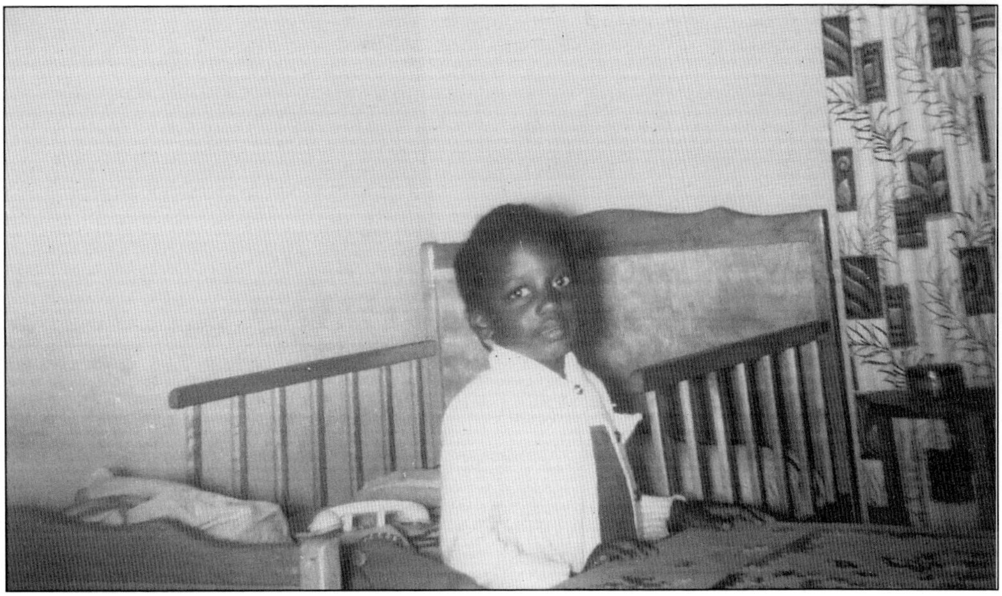

Gail Yvette Howard. Gail is seen here *c.* 1959, at the age of five, in the bedroom of her home on Clinton Road in East Macon. (Courtesy of Jeanne C. Herring.)

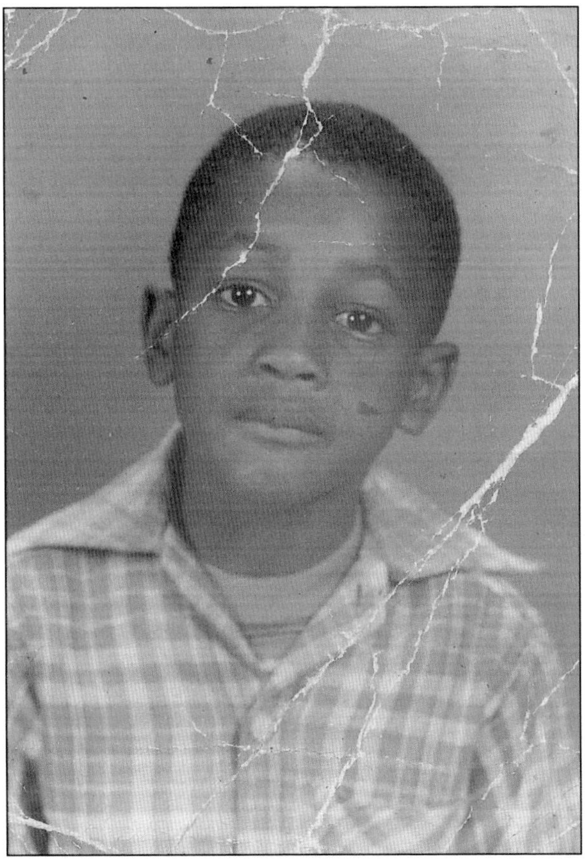

Larry Darnell Howard. Larry was a student at Minnie Butler Elementary School when this this photo was taken in 1956. (Courtesy of Lorena H. Latham.)

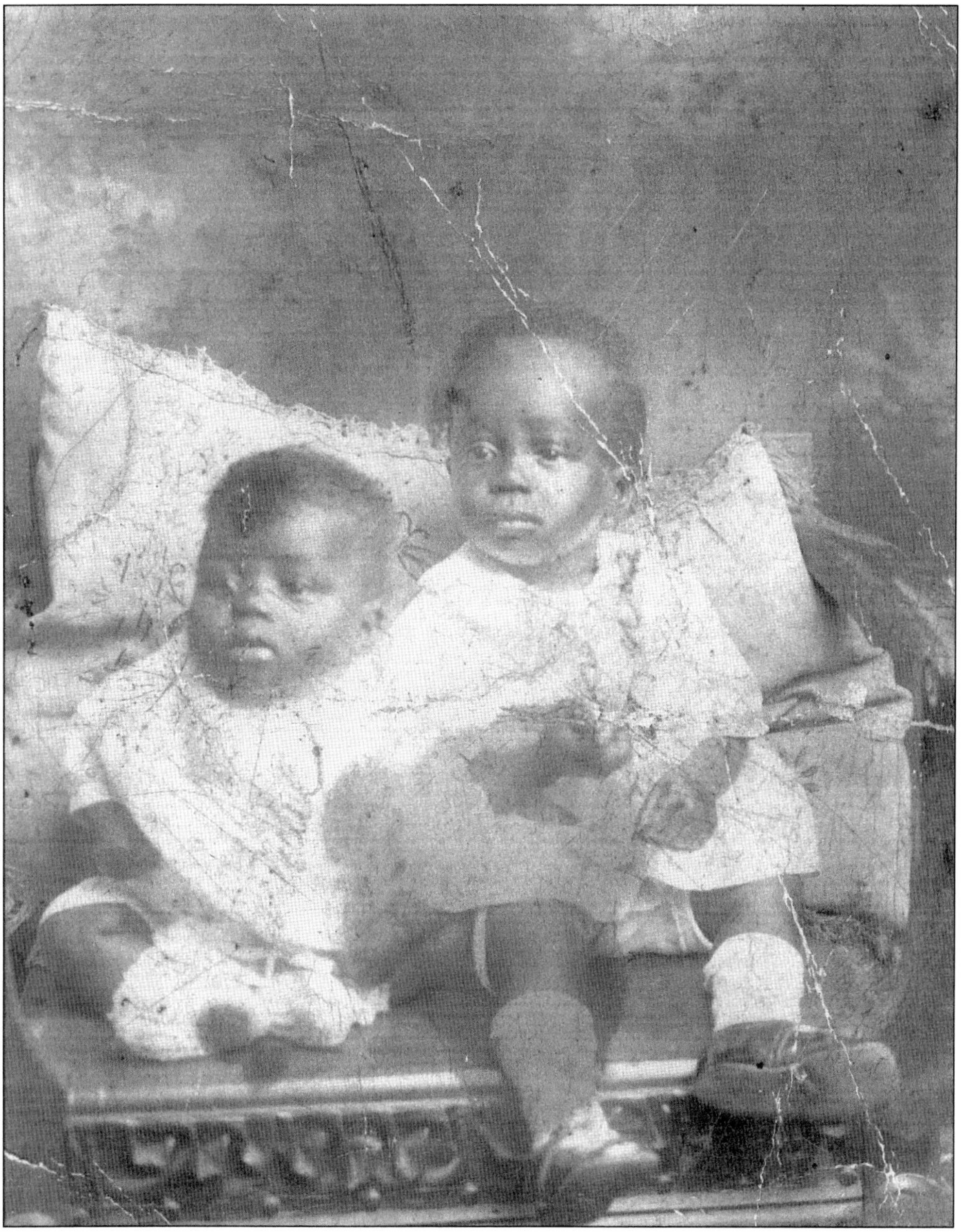

LORENA ANDREW HOWARD AND LOIS HOWARD. Sisters born only 11 months apart, they remain close to this day. They are the daughters of Mr. and Mrs. Emanuel Howard Sr. Lorena's birthday is May 1 and Lois's birthday is May 18. Lois would grow up to be the mother of the author. Lorena received a "special name" from her older sister, Lois. The story goes that often times when they were playing outside some problem would occur in their playtime experiences and Lois would call to her baby sister to go inside. She could not say "baby"—it would come out "bae-be"—and to this day Lorena is still referred to by family members by her special name, "Bae-be." This photo was taken *c.* 1927. (Courtesy of Lois H. Miller.)

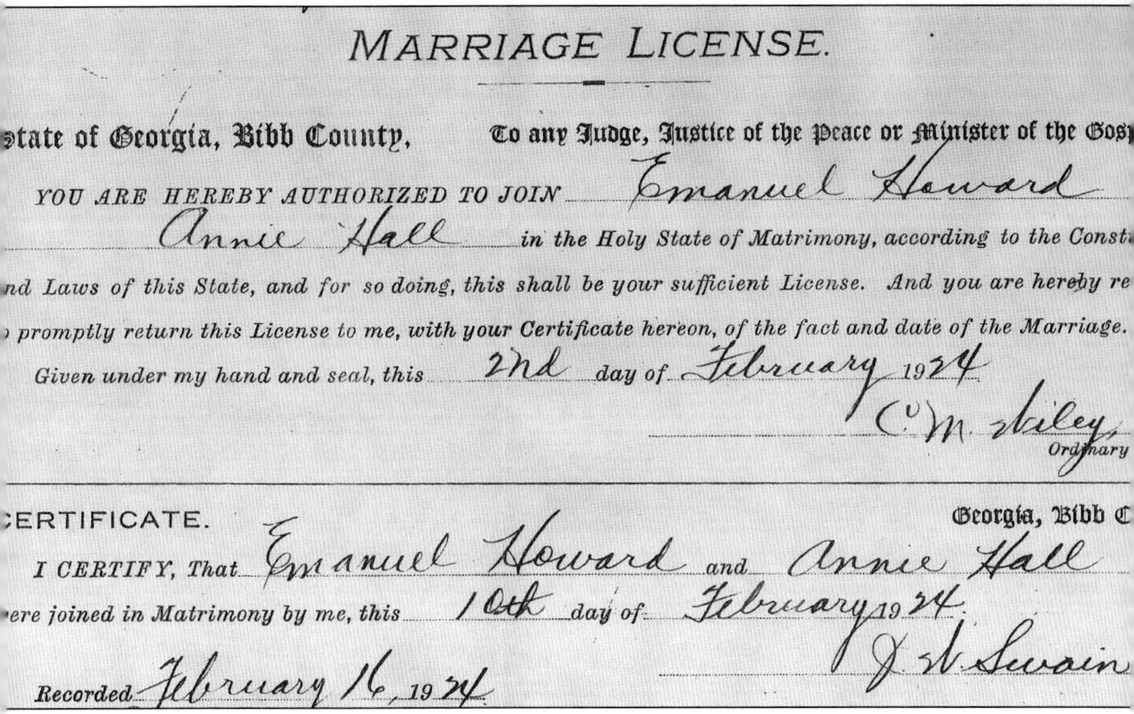

MARRIAGE LICENSE.

State of Georgia, Bibb County, To any Judge, Justice of the Peace or Minister of the Gos

YOU ARE HEREBY AUTHORIZED TO JOIN Emanuel Howard

Annie Hall in the Holy State of Matrimony, according to the Const

nd Laws of this State, and for so doing, this shall be your sufficient License. And you are hereby re

promptly return this License to me, with your Certificate hereon, of the fact and date of the Marriage.

Given under my hand and seal, this 2nd day of February 1924

C. M. Wiley, Ordinary

CERTIFICATE. Georgia, Bibb C

I CERTIFY, That Emanuel Howard and Annie Hall

ere joined in Matrimony by me, this 10th day of February 1924.

J. W. Swain

Recorded February 16, 1924

A Marriage License. This document is a copy of the marriage license of Emanuel Howard and Annie Hall. They were married February 10, 1924. A marriage license was a highly regarded document at this particular time in history for African Americans, mainly because they were not allowed to marry during slavery. "Jumping over the Broom" became the ritual for partnership. Marriage licenses were often framed and displayed in homes for family and visitors to see. Divorce was not even a consideration of these early families. Marriage was an accomplishment, and was encouraged by the elders. (Courtesy of Bibb County Court House Records.)

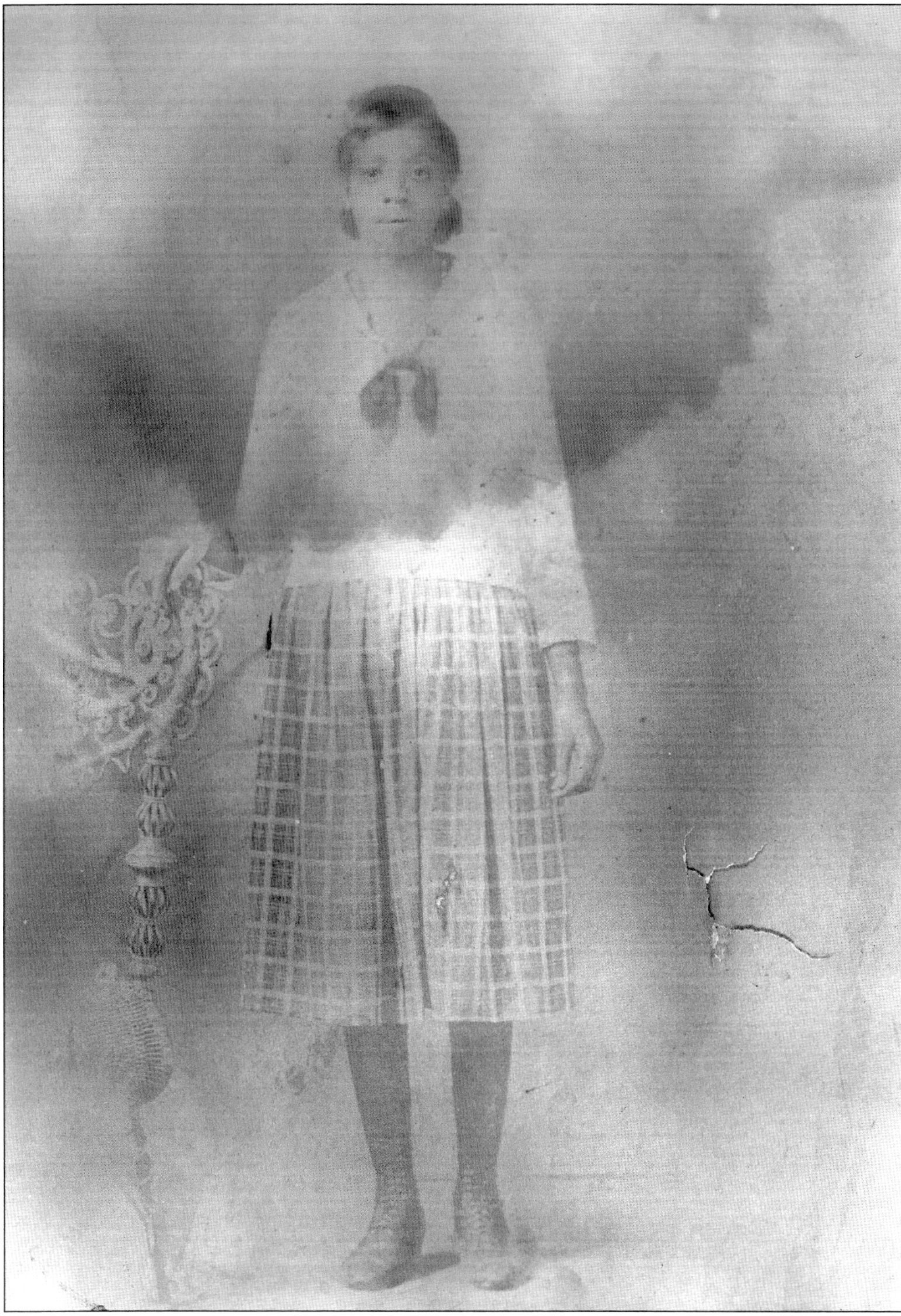

ANNIE CATHERINE HALL HOWARD. The author's maternal grandmother is pictured here *c.* 1920 at the age of 16. She died in 1961 at the age of 54. (Courtesy of Lorena H. Latham.)

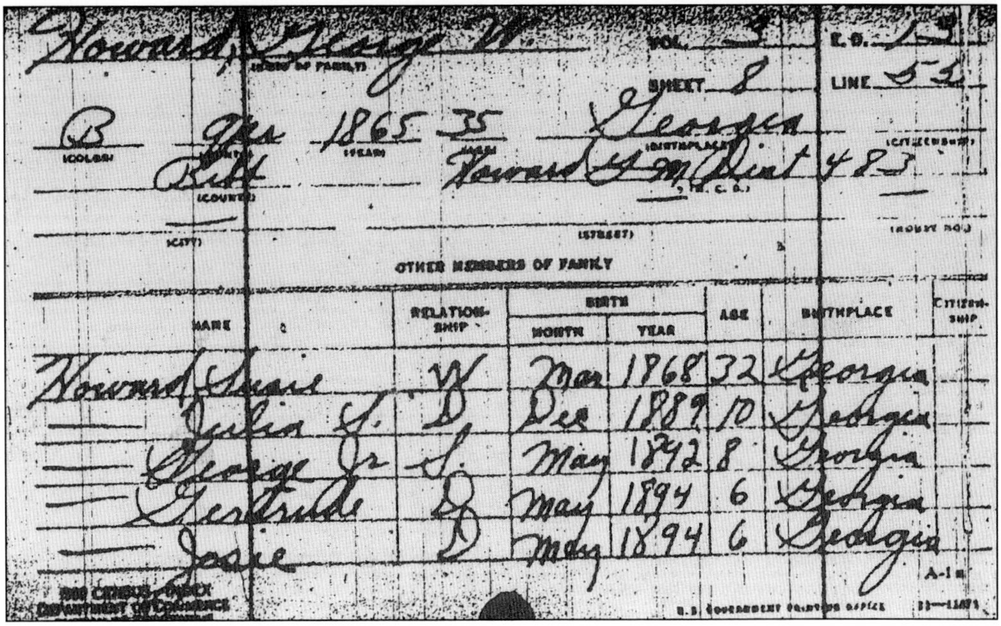

Howard, George W. (HEAD OF FAMILY) VOL. 3 E.D. 13 SHEET 8 LINE 55

B (COLOR) Mar (MONTH) 1865 (YEAR) 35 (AGE) Georgia (BIRTHPLACE) (CITIZENSHIP)

Bibb (COUNTY) Howard G M Dist 483 (M.C.D.)

(CITY) (STREET) (HOUSE NO.)

OTHER MEMBERS OF FAMILY

NAME	RELATIONSHIP	BIRTH MONTH	BIRTH YEAR	AGE	BIRTHPLACE	CITIZENSHIP
Howard Susie	W	Mar	1868	32	Georgia	
— Julia S.	D	Dec	1889	10	Georgia	
— George Jr	S	May	1892	8	Georgia	
— Gertrude	D	May	1894	6	Georgia	
— Josie	D	May	1894	6	Georgia	

1900 CENSUS—INDEX DEPARTMENT OF COMMERCE A-1a U.S. GOVERNMENT PRINTING OFFICE

The 1900 Census. Shown here are copies of the 1900 Census index from the department of commerce. Seven of George Washington Howard's children are listed. His 12 children included the following: Julia, born in December 1889; George Jr., May 1892; Gertrude and Josephine (twins), May 1894; Carrie, January 1896; Isaac, December 1897; and Emanuel, July 1906. Not listed on this report are Roy, Susie Lee, Elnora, Green, and Albert. (Courtesy of Bibb County Court House Records.)

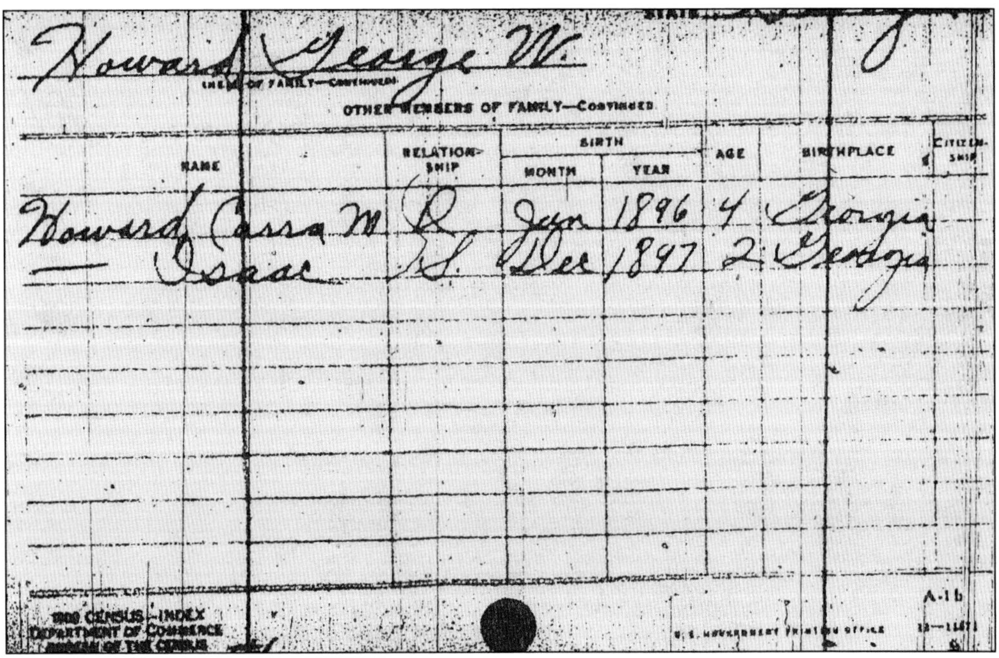

Howard, George W. (HEAD OF FAMILY—CONTINUED)

OTHER MEMBERS OF FAMILY—CONTINUED

NAME	RELATIONSHIP	BIRTH MONTH	BIRTH YEAR	AGE	BIRTHPLACE	CITIZENSHIP
Howard Carra M	D	Jan	1896	4	Georgia	
— Isaac	S	Dec	1897	2	Georgia	

1900 CENSUS—INDEX DEPARTMENT OF COMMERCE BUREAU OF THE CENSUS A-1b U.S. GOVERNMENT PRINTING OFFICE

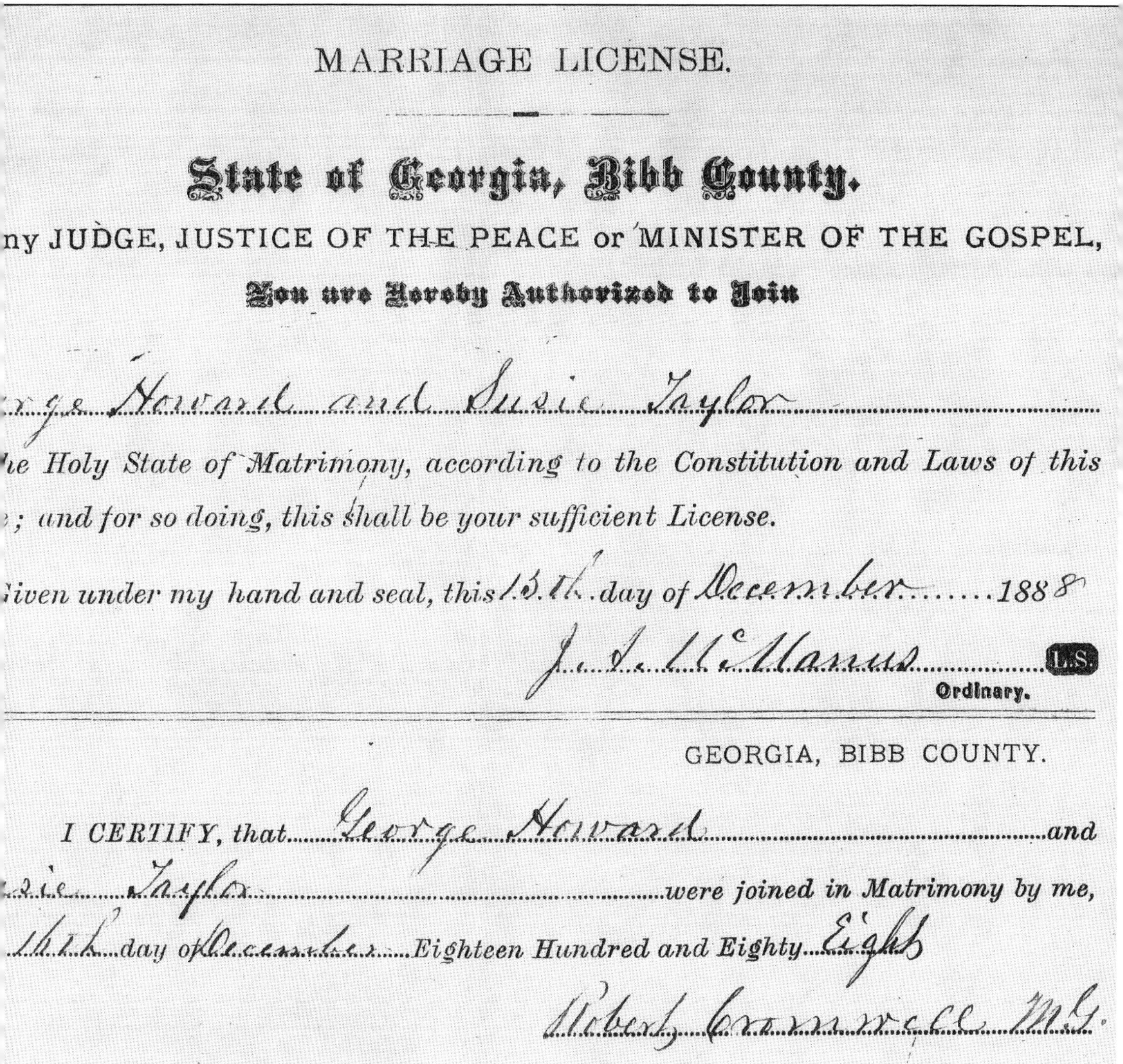

MARRIAGE LICENSE.

State of Georgia, Bibb County.

[A]ny JUDGE, JUSTICE OF THE PEACE or MINISTER OF THE GOSPEL,

You are Hereby Authorized to Join

[Geor]ge Howard and Susie Taylor

[in t]he *Holy State of Matrimony, according to the Constitution and Laws of this*
[State]; *and for so doing, this shall be your sufficient License.*

[G]*iven under my hand and seal, this* 13th *day of* December 1888

J. A. McManus (L.S.)
Ordinary.

GEORGIA, BIBB COUNTY.

I CERTIFY, that George Howard *and*
[Su]sie Taylor *were joined in Matrimony by me,*
[this] 16th *day of* December *Eighteen Hundred and Eighty* Eight

Robert Cromwell M.G.

Holy Matrimony. This document is a copy of the marriage license for George Washington Howard and Susie Taylor. They were married on December 16, 1888. (Courtesy of Bibb County Court House Records.)

Slave Codes

That all and every person and persons whatsoever, who shall hereafter teach, or cause any slave or slaves to be taught to write or read writing, or shall employ any slave in any manner of writing whatsoever, every such person and persons shall for every offense forfeit the sum of twenty pounds sterling.

[Adapted from Slave Code: 1770, Act of May 10, 1770, in Watkins Digest, 163-77.]

Because of the growing number of slaves in the Georgia colony, laws had to be enacted in order to govern the behavior of the slave, and in some cases the slave owner. This law was passed by the colonial Georgia General Assembly . It shows the legal position of Georgia's slave population.

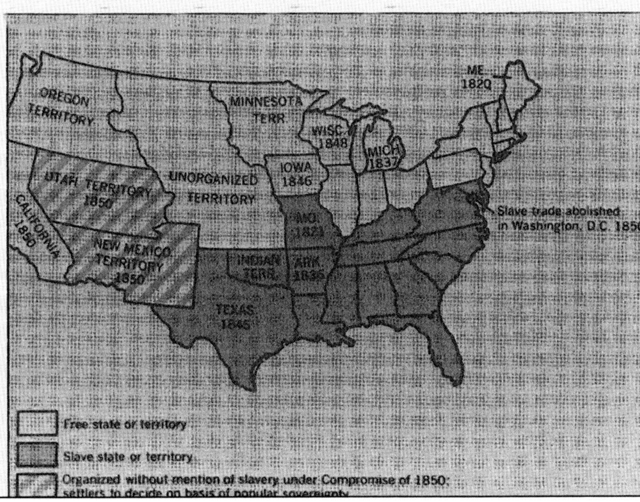

Three

Education:
Communal, Public, and Private

African Americans have always embraced education, because so many other doors were closed in the faces of people of color. The black community created the first learning environment. From the moment the Africans set foot upon the land that would one day be America, education and learning became a goal. Learning then meant doing whatever it took in order to survive.

In the city of Macon during slavery, opportunities for blacks were extremely limited. Even "free blacks" were discriminated against because of attitudes about color and background. On the plantation, slaves learned many jobs. If they became really skilled at their job, then their lives would be somewhat "easier." Communal forms of education in Macon came from preachers, individuals who could read or write, and liberal whites that took risks in order to help educate blacks. Adriadine Sellers started the first school for blacks in 1865. Many other blacks started communal schools. Elizea Miller started a school in a hospital. Ballard Normal and Lewis High came soon after. Neighbors taught children and young adults the skills they knew. Public education first appeared in Macon around 1872. Some of the public schools included Unionville, Bethel, Union Church, Antioch, Swift Creek, and several others. Even though blacks had schools, unfortunately they were still operating below white standards.

In Macon, public school education for black children started off far behind that of white children. Most of the schools were in session only for four to six months. They did not have adequate materials, and there were perhaps 50 students to every teacher. Most classrooms did not have enough heat in winter and not enough seats year-round.

Private schools for blacks began to appear soon after the Civil War. In 1868, the American Missionary Association constructed buildings in Macon to be used by black students. Concerned white liberals secretly donated money for books and materials. The American Baptist Home Mission Board built schools. Even with all this support, many children were not being served however. Consequently, illiteracy and poverty remained rampant in many black communities in Macon for years after the Reconstruction.

Black Maconites had to fight discouragement from the majority of the white population. The whites could not see the reasoning behind blacks striving for higher education. The general consensus was, "They don't need to read or write to be cooks, maids, and ditch diggers." African-American Maconites also took part in the financial physical construction of their own educational needs. Mrs. Minnie Smith, who was a teacher, founded Beda-Etta College in 1921. Mrs. Smith used much of her own money for the building, and named the school for her two deceased sisters. Hudson Industrial High was started in the late 1920s. The main focus of this school was to teach and train students so that they could get a job. Higher learning also came in the form of the Lena Clemons Conservatory of Music and Art. The primary focus of this institution was to promote the arts and music. The school championed cultural activities, art exhibits, and it sponsored recitals often. Ballard Normal School opened to continue higher academic achievement for African Americans in Macon and the surrounding area in the late 1880s.

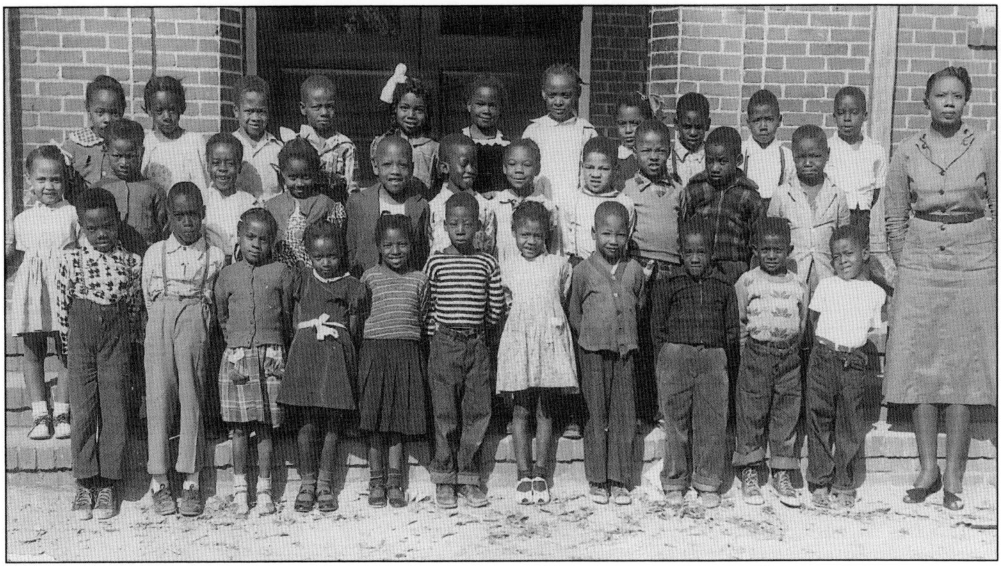

A Class Photo. A teacher and her first grade class are pictured at G.W. Carver School, *c.* 1939 (Courtesy of Booker T. Washington Center.)

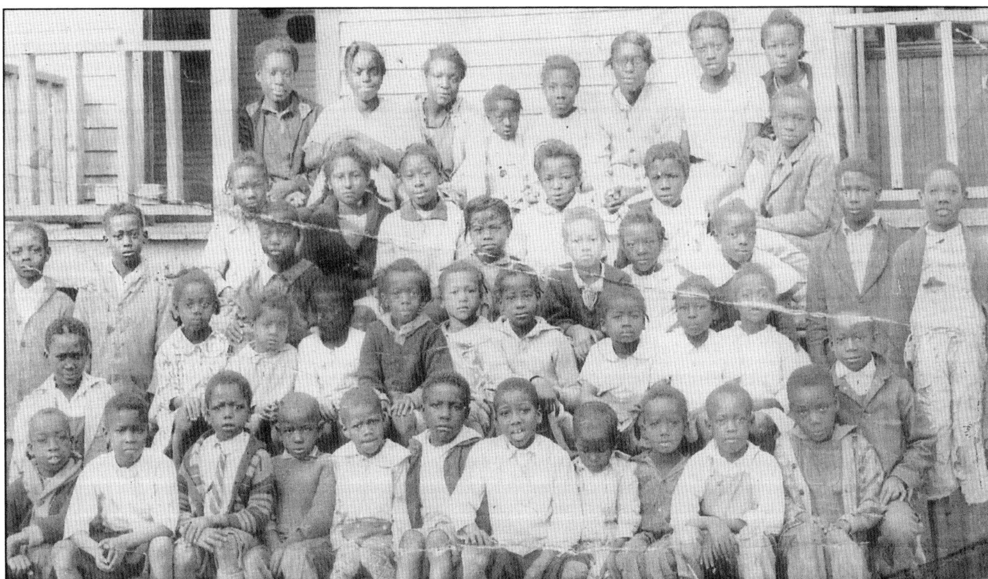

Summerfield School. This school was located on Old Lundy Road, which is presently Forest Hill Road. The children are assembled in front of the wooden dwelling for a class photograph, *c.* 1924. They are, from left to right, as follows: (front row) unidentified, unidentified, George Taylor, unidentified, Edward Tolliver, Warren Ussery, unidentified, Eddie Hall, unidentified, and John Pope; (second row) Beatrice Hall, unidentified, Mozelle Hall, Frances Tolliver, Isabelle Dumas, unidentified, unidentified, and unidentified; (third row) Ellis Davis, unidentified, unidentified, Lizzie Hollis, Laura Pope, Jessie Hall, unidentified, Narciss Hall, and John Simmons; (back row) unidentified, Wesley Mitchell, Polly Lockett, Julia Jarrell, Georgia Mae Simmons, Camilla Ussery, Rosa Hutchins, and unidentified. (Courtesy of Susie P. Ussery.)

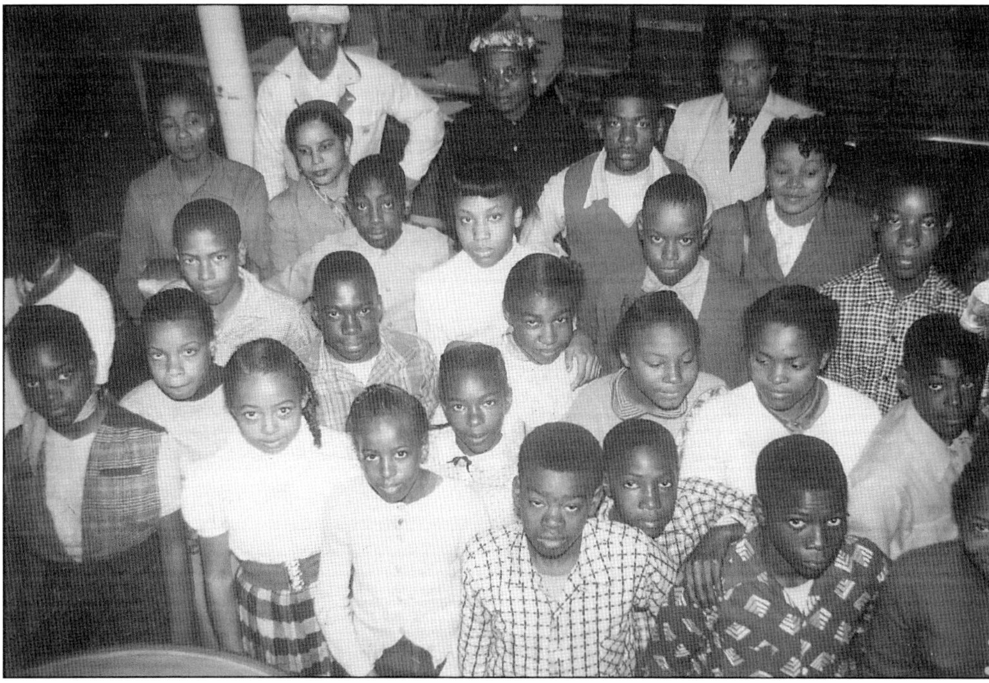

A Field Trip. A group of second graders are shown here on a field trip with their teachers to the American Bakeries Company, *c.* 1950s. They learned how bread was made as two bakery workers gave a demonstration. (Courtesy of Booker T. Washington Center.)

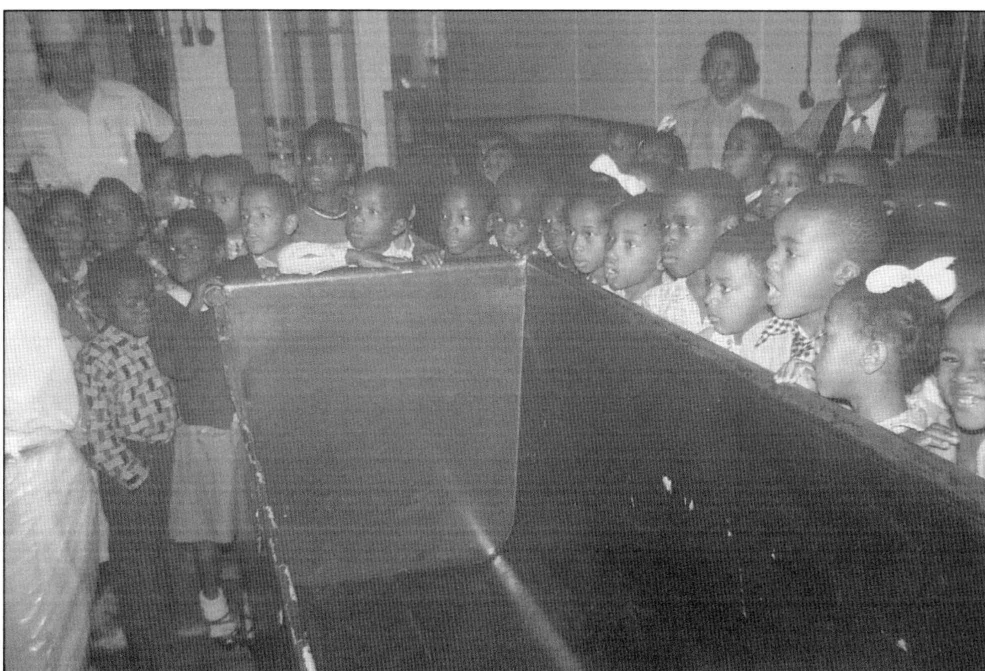

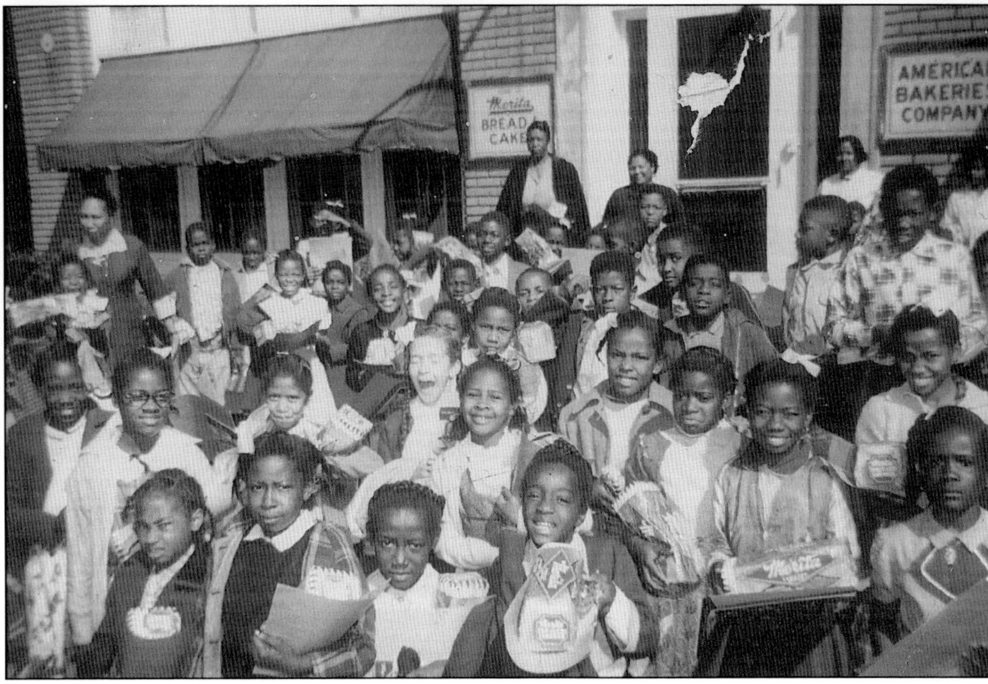

OUTSIDE THE BAKERY. Children and teachers pose outside American Bakeries Company for class pictures, *c.* 1950s. The company produced Merita bread, and each child received a loaf of bread during the field trip. (Courtesy of Booker T. Washington Center.)

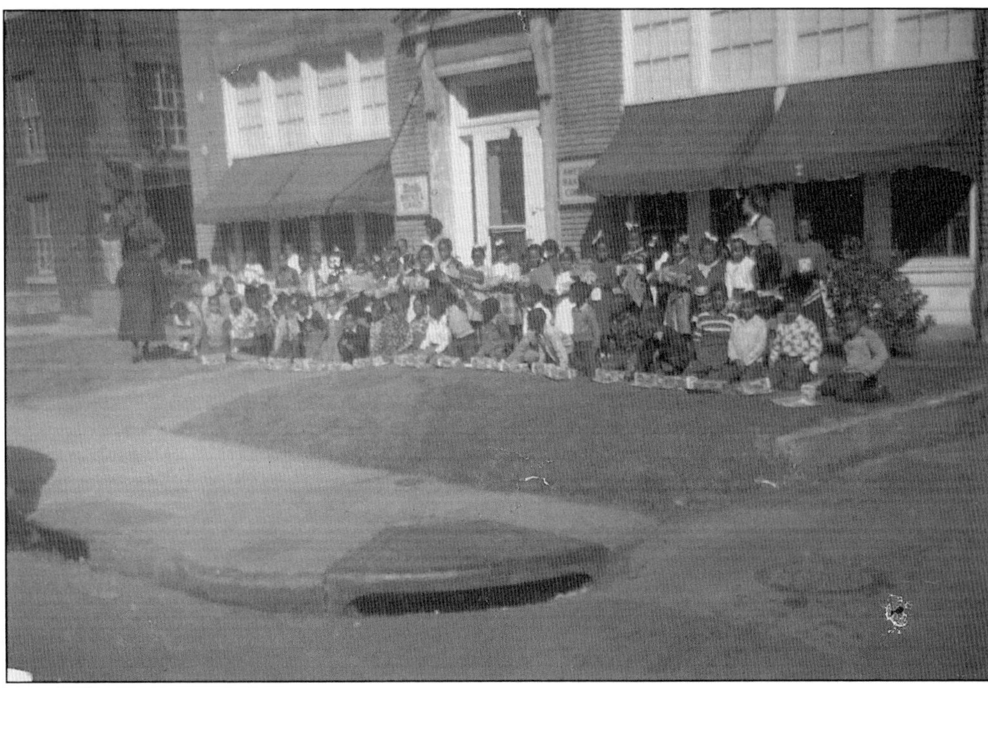

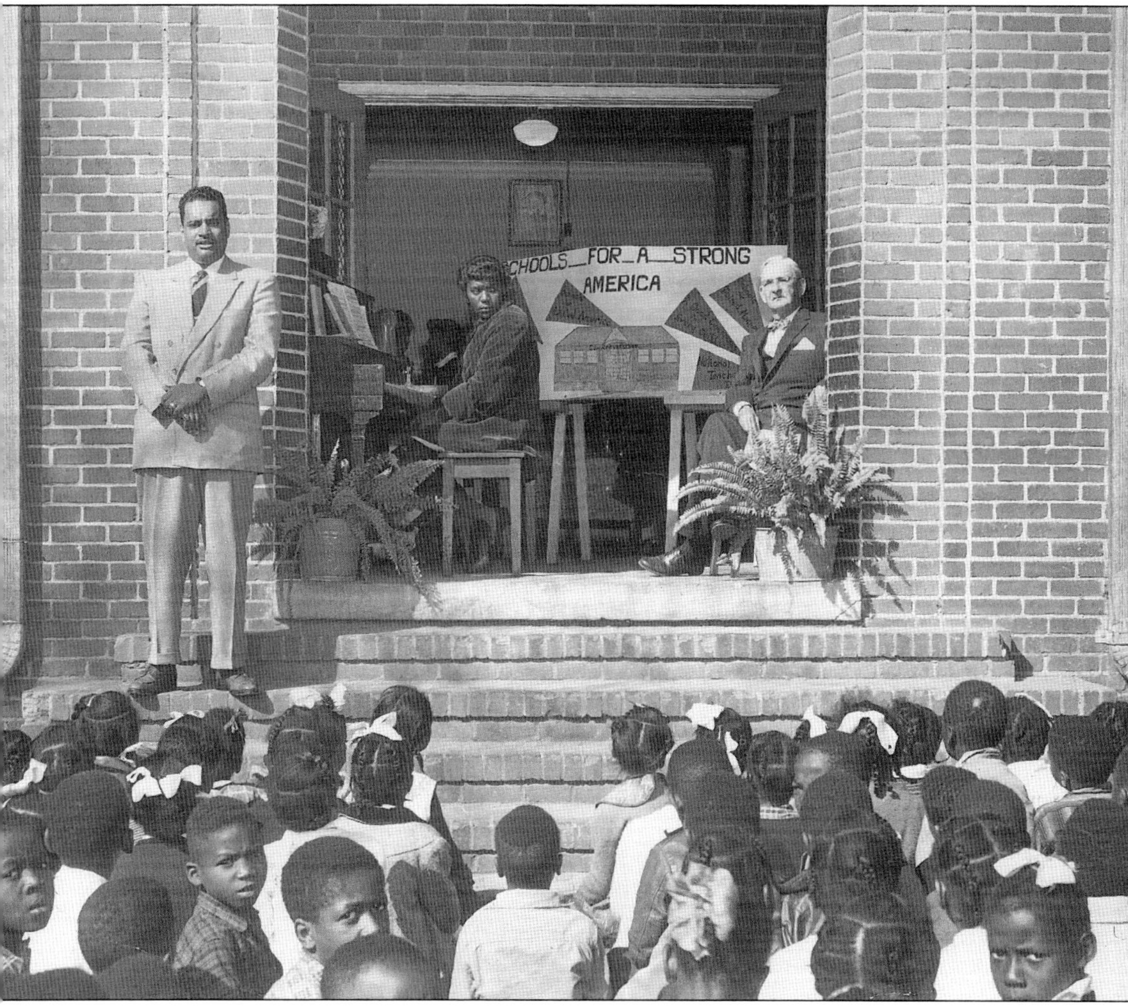

G.W. CARVER ELEMENTARY SCHOOL. Dr. Nixon, a piano player, an unidentified male member of the platform, and a group of young student s are pictured in the audience of G.W. Carver Elementary School. They are listening to a program highlighting a school for a strong America, *c.* 1940 (Courtesy of Booker T. Washington Center.)

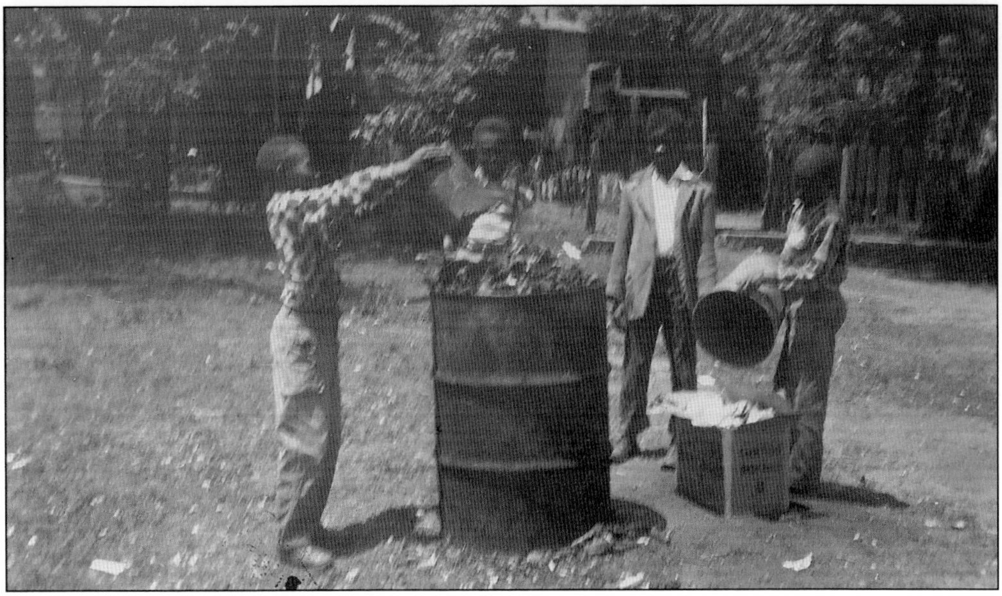

Yard Cleanup. In the photograph above, trash has been gathered and placed in a barrel to be burned, *c.* 1940s In the image below, five youngsters are pictured standing around a barrel of burning debris. They helped keep the schoolyard clean, *c.* 1948. At the time, students were expected to help keep the building and grounds clean, as there was no money available to hire janitors. (Both images courtesy of Booker T. Washington Center.)

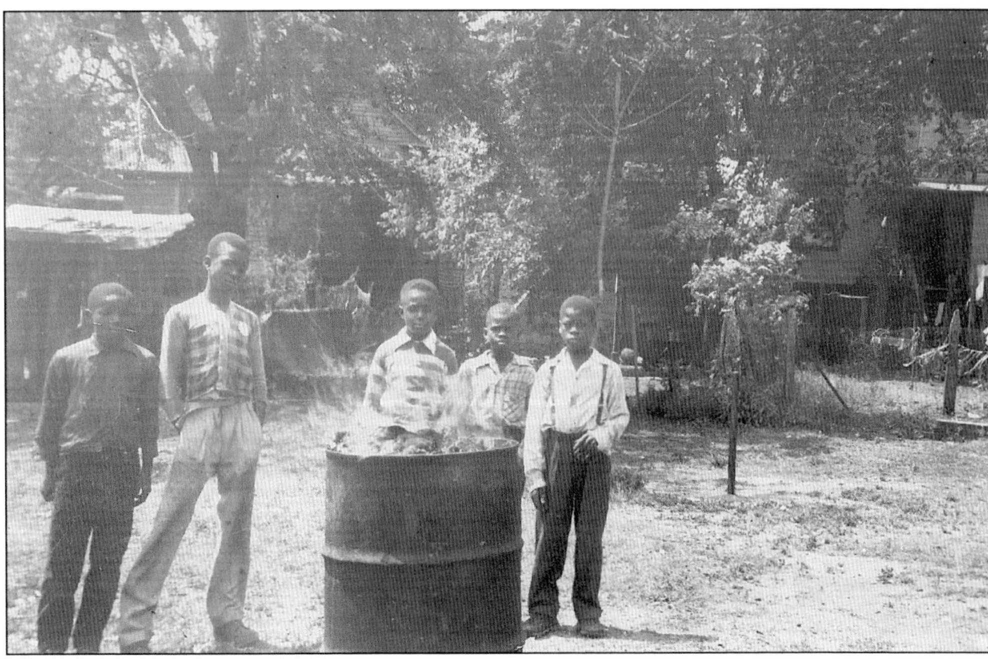

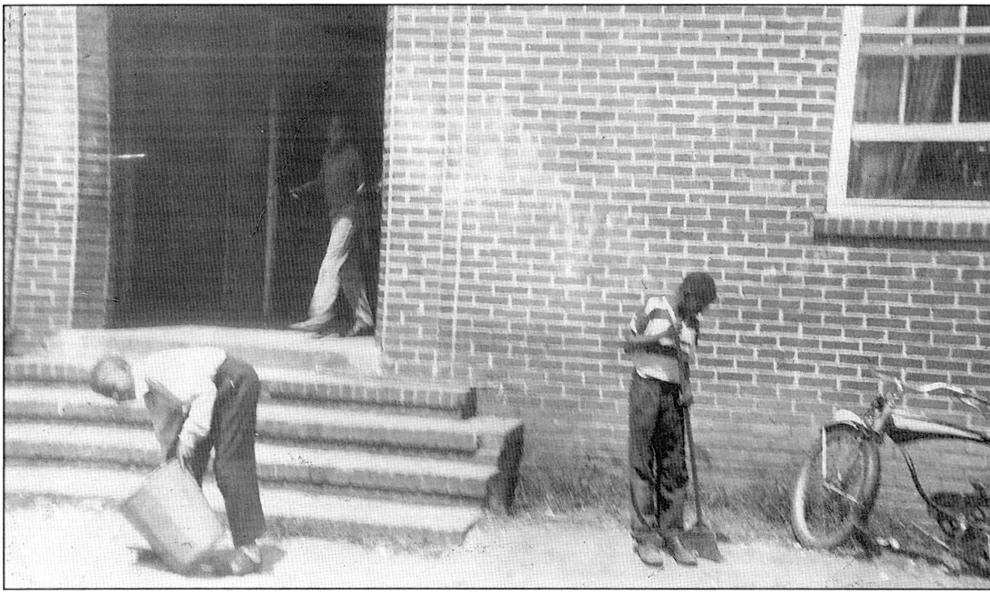

Maintaining the School. Young boys clean up outside of G.W. Carver, probably in the spring or summer. The windows are open as there was no air conditioning. This photo was taken *c.* 1948. (Courtesy of Booker T. Washington Center.)

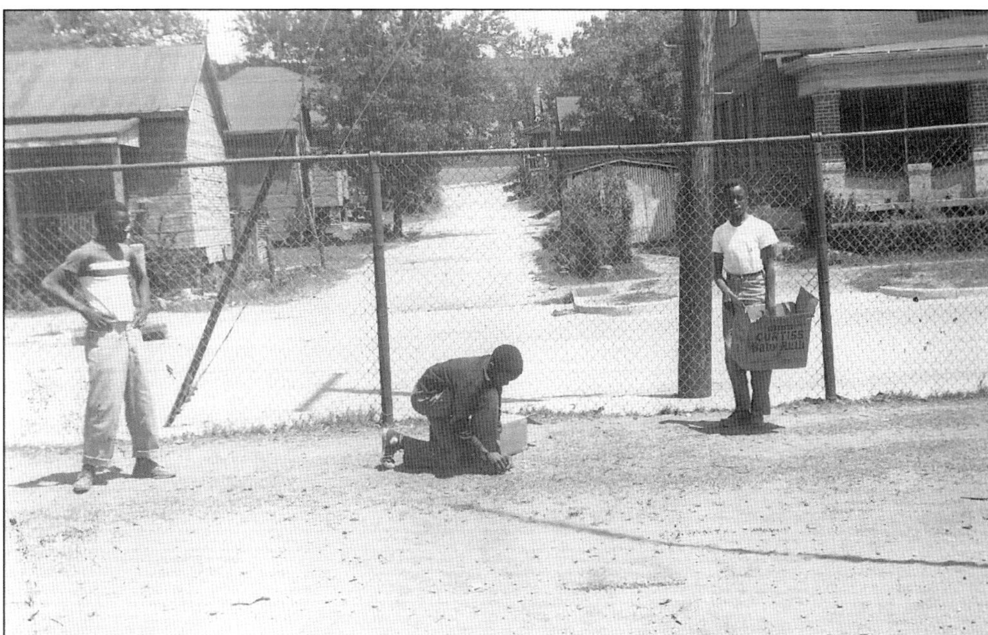

Keeping the Schoolyard Clean. Young men are pictured cleaning up Carver's playground, *c.* 1950s. A Rio Grande fence separates the school property from the unpaved street and the neighborhood. (Courtesy of Booker T. Washington Center.)

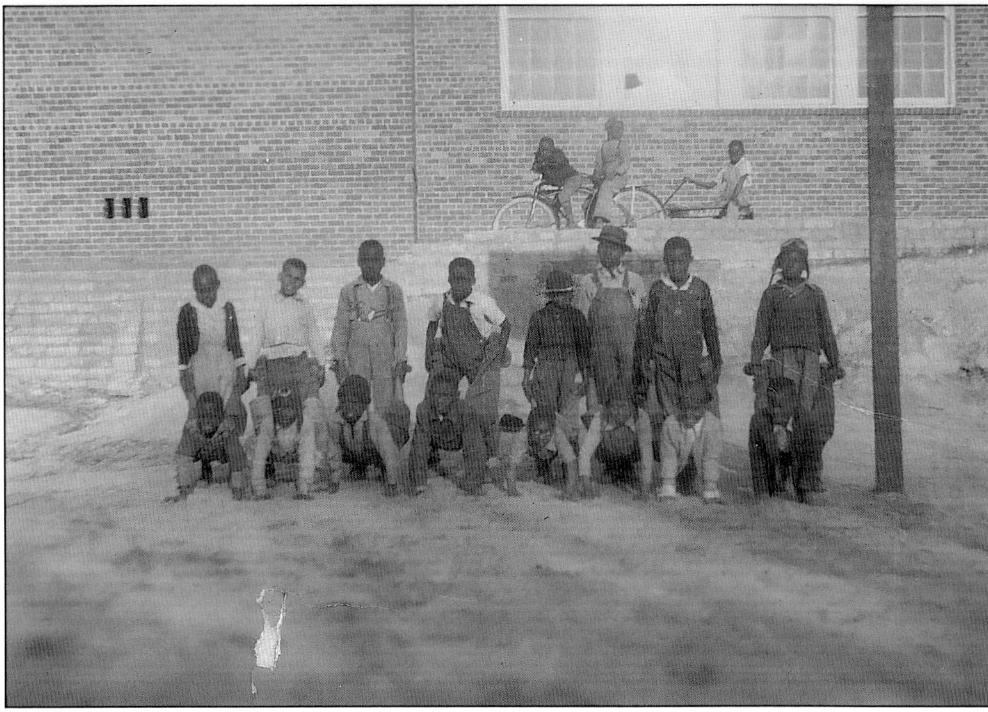

Children at Play. These children are pictured on the grounds of G.W. Carver School, *c.* 1950s. (Courtesy of Booker T. Washington Center.)

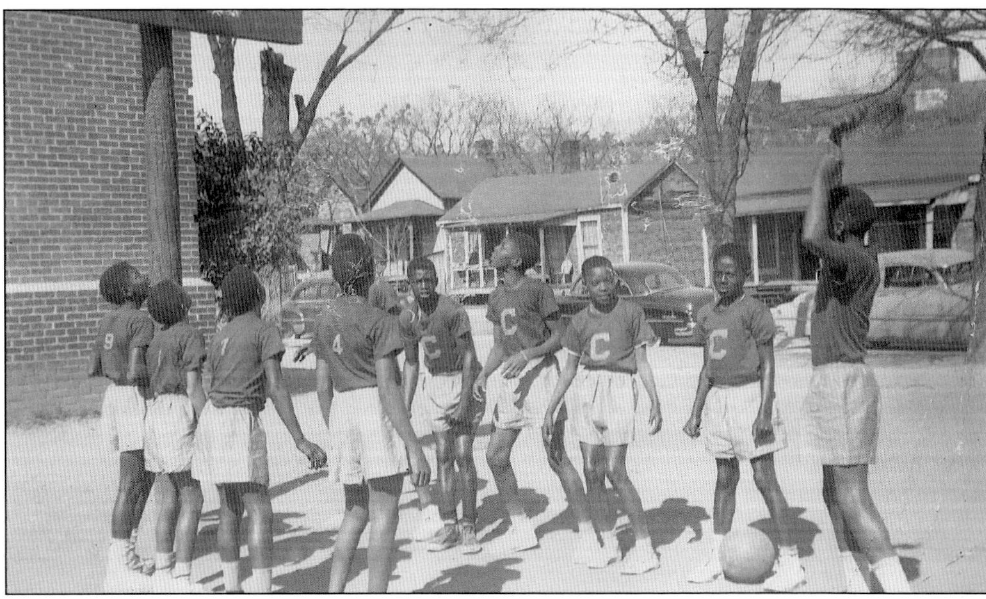

Practice. These young men are practicing for an upcoming game. They have the letter "C" on their shirts, representing G.W. Carver School. Cars parked along the curb show that the photo was taken *c.* 1950s. The homes in the background are constructed of wood and a type of siding used for outside protection from the elements. (Courtesy of Booker T. Washington Center.)

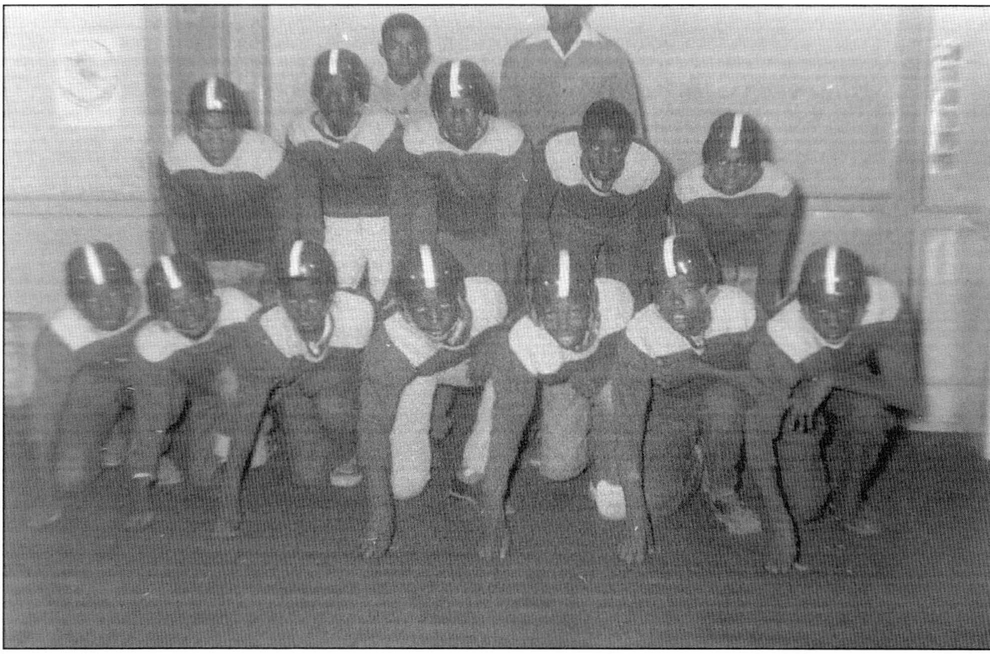

The G.W. Carver Football Team. Two young men in the rear are not suited up. Legend has it that this was a pretty good team. They are pictured *c.* 1956 (Courtesy of Booker T. Washington Center.)

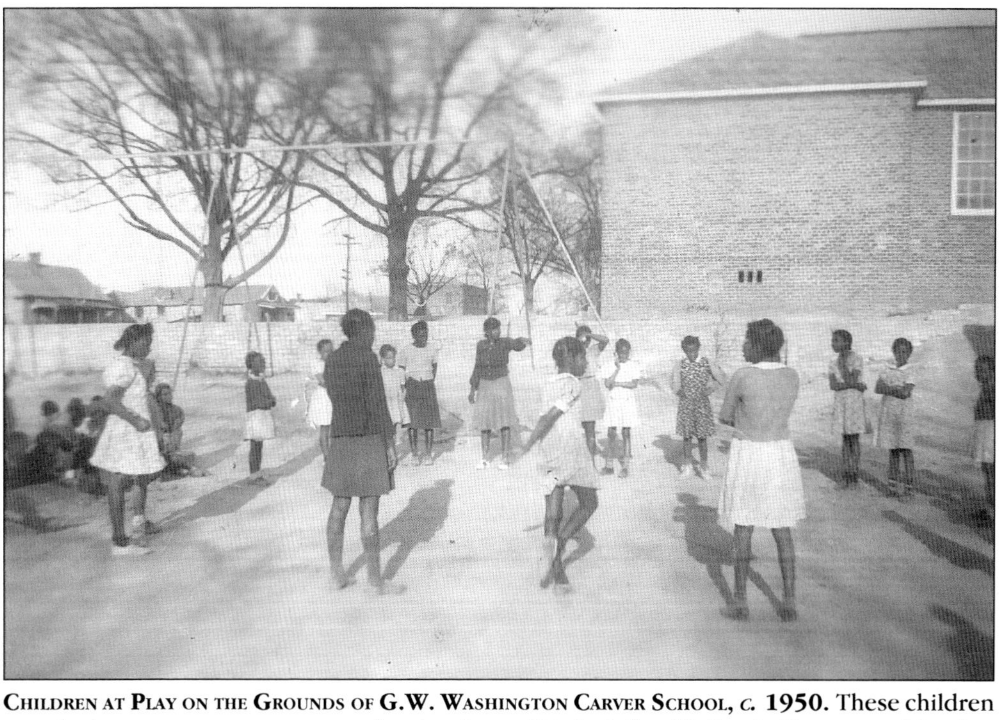

Children at Play on the Grounds of G.W. Washington Carver School, *c.* 1950. These children are playing a game very common for the times: "Little Salley Walker." (Courtesy of Booker T Washington Center.)

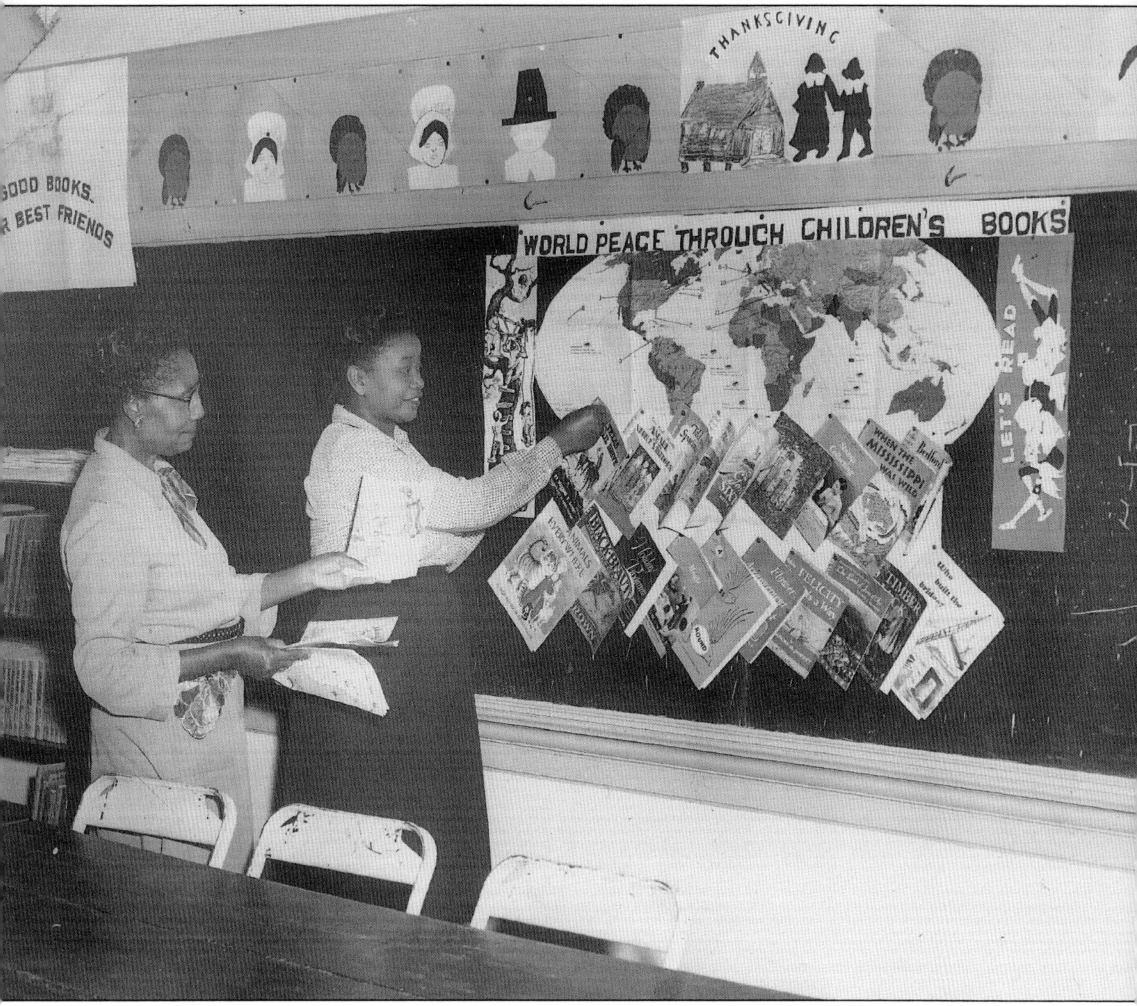

Librarians. These ladies were librarians at G.W. Carver School. Pictured from left to right are Mrs. E.L. Price and Mrs. C.C. Dickey. The school was participating in "Books About Children from Around the World." Emphasis is being placed upon the cultivation of reading skills, grammar, and a tolerance of other cultures. This photo was taken *c.* 1939 (Courtesy of Booker T. Washington Center.)

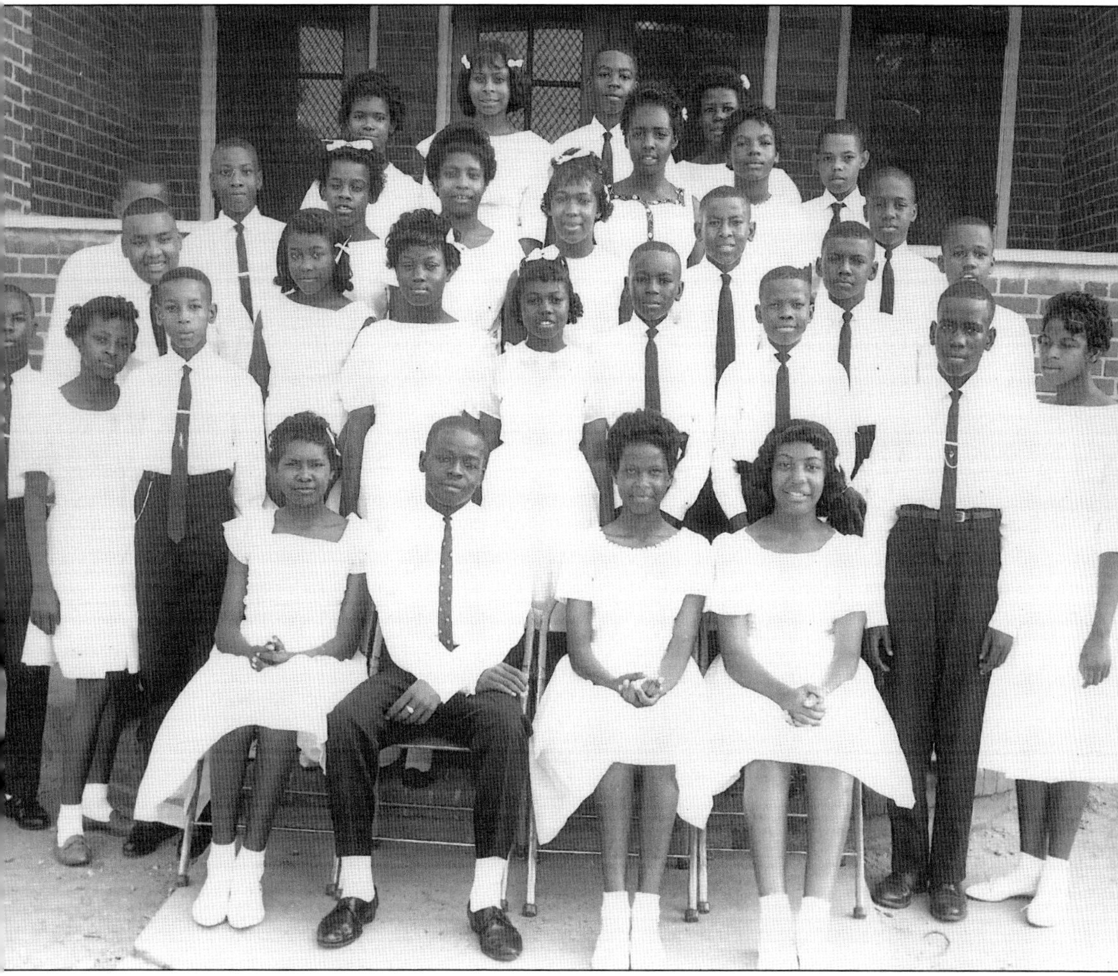

STUDENTS AT G.W. CARVER ELEMENTARY SCHOOL. An unidentified group of students from G.W. Carver Elementary School are pictured at their seventh grade graduation, *c.* 1940. They are wearing traditional colors and styles for this ceremony—boys are in black trousers, with white long-sleeved shirts and ties, and girls are wearing white dresses and white fold-down socks. (Courtesy of Booker T. Washington Center.)

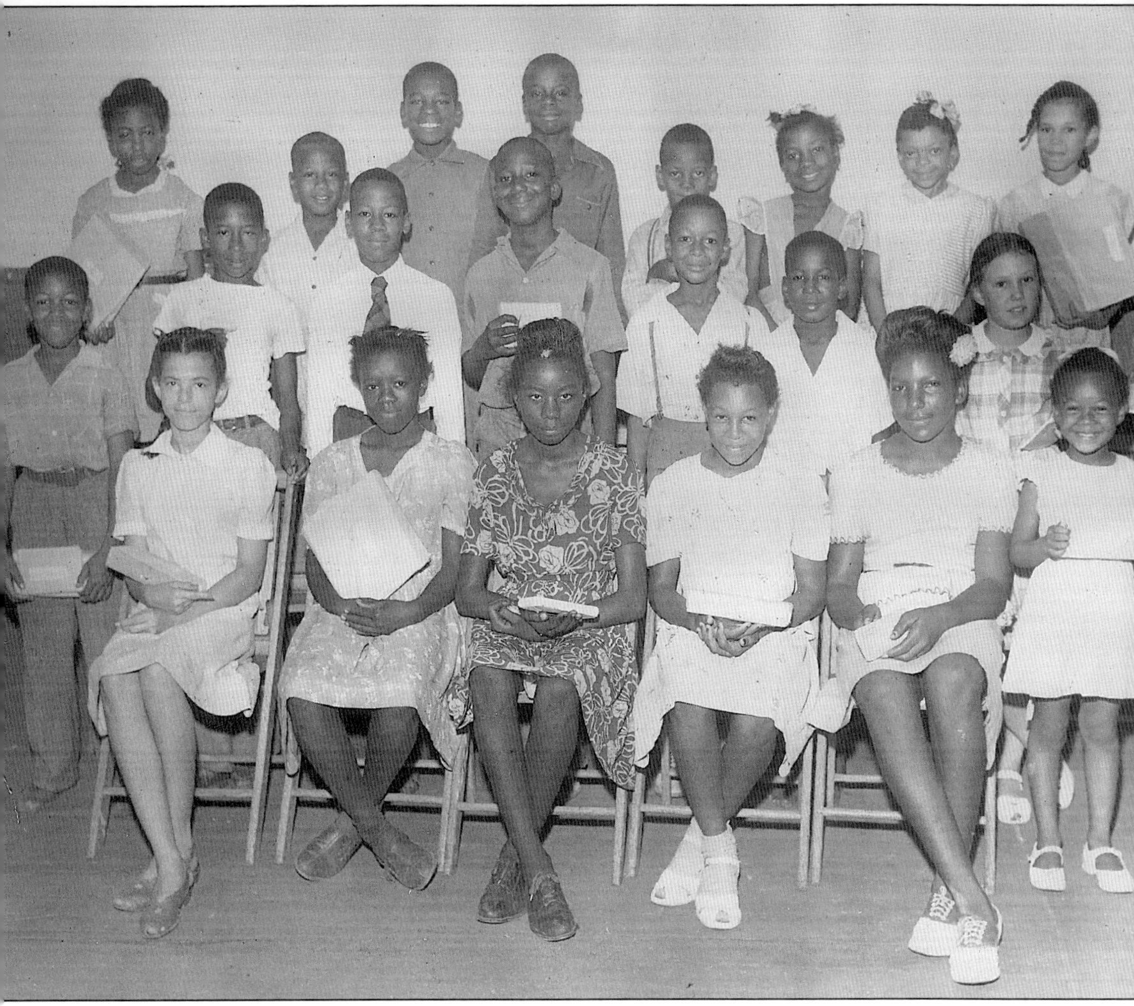

Awards Day. Pictured here is a group of youngsters who received awards for participating in the summer program at the Booker T. Washington Center's Junior Recreation Department, *c.* 1947. Young boys and girls often took sewing, cooking, art, and music classes here. Academic summer tutoring sessions were offered. (Courtesy of Booker T. Washington Center.)

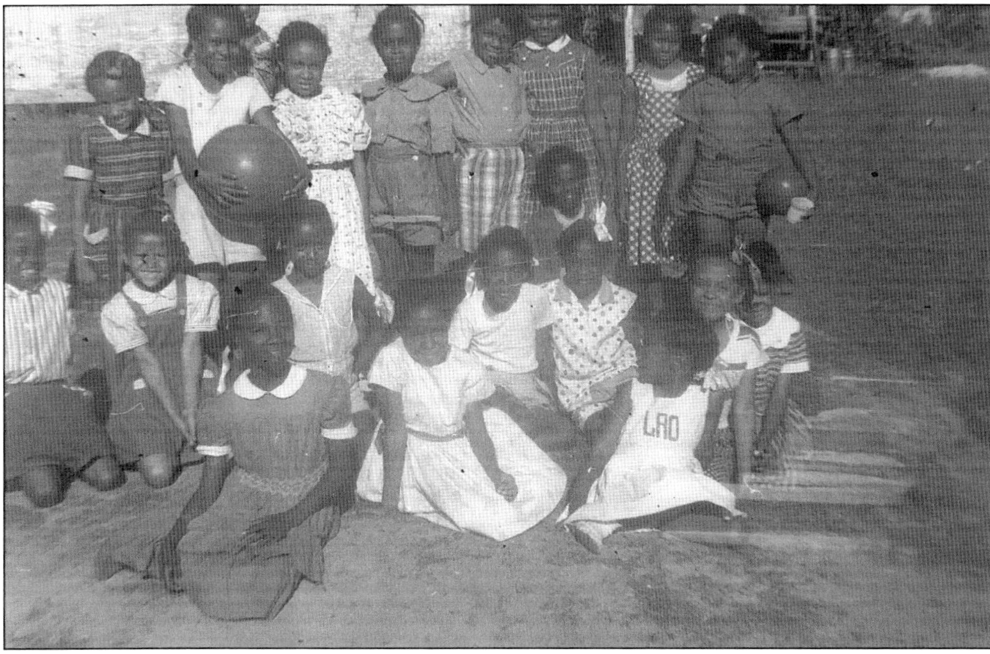

Games. These neighborhood girls have just finished playing dodge ball, *c.* 1956 (Courtesy of Booker T. Washington Center.)

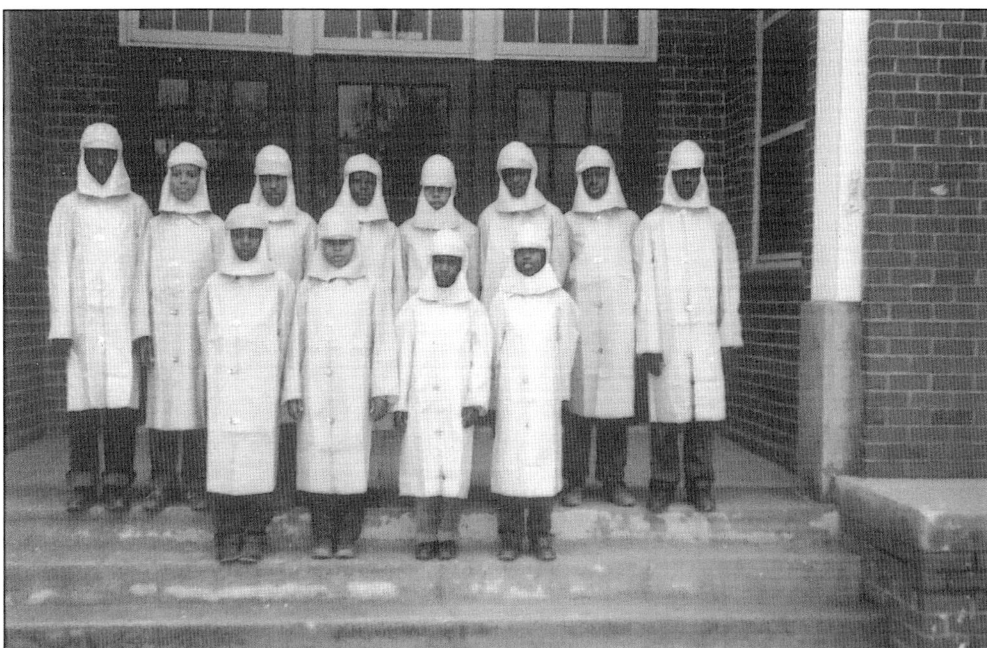

Junior Guards. Twelve youngsters from G.W. Carver pose on the steps in their yellow rain slickers. They served as junior crossing guards, *c.* 1953 (Courtesy of Booker T. Washington Center.)

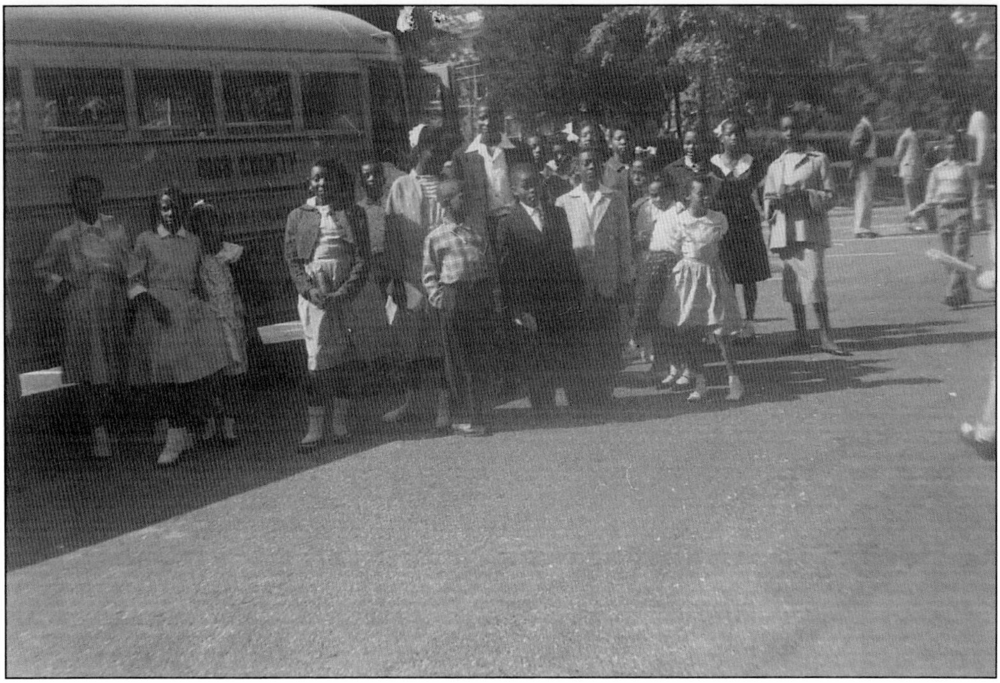

Riding the Yellow Bus Wasn't So Bad. These students have just dismounted a Bibb County bus and are ready to explore, *c.* 1950 (Courtesy of Booker T. Washington Center.)

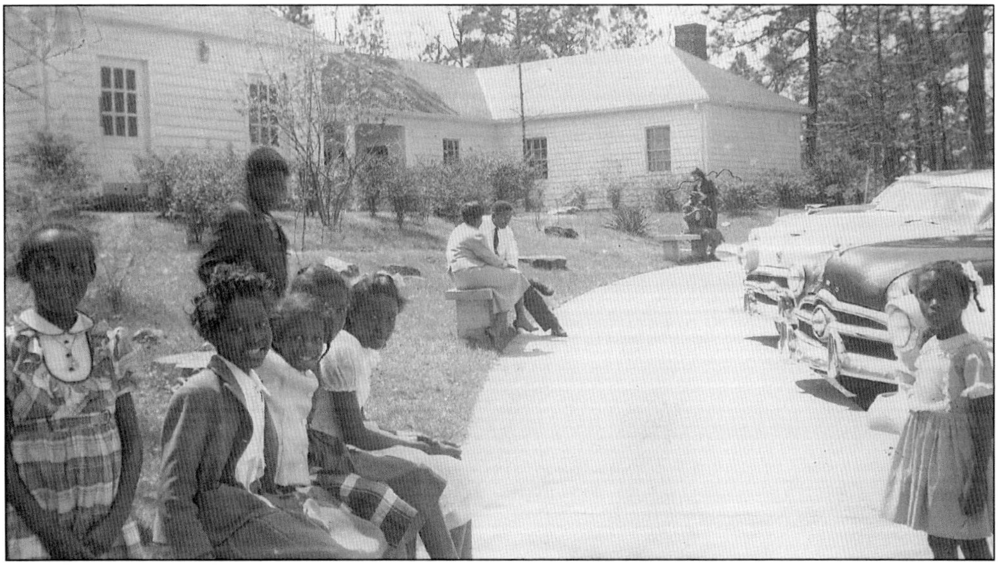

Field Trip. A group of elementary school students and their teachers are pictured on a field trip to Warm Springs, GA, *c.* 1950 (Courtesy of Booker T. Washington Center.)

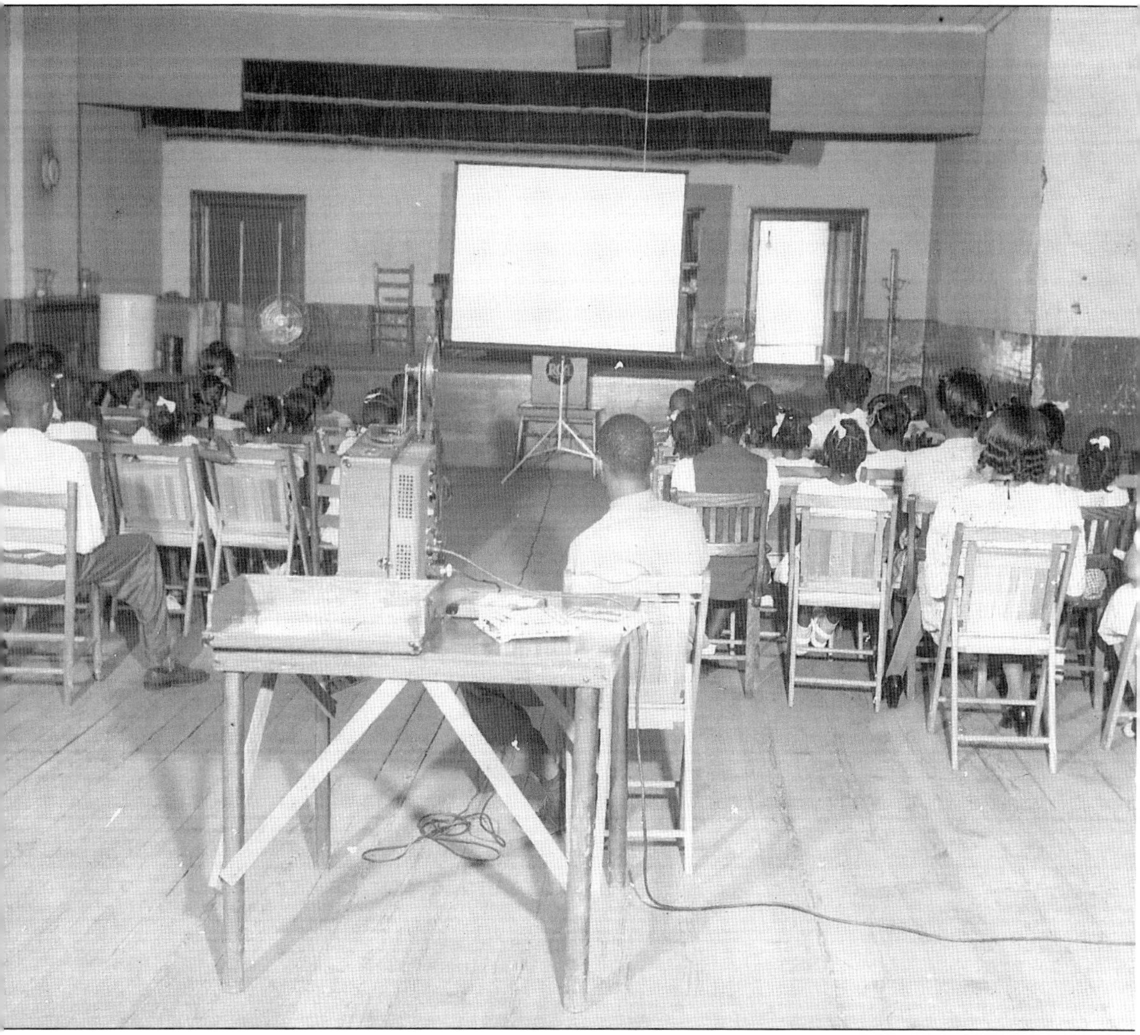

The Booker T. Washington Center. These youngsters are getting ready to view a movie at the Booker T. Washington Center, *c.* 1947. They are a part of the Junior Department. The two young men sitting in the back served as helpers, and two female teachers are also seated in the rear. The fans running in the foreground indicate that it is summer. There are cracks in the floor and no rugs to cushion their feet. (Courtesy of Booker T. Washington Center.)

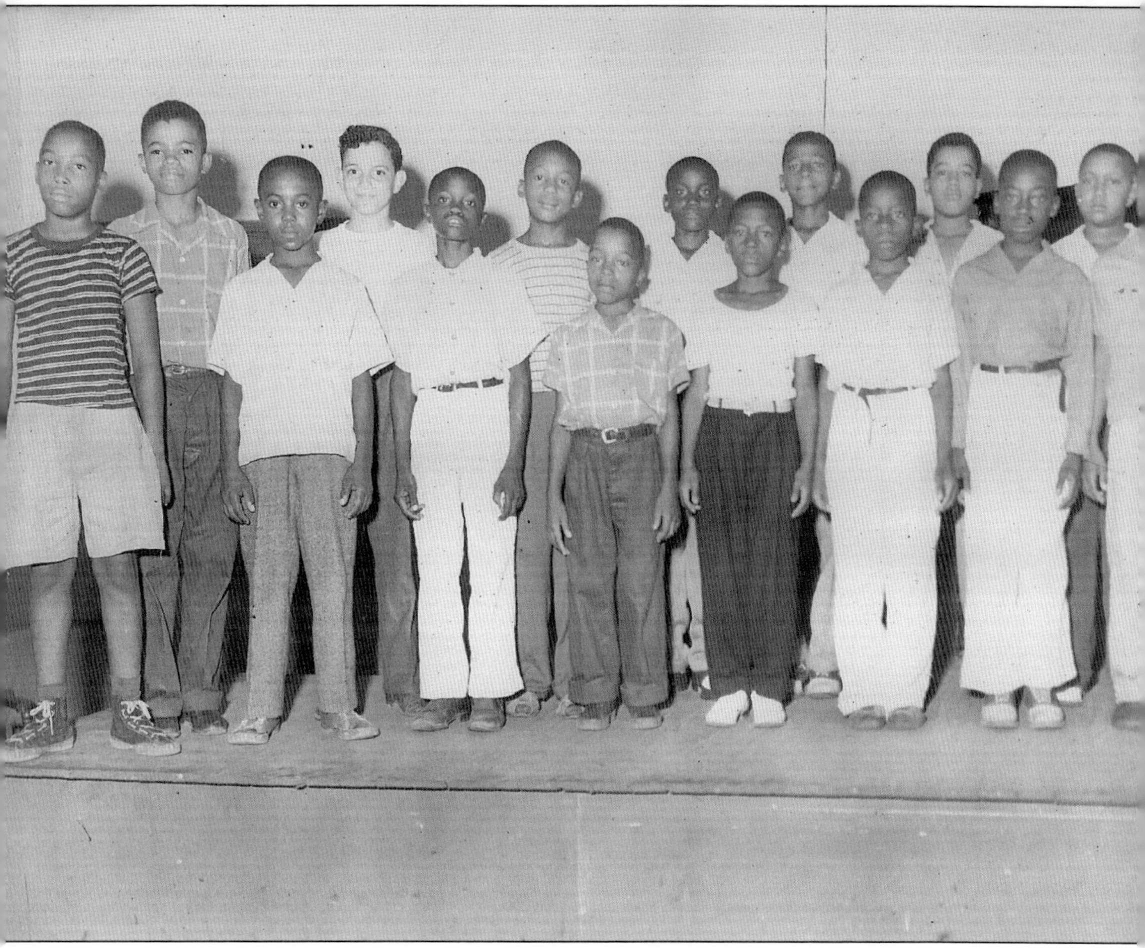

The Boys Glee Club. The glee club is shown here shortly after its first meeting at the Booker T. Washington Center. The club was organized June 11, 1946. These young men were selected for the specific purpose of singing and performing at the center, churches, and at school functions. (Courtesy of Booker T. Washington Center.)

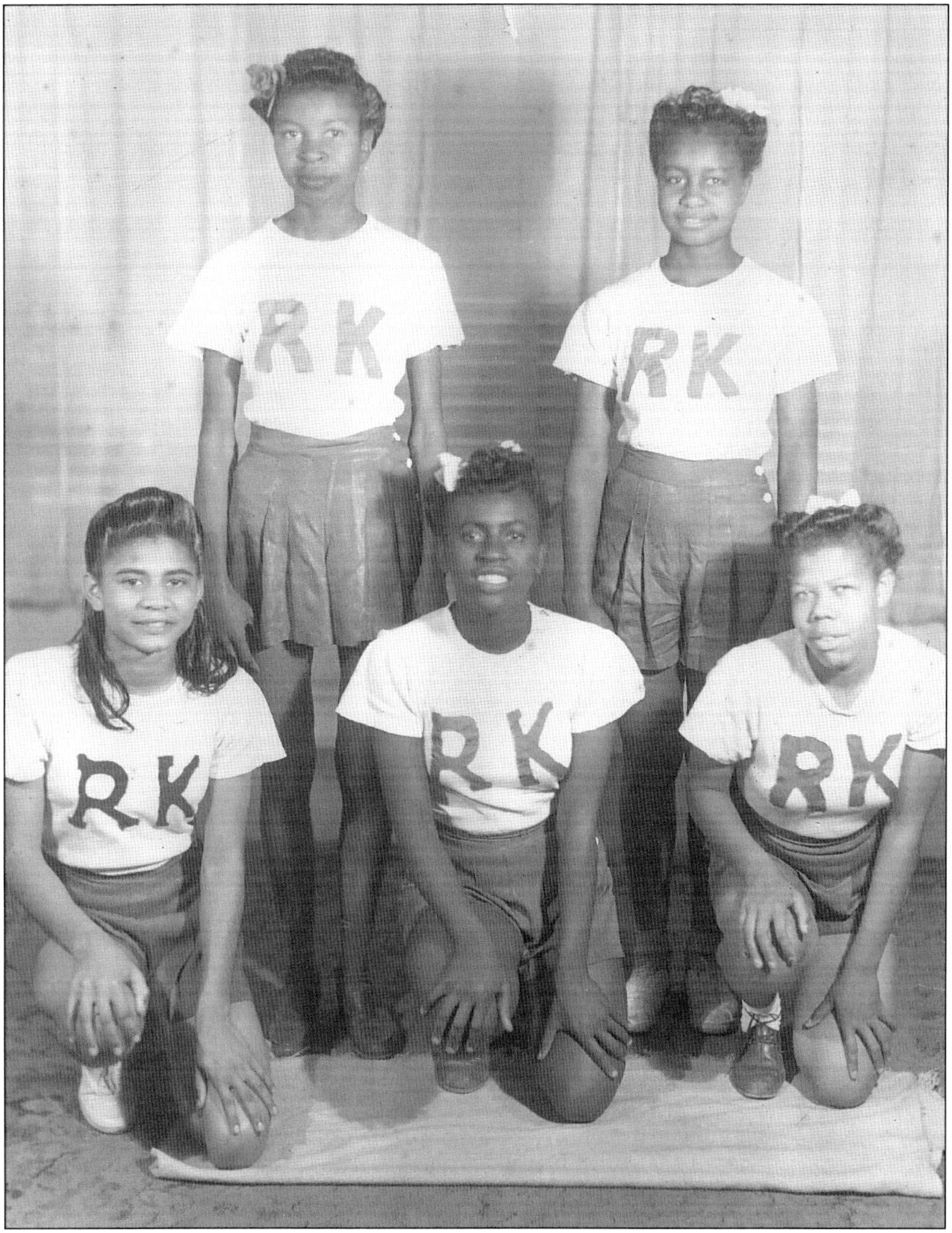

A Basketball Team. A group of high school girls pose for their basketball team picture, *c.* 1945. On their shirts are the letters "RK." (Courtesy of Booker T. Washington Center.)

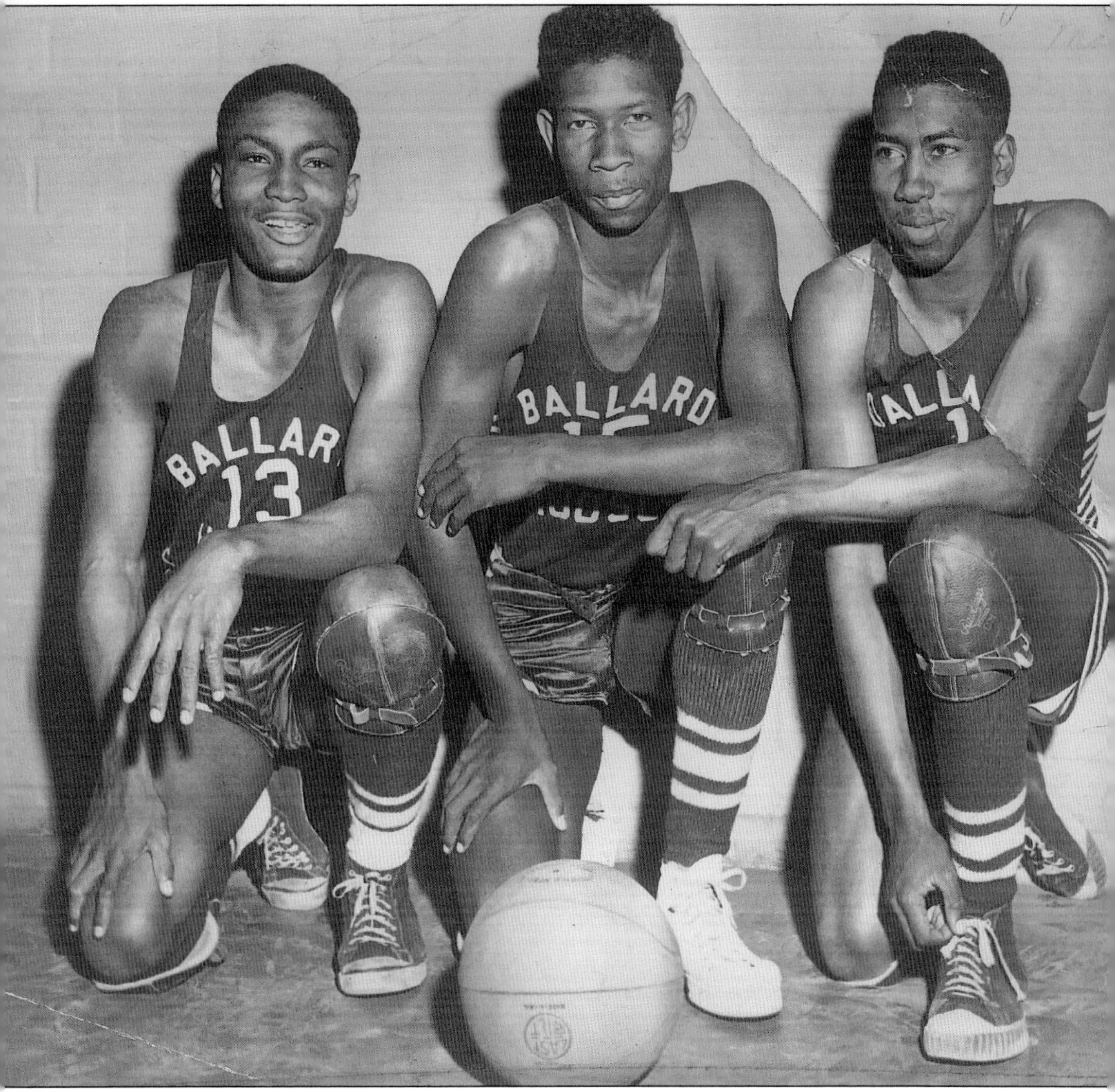

Let the Games Begin. These three unidentified basketball players are members of the first team at Ballard Hudson Sr. High School, *c.* 1949. They were the starters for the team and were all smiles, ready to defeat their opponents. Ballard Hudson Sr. High athletes would go on to set a high standard in football, basketball, and track, a reputation that surrounding schools viewed with much respect. (Courtesy of Booker T. Washington Center.)

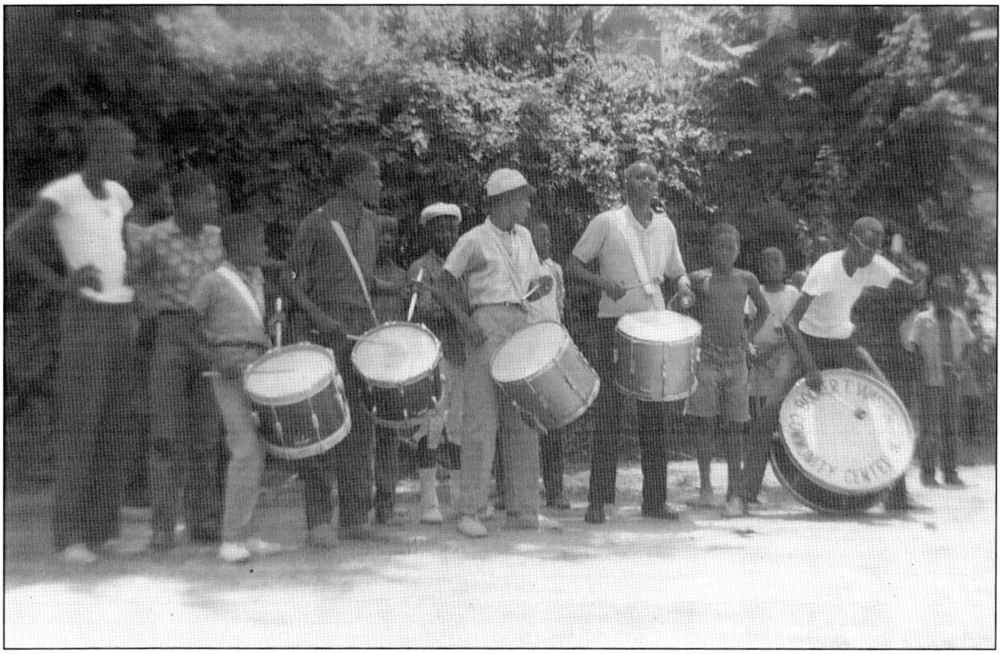

BOOKER T. WASHINGTON CENTER'S BAND. These young boys were drummers in the Booker T. Washington Center band, pictured on a summer day, *c.* 1960 (Courtesy of Booker T. Washington Center.)

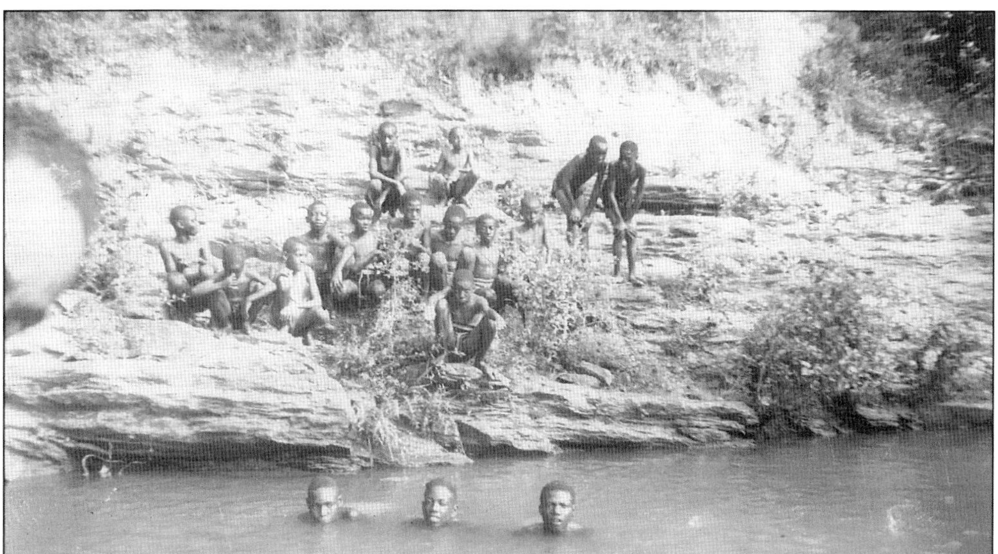

FUN IN THE SUN. A large group of young boys are having a day of fun and swimming at the rock quarry, *c.* 1939 (Courtesy of Booker T. Washington Center.)

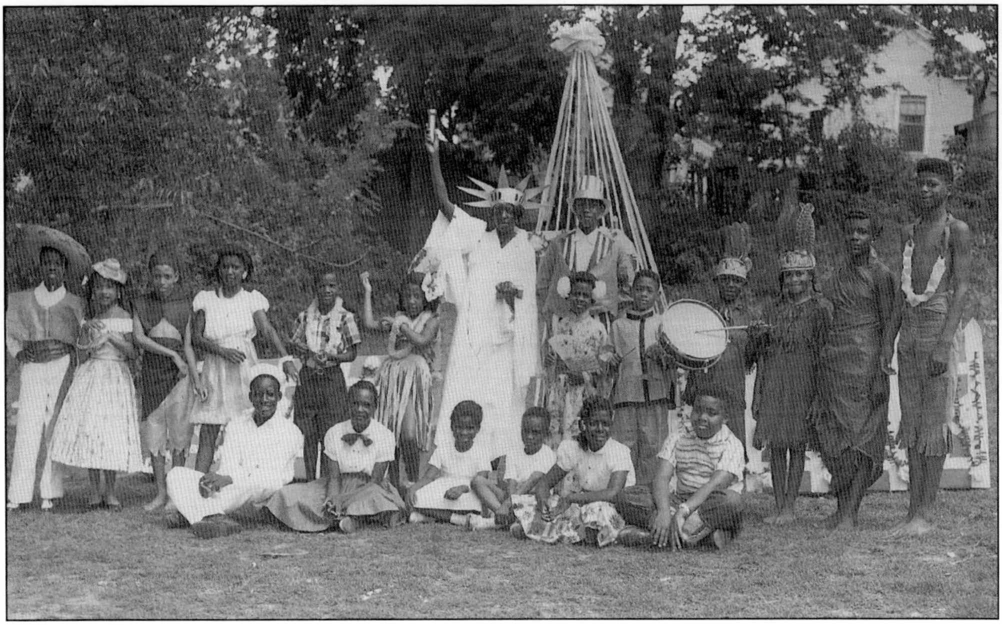

Students. A group of young students from G.W. Carver Elementary School are dressed for a spring festival, *c.* 1939, celebrating the birth of the American Republic. The children took great pride in designing and making their costumes. (Courtesy of Booker T. Washington Center.)

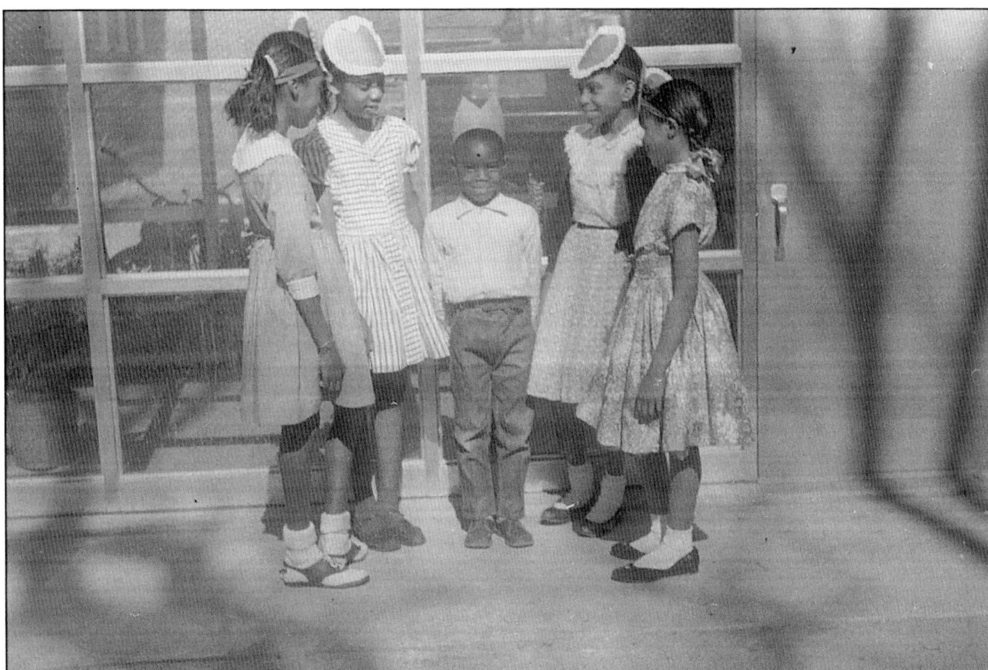

Be My Valentine! Surrounded by four smiling young ladies, this young man can't help feeling special. He is the "king of hearts," *c.* 1952 (Courtesy of Booker T. Washington Center.)

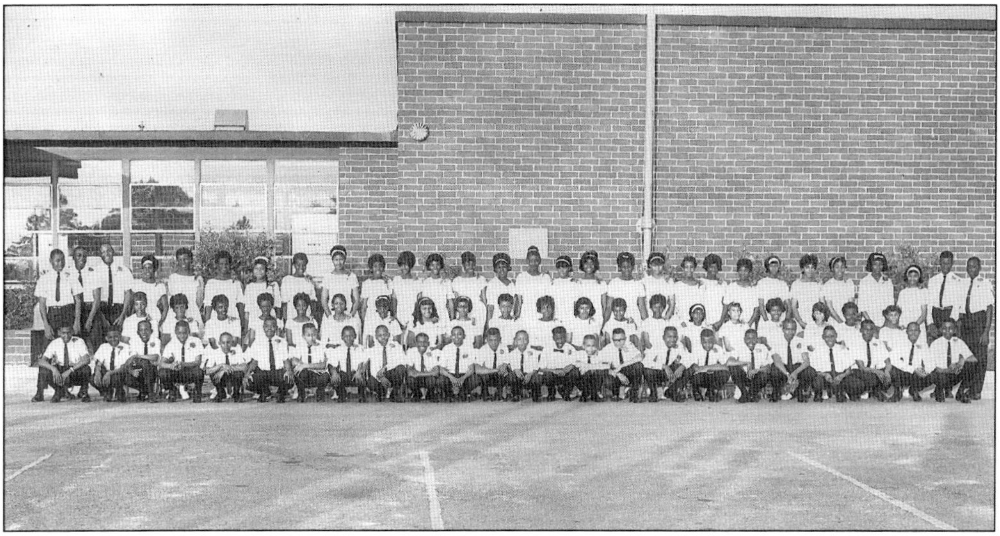

Graduation Day at Minnie Butler Elementary School. Once located in the Bellvue area of Macon, this school was named for one of Macon's outstanding educators, Minnie Butler. Miss Butler began her personal educational journey in Jeffersonville, GA. She later moved to Macon and began attending Ballard Normal School. To further her education, she enrolled in Central City College. Miss Butler was always seeking ways to improve the quality of learning for her students. She organized the first schoolboy patrol in Macon, and served as principal of G.W. Carver and B.S. Ingram. This photo was taken in the 1950s. (Courtesy of Susie P. Ussery.)

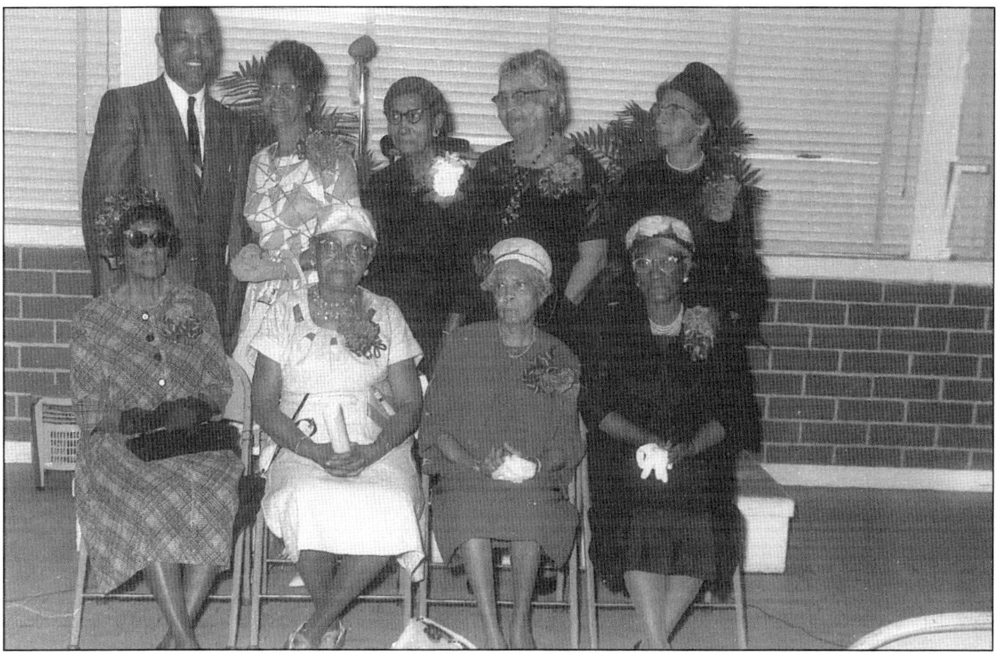

G.W. Carver Elementary School. The principal and a group of retired teachers from G.W. Carver Elementary School are pictured in the 1950s. (Courtesy of Booker T. Washington Center.)

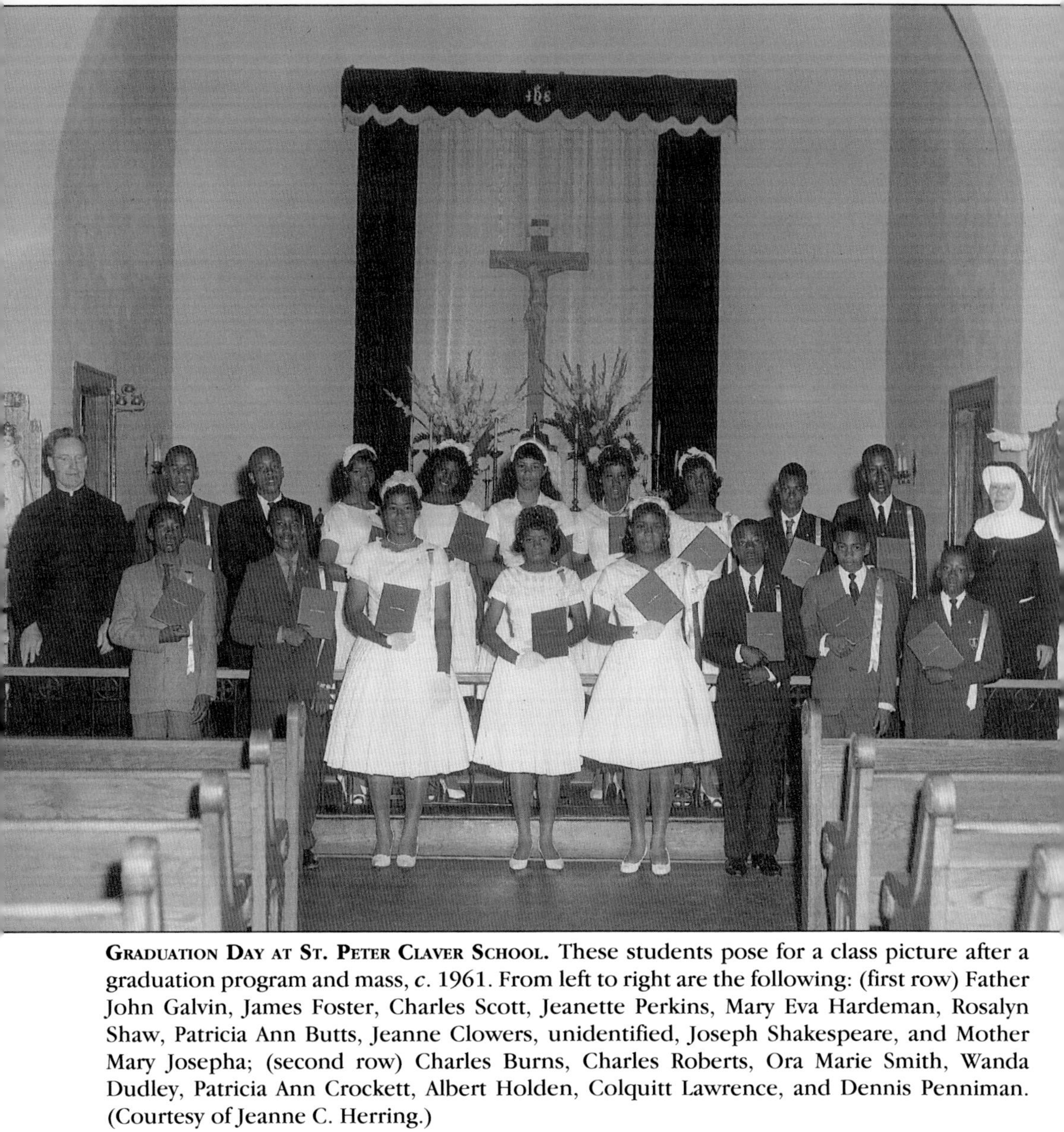

Graduation Day at St. Peter Claver School. These students pose for a class picture after a graduation program and mass, *c.* 1961. From left to right are the following: (first row) Father John Galvin, James Foster, Charles Scott, Jeanette Perkins, Mary Eva Hardeman, Rosalyn Shaw, Patricia Ann Butts, Jeanne Clowers, unidentified, Joseph Shakespeare, and Mother Mary Josepha; (second row) Charles Burns, Charles Roberts, Ora Marie Smith, Wanda Dudley, Patricia Ann Crockett, Albert Holden, Colquitt Lawrence, and Dennis Penniman. (Courtesy of Jeanne C. Herring.)

A Diploma. This document certifies completion of kindergarten through eighth grade at St. Peter Claver School, *c.* 1961

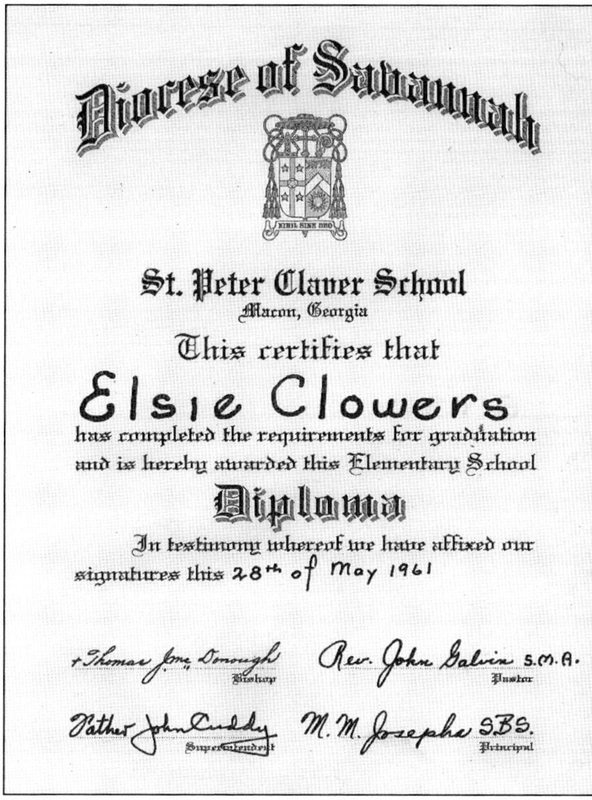

Diocese of Savannah

St. Peter Claver School

Macon, Georgia

This certifies that

Elsie Clowers

has completed the requirements for graduation and is hereby awarded this Elementary School

Diploma

In testimony whereof we have affixed our signatures this 28th of May 1961

+Thomas J. Mc Donough, Bishop

Rev. John Galvin S.M.A., Pastor

Father John Cuddy, Superintendent

M. M. Josepha SBS., Principal

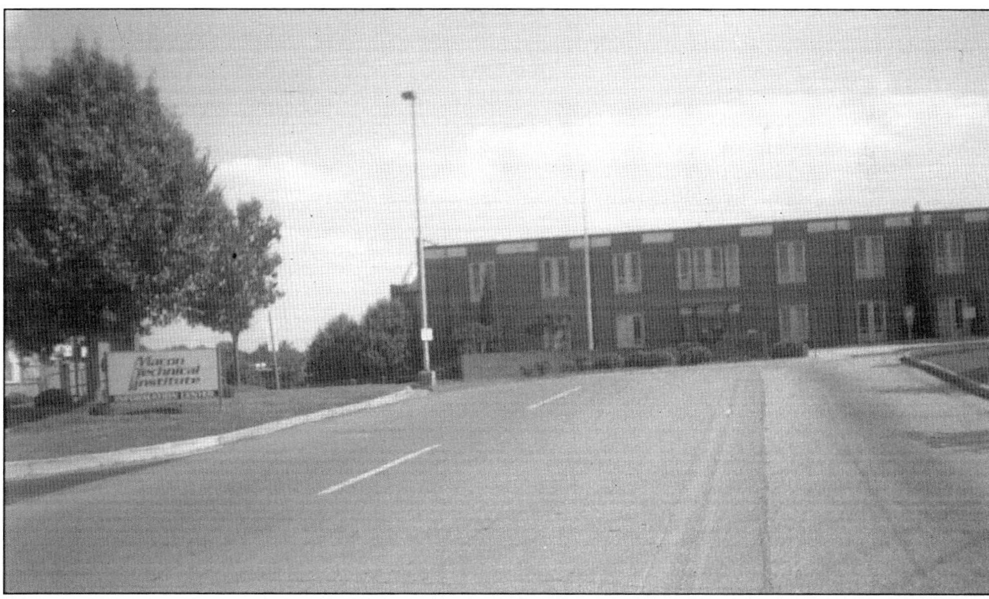

Macon's Technical Institute. This educational facility is located off Eisenhower Parkway. Students come here to learn various technical and vocational skills that will enhance their marketability in the public sector. Many African Americans used this institution to become gainfully employed.

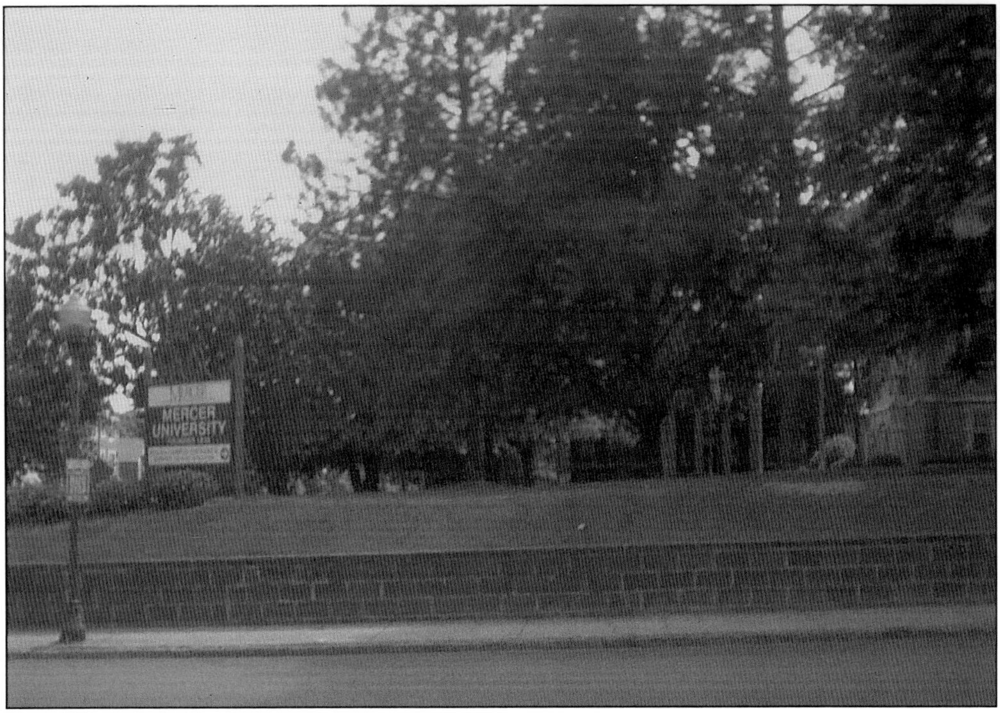

Mercer University. Located on Coleman Avenue, Mercer boasts a very beautiful campus. Black students began attending this school in the late 1960s and early 1970s after desegregation.

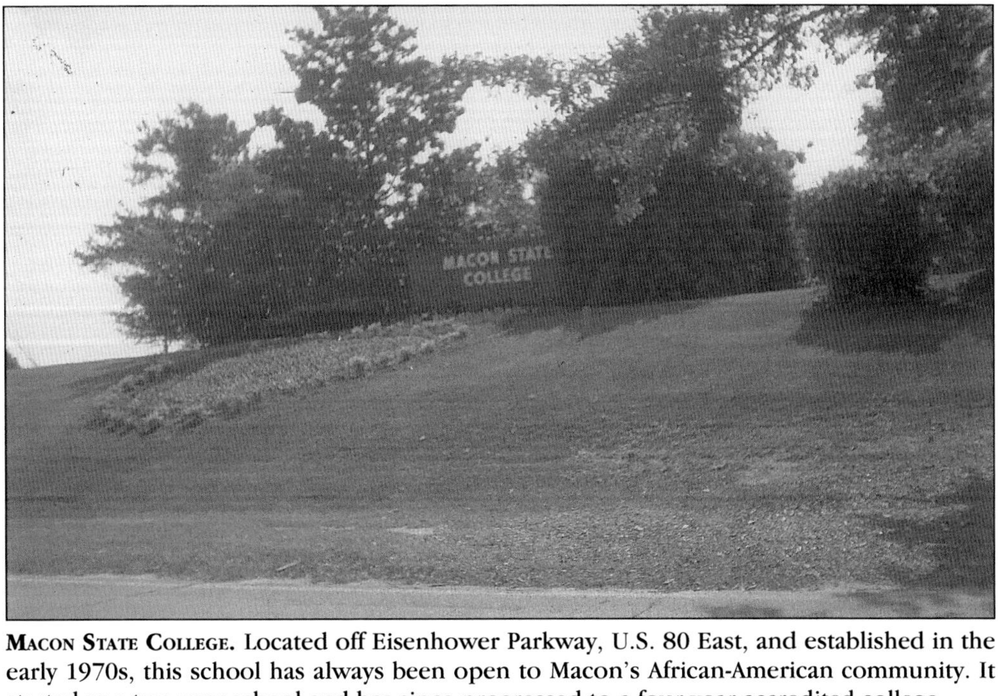

Macon State College. Located off Eisenhower Parkway, U.S. 80 East, and established in the early 1970s, this school has always been open to Macon's African-American community. It started as a two-year school and has since progressed to a four-year accredited college.

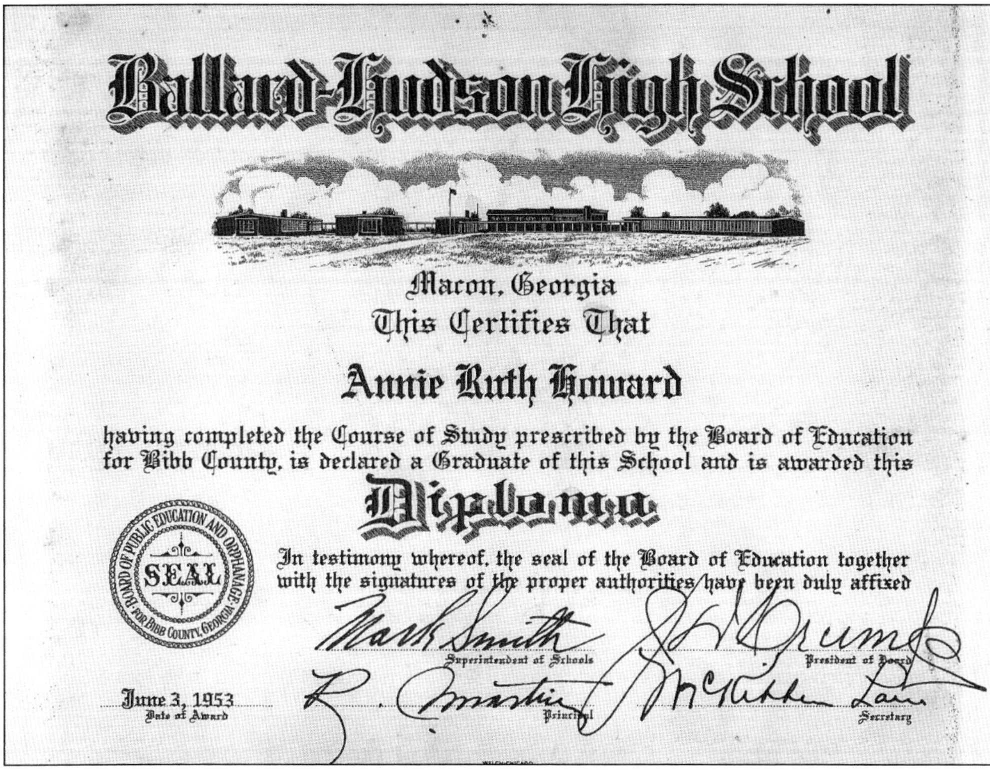

Ballard-Hudson High School

Macon, Georgia

This Certifies That

Annie Ruth Howard

having completed the Course of Study prescribed by the Board of Education for Bibb County, is declared a Graduate of this School and is awarded this

Diploma

BOARD OF PUBLIC EDUCATION AND ORPHANAGE FOR BIBB COUNTY, GEORGIA
SEAL

In testimony whereof, the seal of the Board of Education together with the signatures of the proper authorities have been duly affixed

Superintendent of Schools — President of Board

June 3, 1953
Date of Award

Principal — Secretary

A Diploma. Pictured is a diploma from Ballard Hudson Sr. High School, which was a segregated facility. This diploma was awarded to Annie Ruth Howard on June 3, 1953. Professor R.J. Martin was the principal and Mark Smith was superintendent of schools. (Courtesy of Lorena H. Latham.)

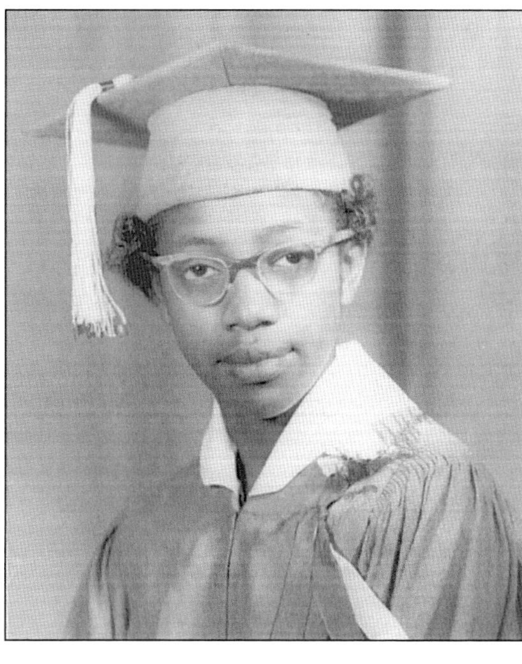

The Graduate. Annie Ruth Howard is seen in her cap and gown, *c.* 1953. (Courtesy of Lorena H. Latham.)

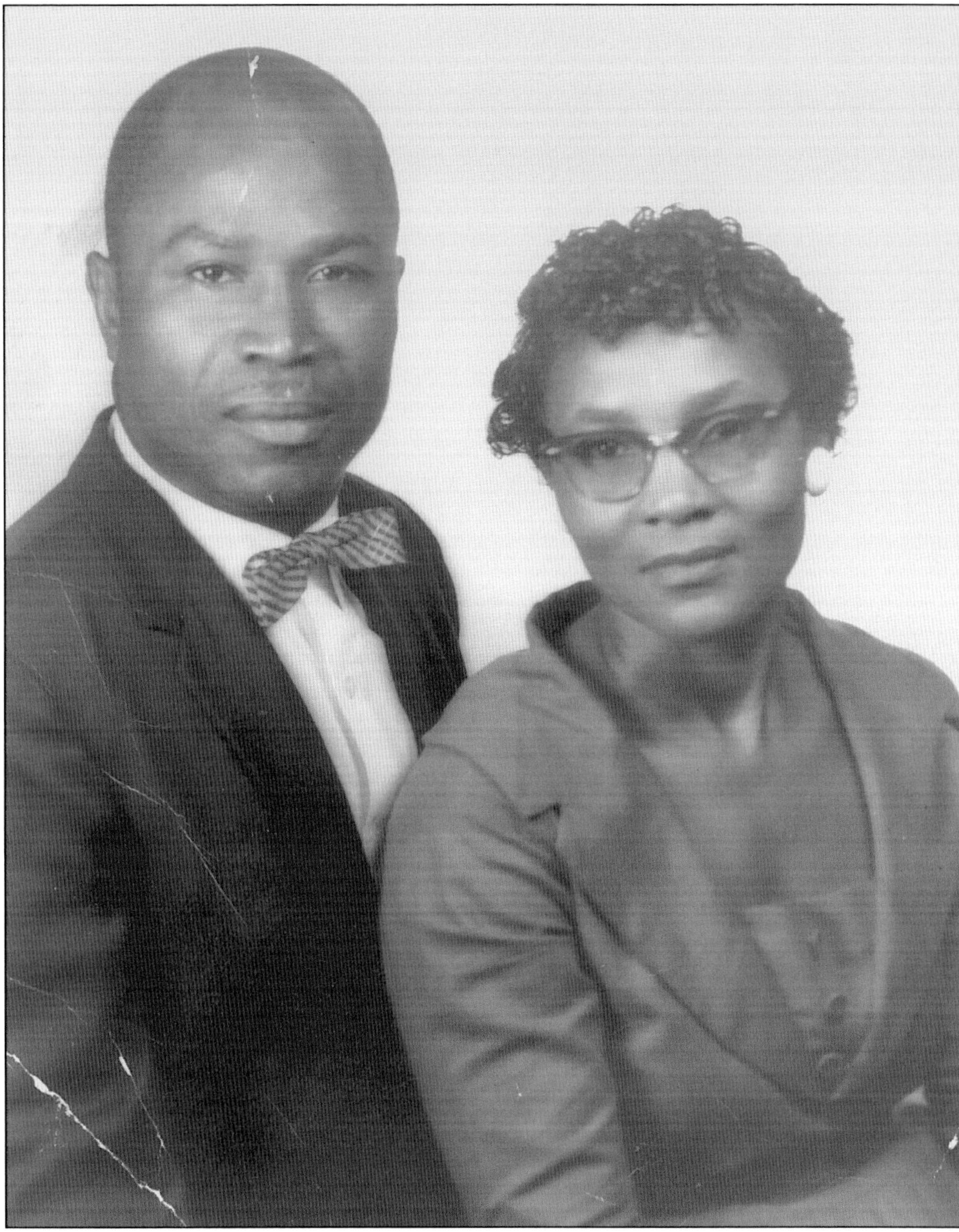

Bryant Herring Jr. and Ruth Butler Herring, Longtime Residents of Macon. The father-in-law and mother-in-law of the author are shown here *c.* 1940s. The two raised a family of five children: Elijah, Moses, Bonnie Ruth, Wallace Jr., and James. Mr. Herring is deceased; Mrs. Herring still lives in the family home.

John T. Jordan Sr. Mr. Jordan worked for many years as an employee of Bibb Mills. He is the father of Lena Jordan (below), and is pictured here *c.* 1959.

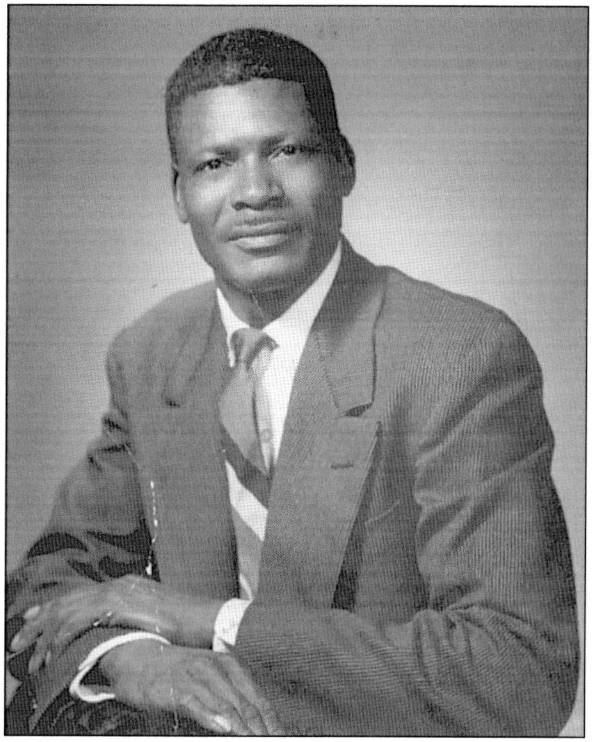

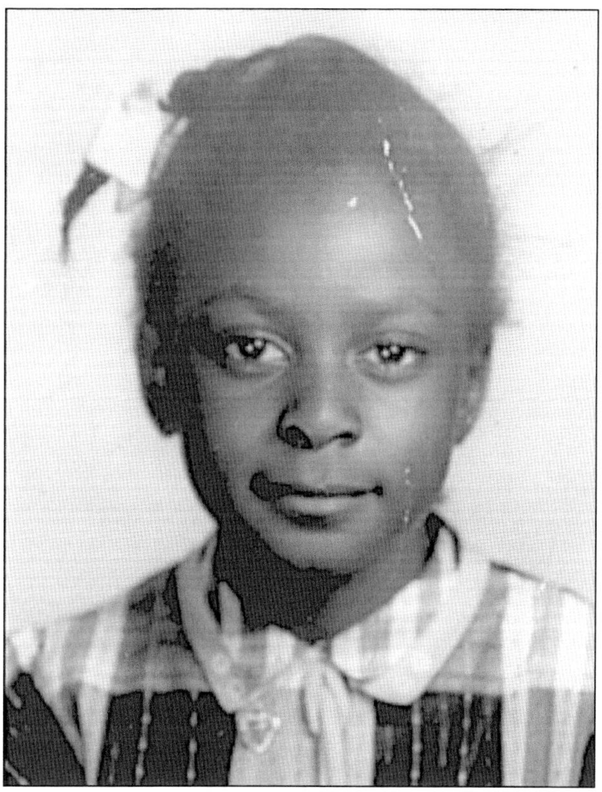

Lena Jordan. This school photo was taken in 1958, when Lena was in third grade.

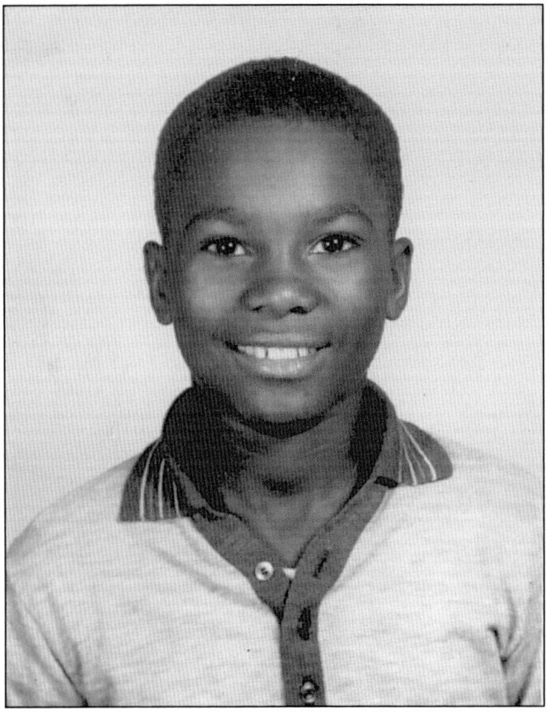

James Richard Herring Sr. Shown here at the age of ten, James was a student at Eugenia Hamilton Elementary School on Pio Nano Avenue. He is the son of Bryant and Ruth Butler Herring. This photo was taken *c.* 1956. (Courtesy of Ruth B. Herring.)

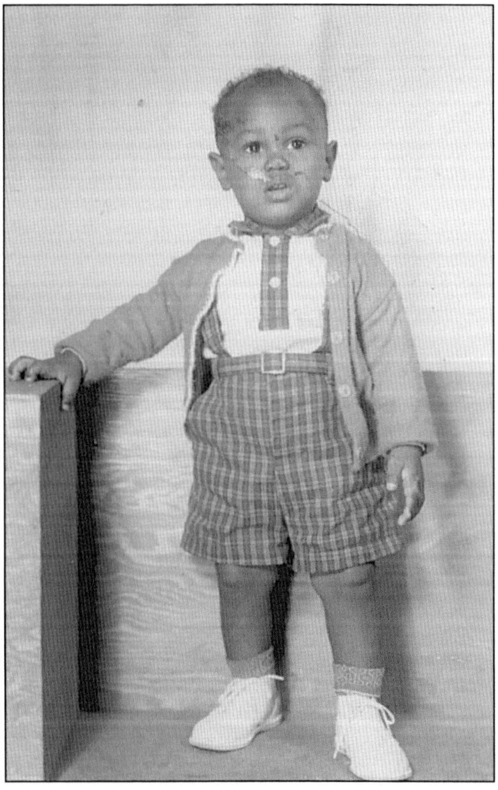

Darryl Robinson. Robinson is pictured all dressed up and ready to go, *c.* 1958. He is currently living and working in Atlanta, but continues to visit friends and family in Macon. (Courtesy Ruth B Herring.)

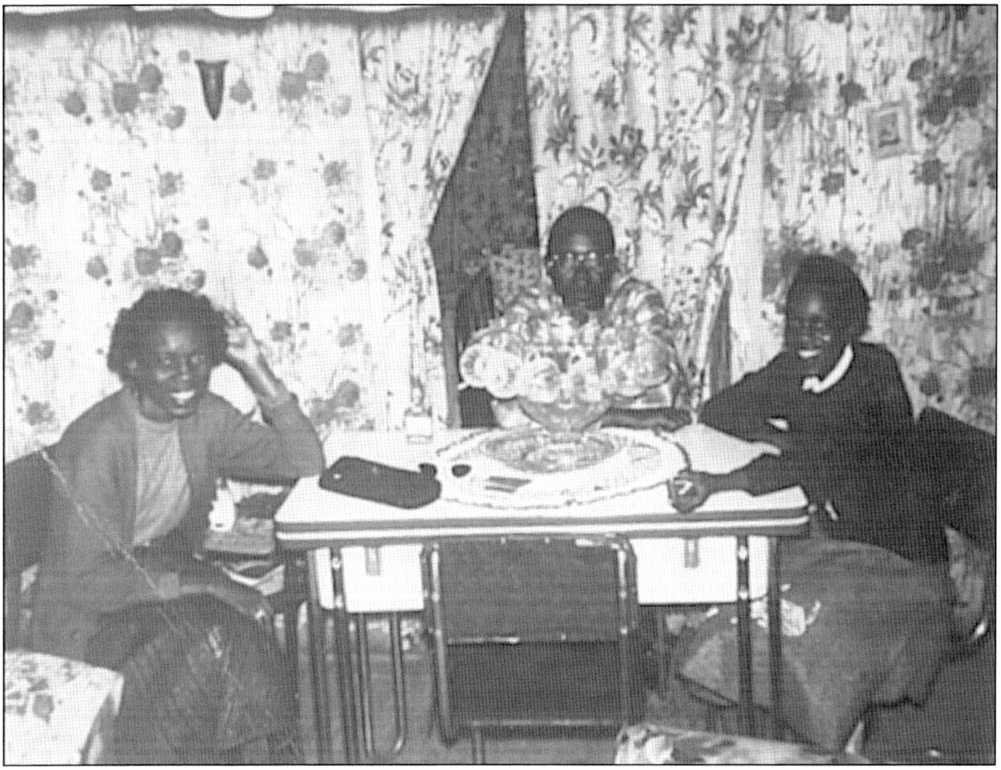

Three Friends. These friends are pictured sharing some time together, *c.* 1959 (Courtesy of Booker T. Washington Center.)

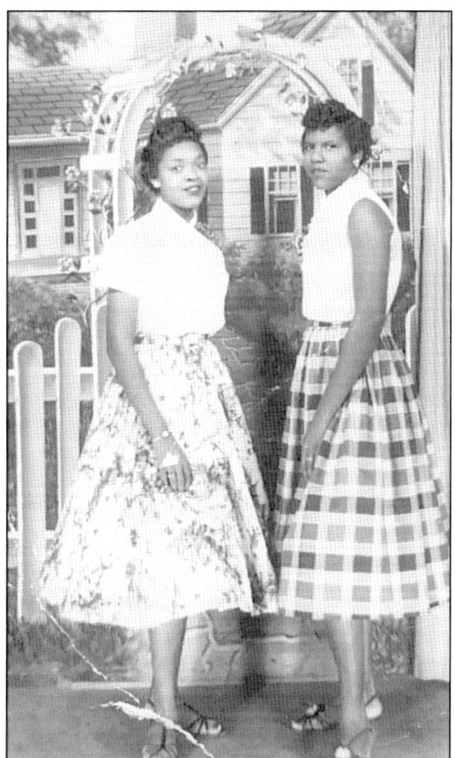

Doretha Wright and Friend. This photograph is from the 1940s. The young ladies are wearing full or flared skirts and blouses. The style of the sandals and the blouse worn by the young lady to the right can be found in stores today. What was old is "new" again. (Courtesy Ruth B Herring.)

A Faculty Member of G.W. Carver School. This faculty member is pictured *c.* 1949 (Courtesy of Booker T. Washington Center.)

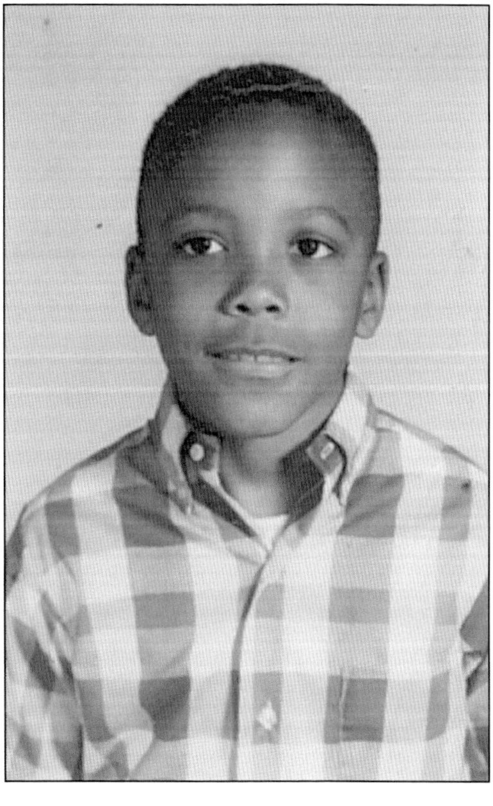

Veotis Williams. This young man posed for his school picture, *c.* 1950.s (Courtesy of Lena J. Herring.)

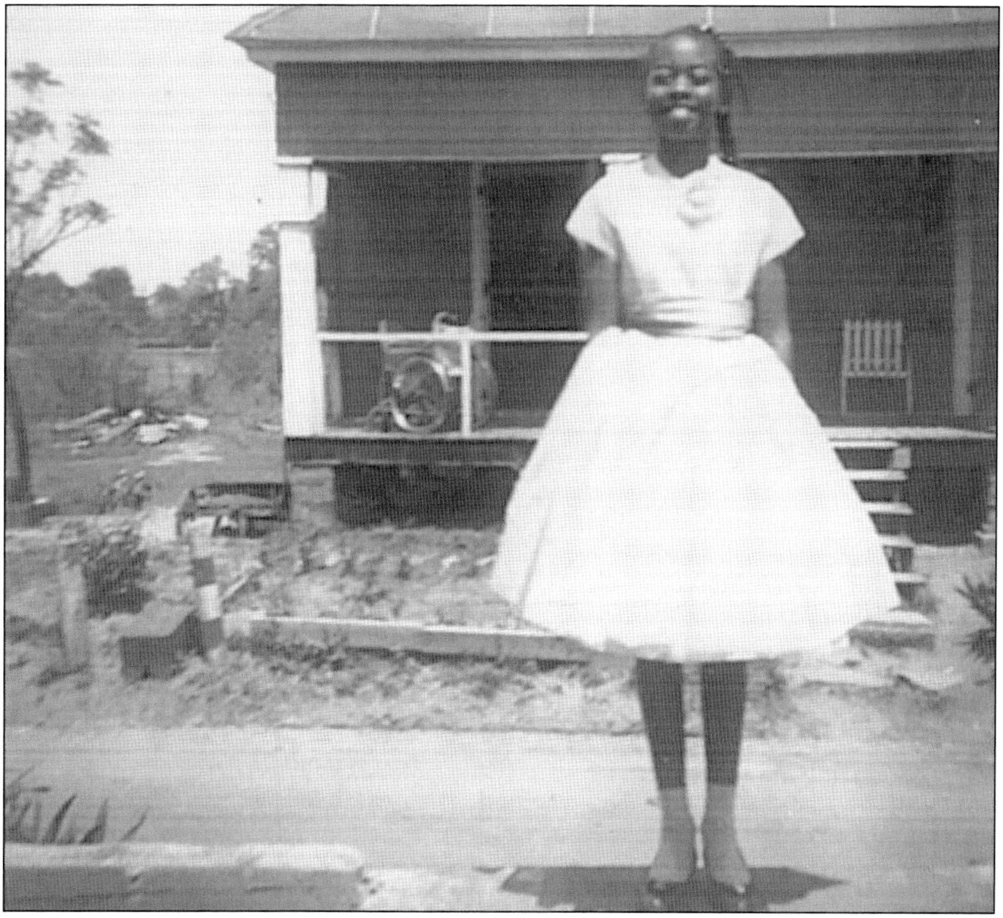

Cynthia Jeanette Perkins. She is shown here in front of her home in West Macon, dressed up in her Sunday best, *c.* 1959 (Courtesy of Jeanne C. Herring.)

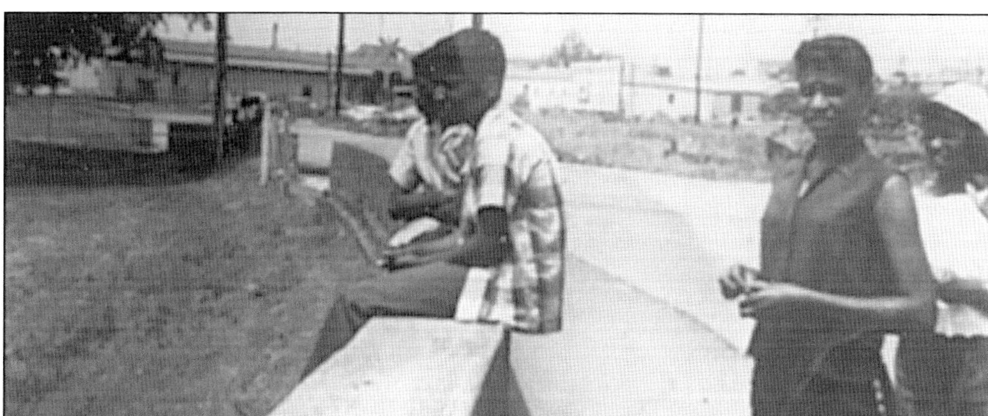

A Field Trip. A group of youngsters are pictured at Central City Park. The students are on a field trip with St. Peter Claver Catholic School. From left to right are Timothy Johnson, unidentified, Rosalyn Shaw, and Jeanette Perkins, *c.* 1960 (Courtesy of Jeanne C. Herring.)

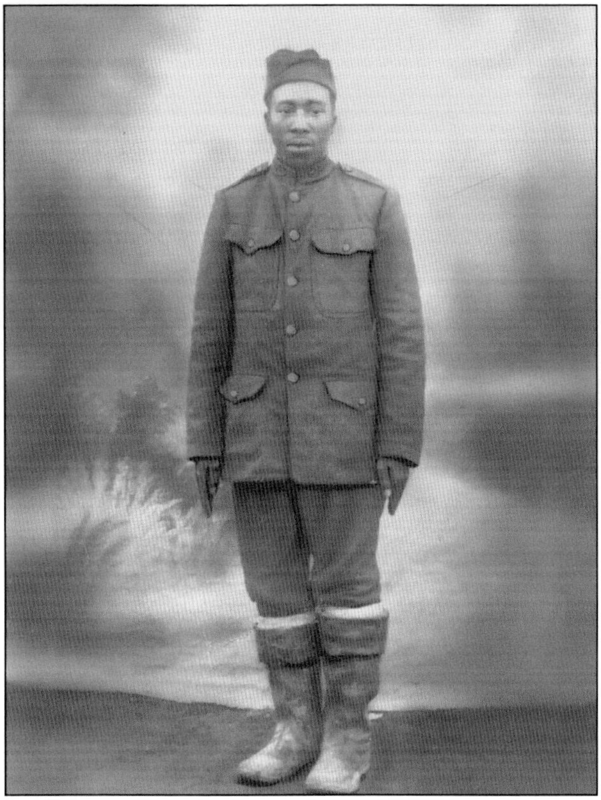

John Pope. Pope married Carrie Howard and had 12 children. This photo shows him in his World War I uniform, *c.* 1917. The U.S. Army was very much segregated at this time. African Americans were assigned menial tasks to perform and shown little courtesy or respect. (Courtesy of Susie P. Ussery.)

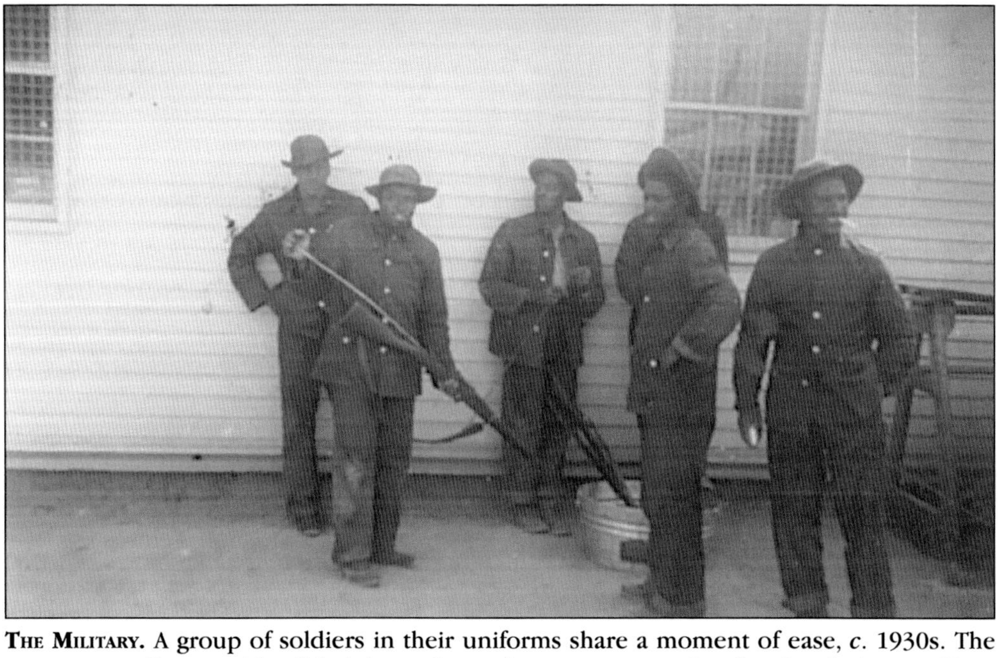

The Military. A group of soldiers in their uniforms share a moment of ease, *c.* 1930s. The men are standing outside of their barracks, and some appear to be cleaning their guns. Note the tin tub serving as a storage place. (Courtesy of Booker T. Washington Center.)

Four

Education: Military, Vocational, and Craftsmen

The military was an area where men and women of color thought they could receive dignity at last. In the early years (the Civil War for example), blacks fought on both sides. The Confederacy allowed blacks into aid their masters. The Union forces allowed blacks in as well, but the service was the same—to cook, clean, and fetch. Life in the armed forces was difficult, and African-American soldiers were occasionally even attacked by white soldiers in their own army. If they attempted to fight back, they were jailed. Segregation did not end in the armed forces until 1948. By then, African Americans had won many medals for the work they had rendered. Subtle discrimination continued for some time, but they had won the right to fight for their country. They participated in all wars—from the American Revolution to present skirmishes around the world.

To learn vocationally meant learning a survivable skill that could afford one a living. The contributions of African-American craftsmen can still be seen in various places around Macon to this day. Even though their work was not held in high regard by whites (in the early years, blacks were looked on more as helpers), oral history still gives accounts of blacks and their work, and their expertise was eventually appreciated. One of the most beautiful antebellum homes in the Macon area, the Hay House, was partially constructed by black artisans. Craftsmen held a variety of occupations in the area, working as plasterers, ironworkers, blacksmiths, street layers, painters, tanners, and toolmakers.

Many African-American men and women also went into the food service industry. There were many great cooks and bakers in the Macon area. They occasionally received praise from their employers, and sometimes went home with full stomachs at the end of the day. If you were a good cook, you had a job in Macon.

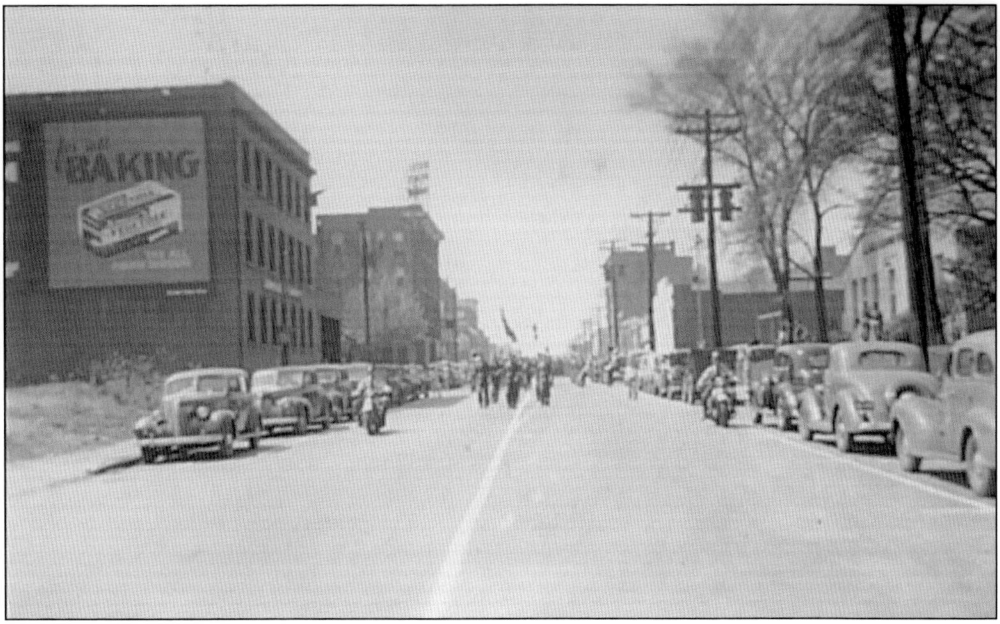

A 1930s Military Parade. In the above photograph, motorcycle police clear the way for the parade. In the photograph below, a band marches along as other squadrons bring up the rear. Cars line both sides of the street. Camp Wheeler soldiers participated in the parade. Vintage advertisements pop out at the reader about Smoked Ham and Lard. (Both images courtesy of Booker T. Washington Center.)

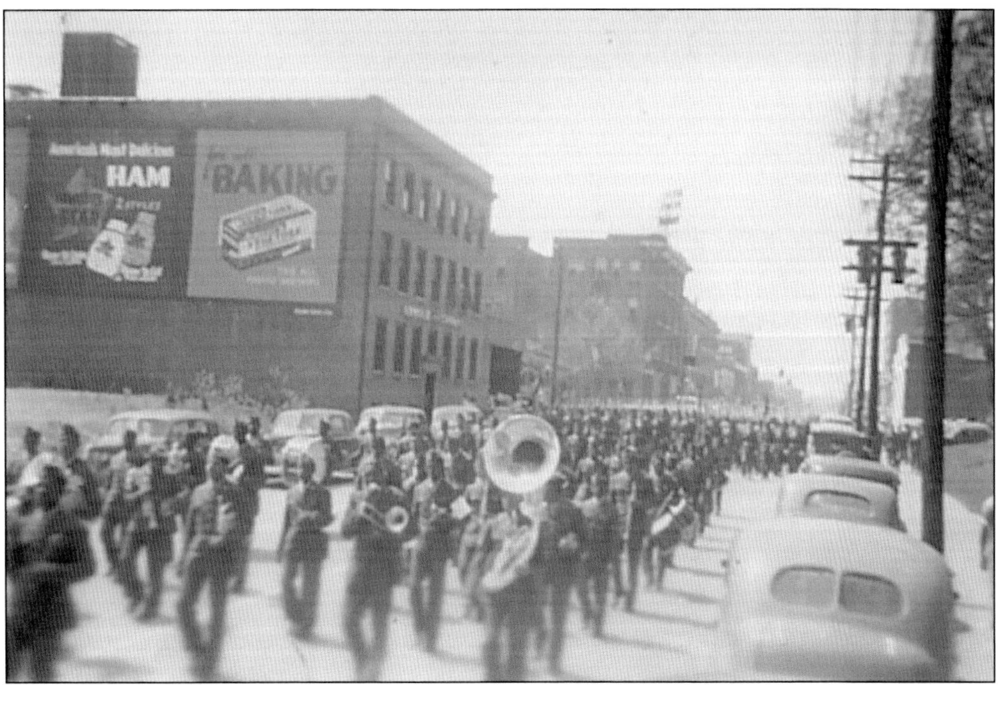

JOSEPH USSERY. Ussery is pictured performing his duties as a member of the U.S. Navy, *c.* 1940s (Courtesy of Susie P. Ussery.)

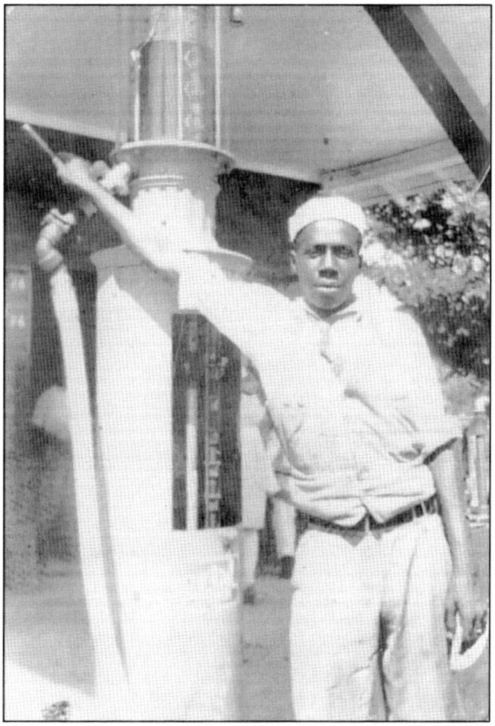

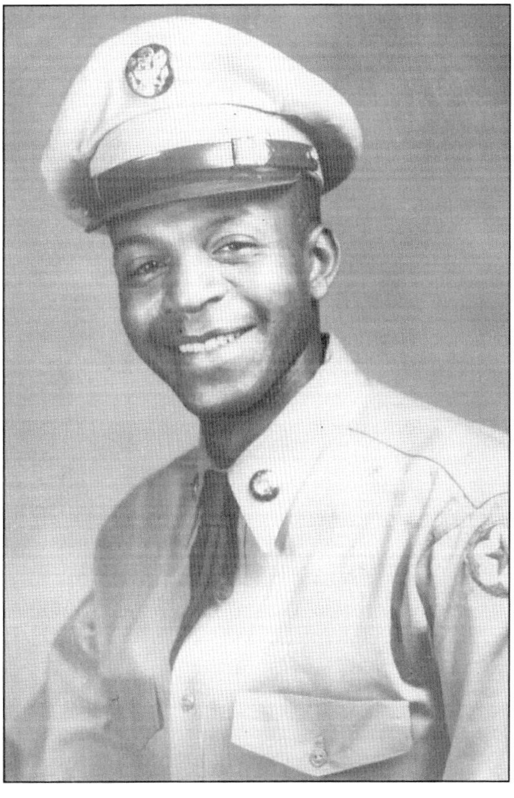

WALTER LATHAM. Latham grew up on Fourth Avenue in Pleasant Hill. He joined the U.S. Army in his early twenties, and married Lorena Andrew Howard. This photo was taken *c.* 1942. (Courtesy of Lorena H. Latham.)

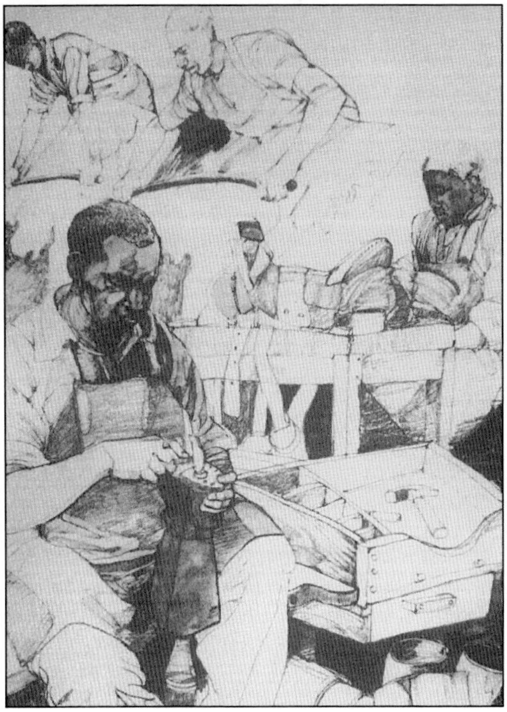

Shoe Cobblers. This sketch shows male slaves making and repairing shoes. Craftsmen of this caliber were prevalent on many plantations around Macon.

Repairing Shoes. James Ragland and his helper are pictured outside his shoe repair shop located in Napier Square, *c.* 1960. Mr. Ragland's shop is currently located on Pio Nono Avenue. (Courtesy of James Ragland.)

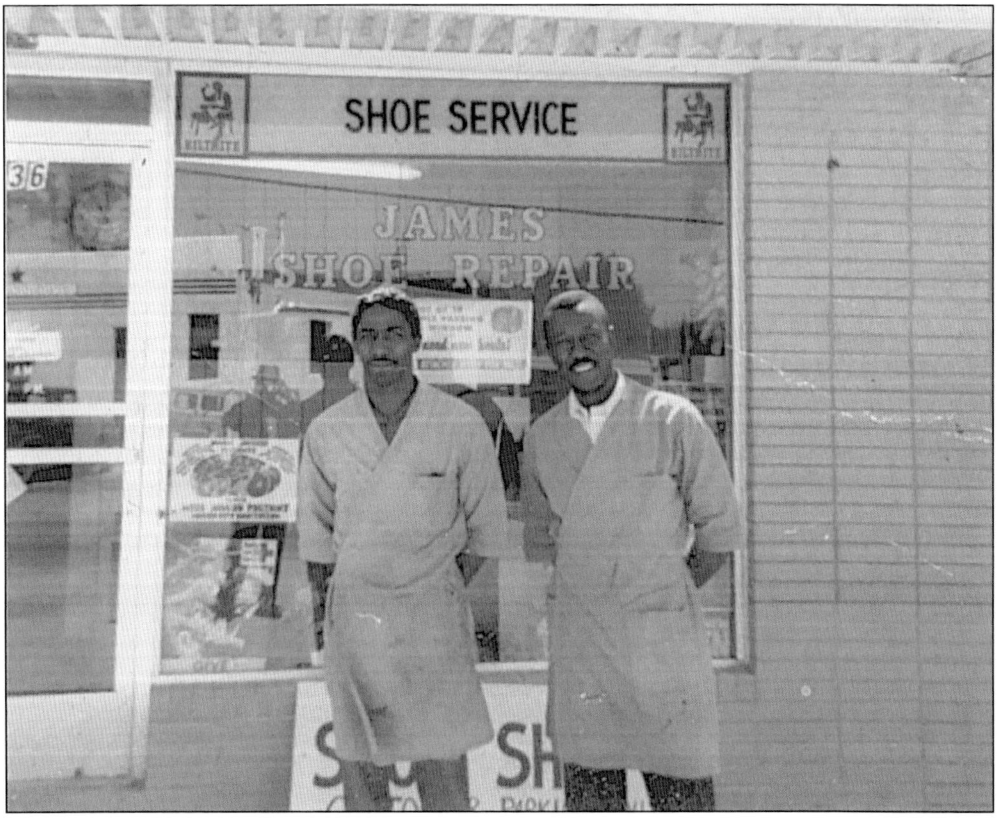

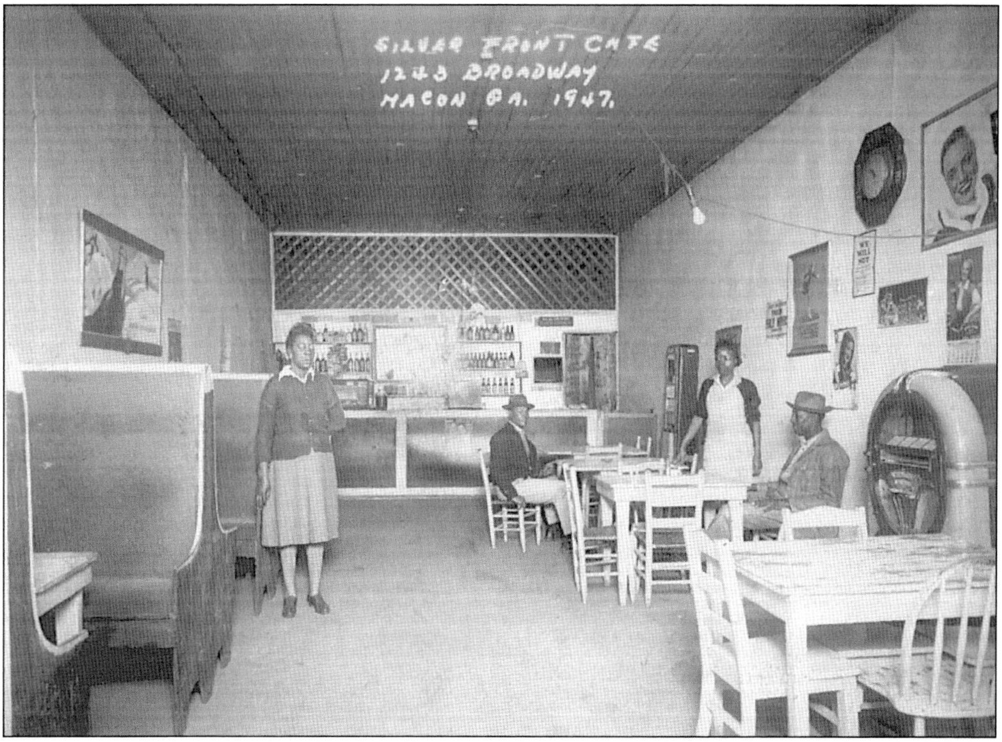

SILVER FRONT CAFE. The Silver Front Cafe was located on Broadway Street. Pictured here are three patrons and a waitress, *c.* 1947. Good food and music make the visit worthwhile. (Courtesy of George W. Crawley Jr.)

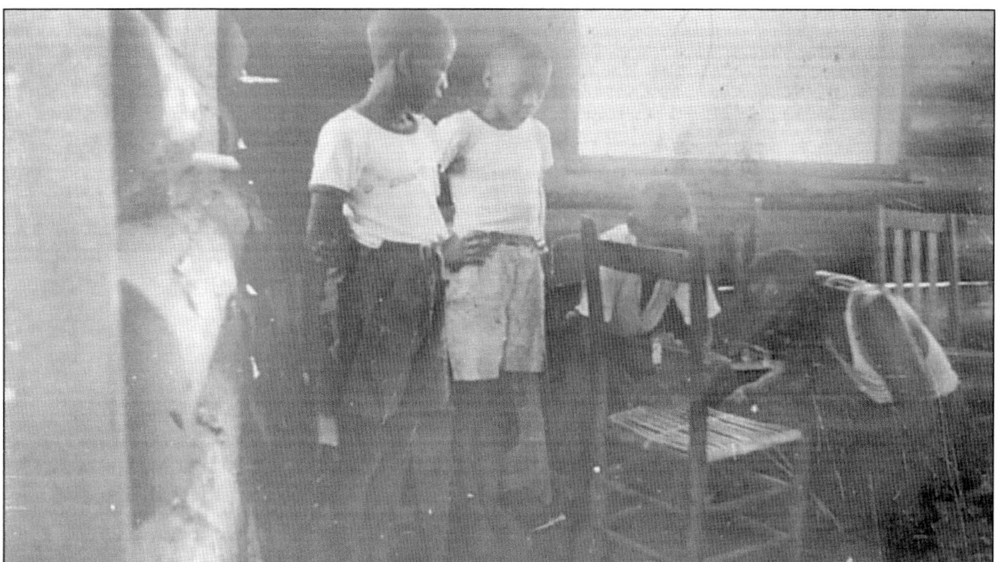

REPAIR DAY. Three young boys observe an older man repairing a cane bottom chair, *c.* 1938 (Courtesy of Booker T. Washington Center.)

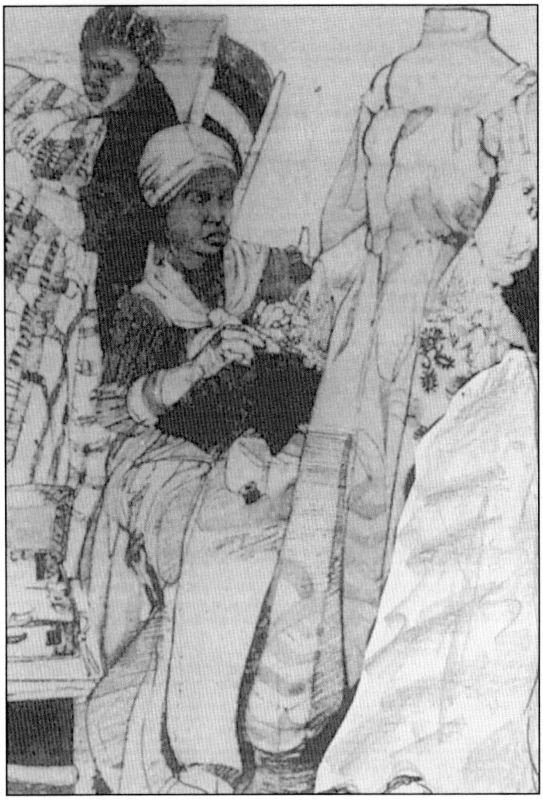

SLAVE COUPLE SEWING. The male slave appears to be working on a quilt, and the female slave is working on a dress for her mistress.

KARLA'S SHOE BOUTIQUE. Located on Cherry Street, this is another African-American business in Macon. The boutique is owned by the Redding family. Otis Redding was a rhythm and blues singer.

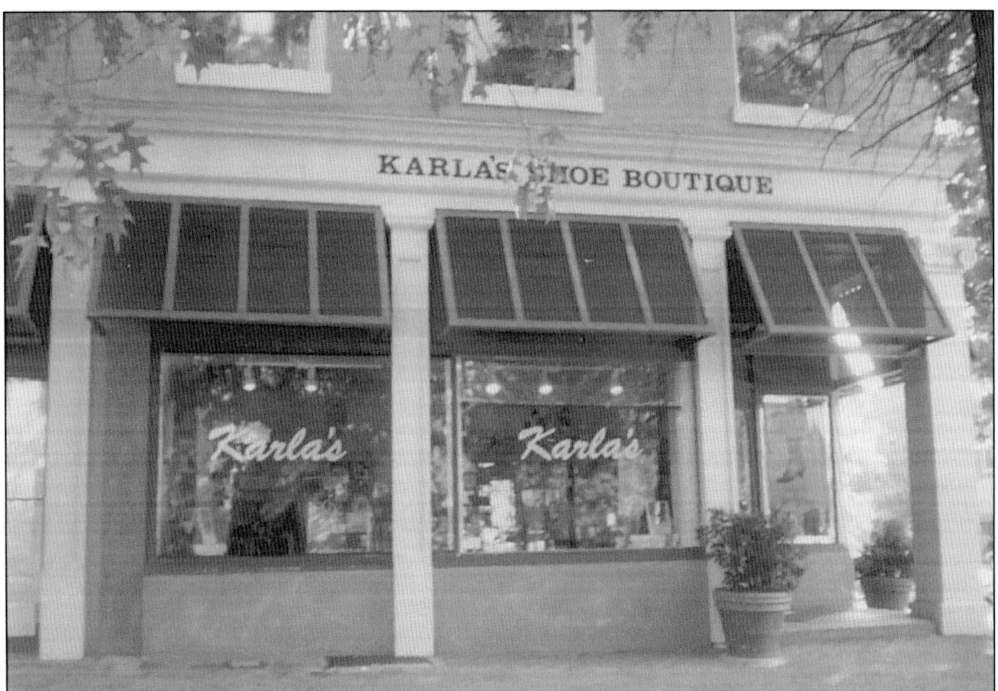

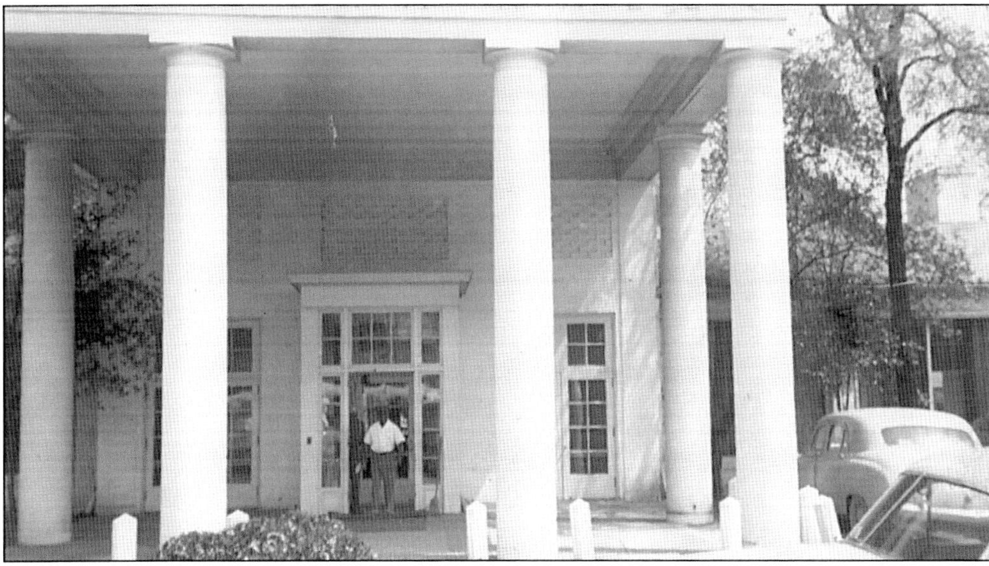

Warm Springs, GA. Two drivers are pictured coming out of an antebellum home in Warm Springs, GA, *c.* 1950 (Courtesy of Booker T. Washington Center.)

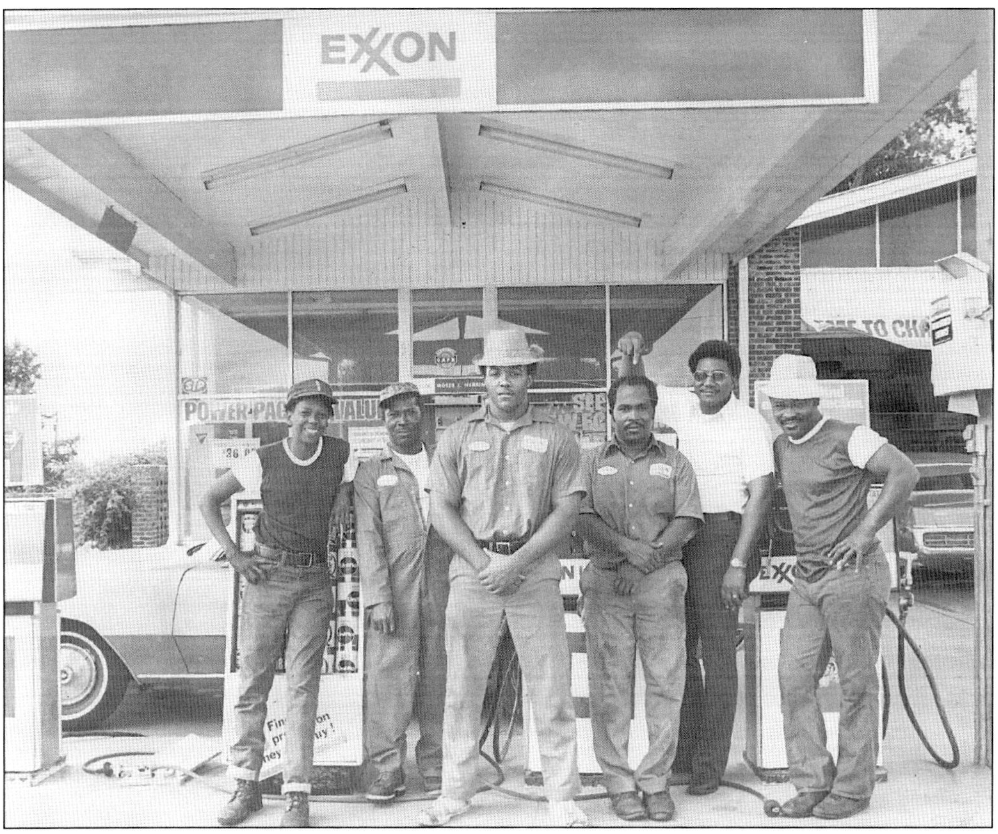

Men at Work, *c.* 1970s. This Exxon service station was located on Dempsey Avenue. It was owned and operated by the Herring family. (Courtesy of W.B. Herring.)

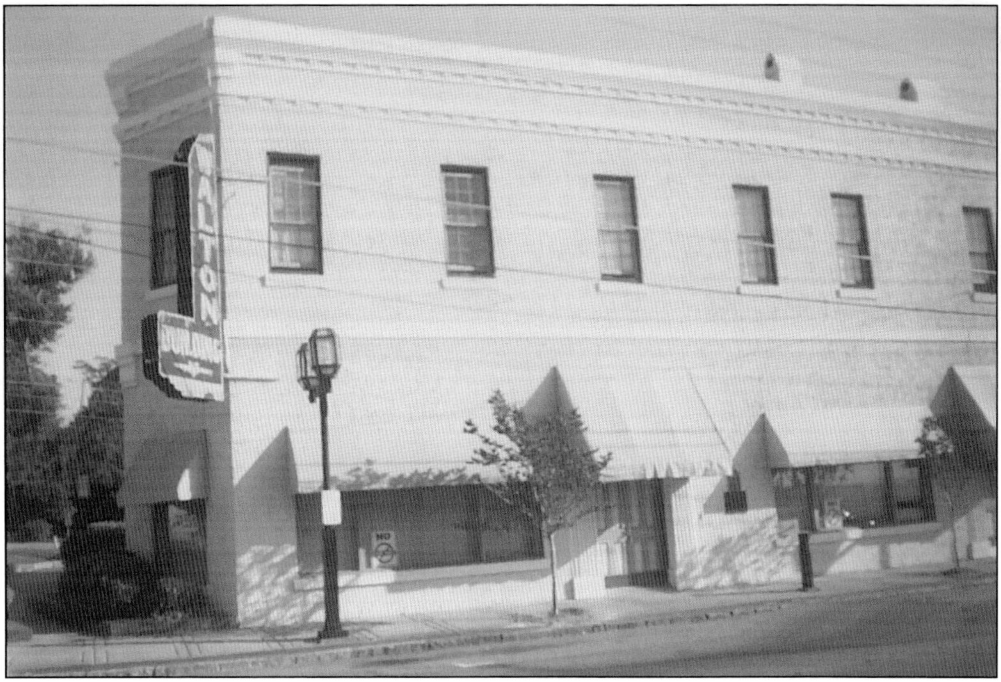

The Walton Building. Named for Dr. D.T. Walton, a local dentist who opened his practice here, this building was purchased in the 1930s. It is located on Cotton Avenue.

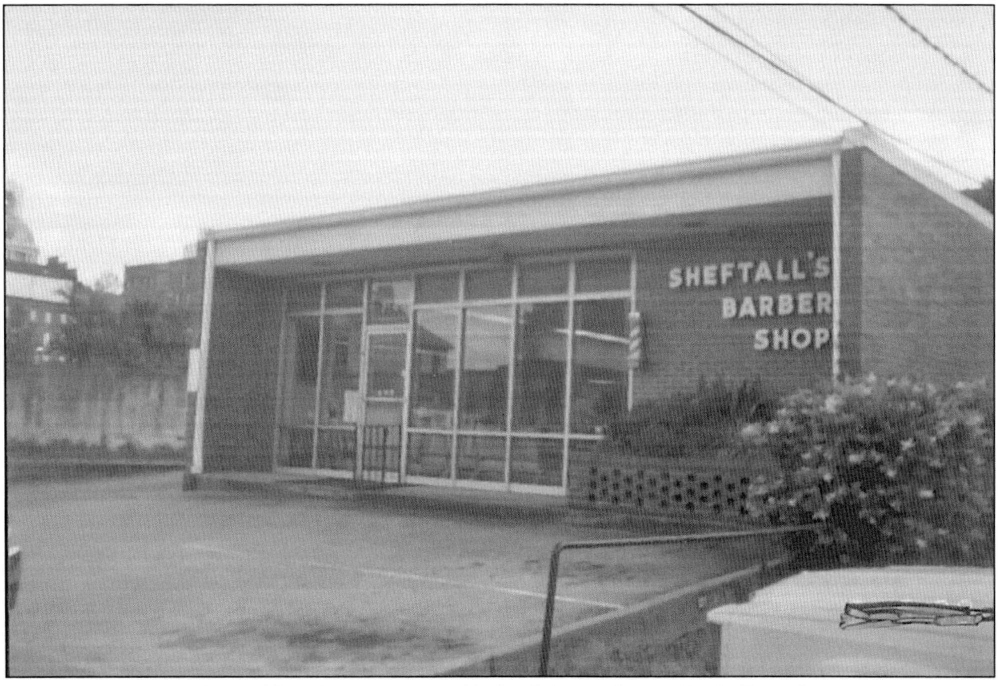

Sheftall's Barber Shop. The shop was established by Willis B. Sheftall in the 1950s.

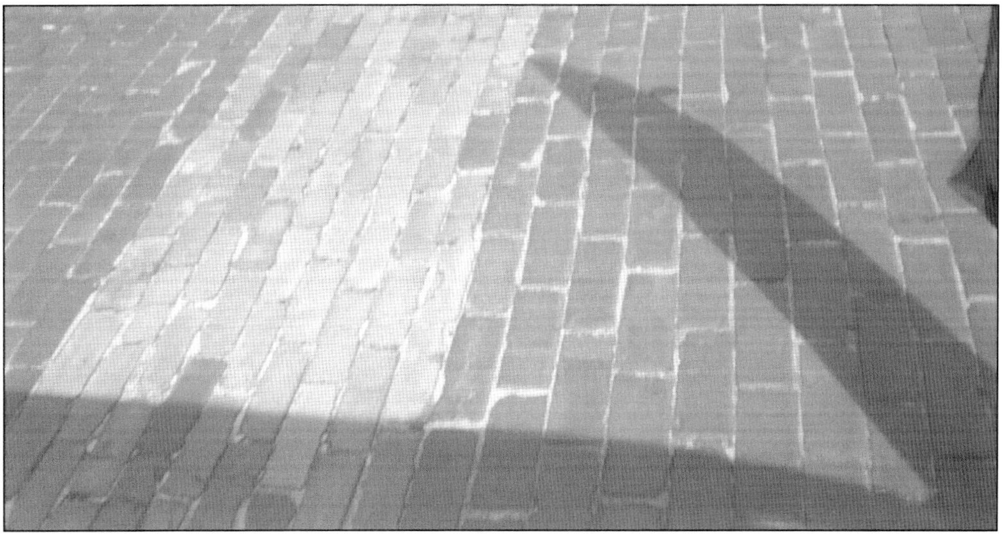

Streets Paved in Brick, not Gold. This picture shows a representation of a street paved with bricks (a cobblestone-type work). Stone walls are also featured on this street. Oral history gives an account of a stonemason by the name of Charlie Peyton who worked in this area. Some of his work can be seen on Riverside Drive.

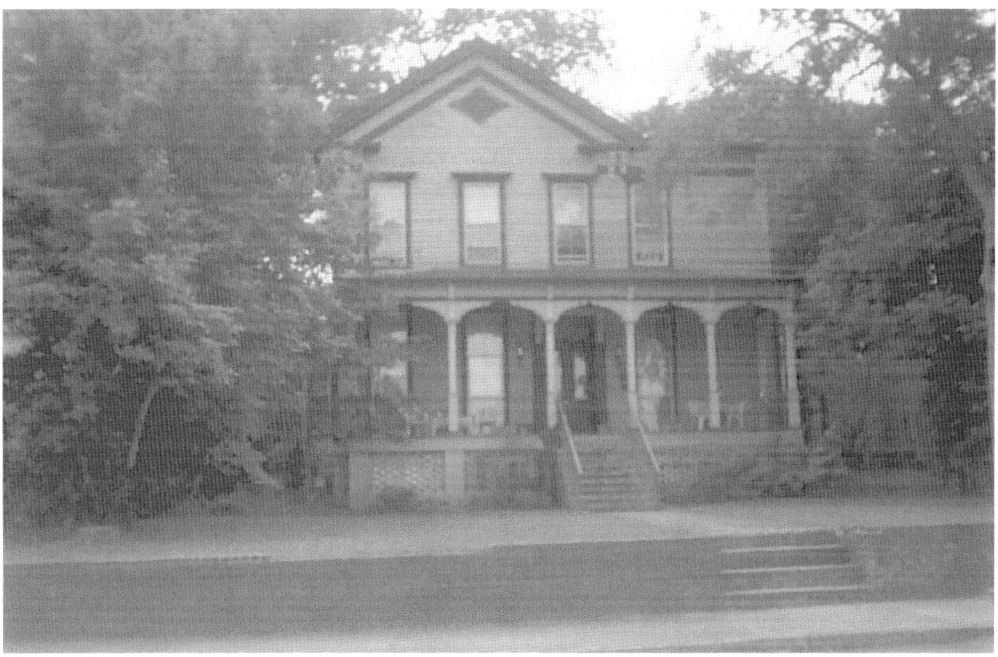

A Two-Story Wooden Home. This two-story frame home features an asymmetrically placed entry way. It has elongated windows, and is a combination of Victorian and Queen Anne influences. The house also features ornate trim. It is located in one of Macon's historic neighborhoods. African-American brick masons, carpenter, roofers, and partners built many of these homes. The street in front of this particular house is laid out in bricks. Careful scrutiny will reveal the approximate age of the work. A local company that employed many African Americans produced the bricks in the late 1800s and early 1900s.

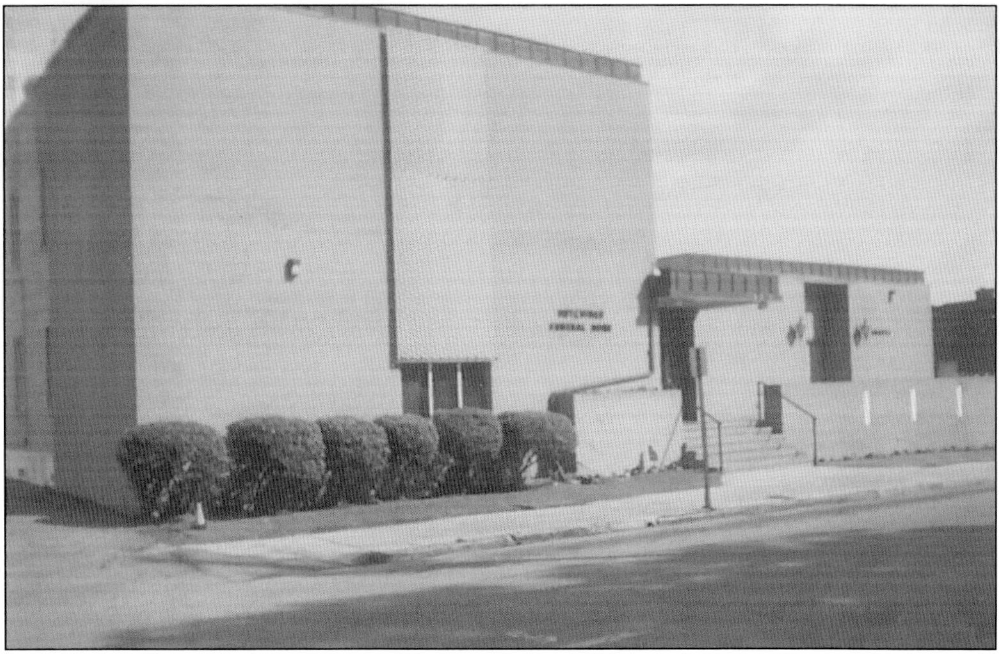

Hutchings Funeral Home. This funeral home was established as a family business by Frank J. Hutchings Sr. in the 1950s.

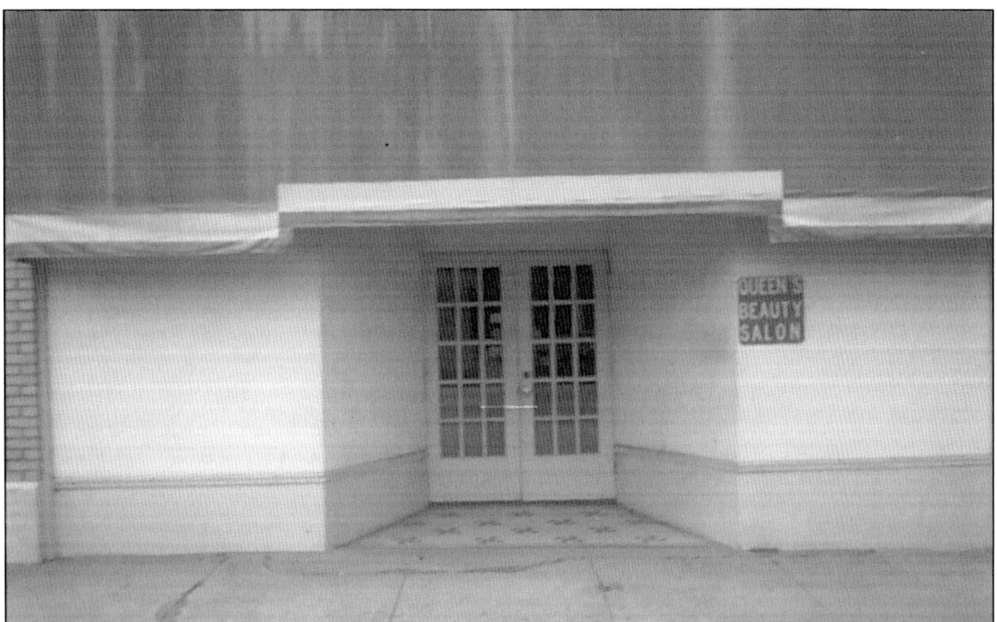

Queen's Beauty Shop. This hair salon is located on Forsythe Street and operated by Louise Hall. Mrs. Hall has been a hairstylist for over 40 years. Many of her customers come from out of town in order to have their hair done especially by her. Now that Mrs. Hall is semi-retired, the business is managed by her daughter.

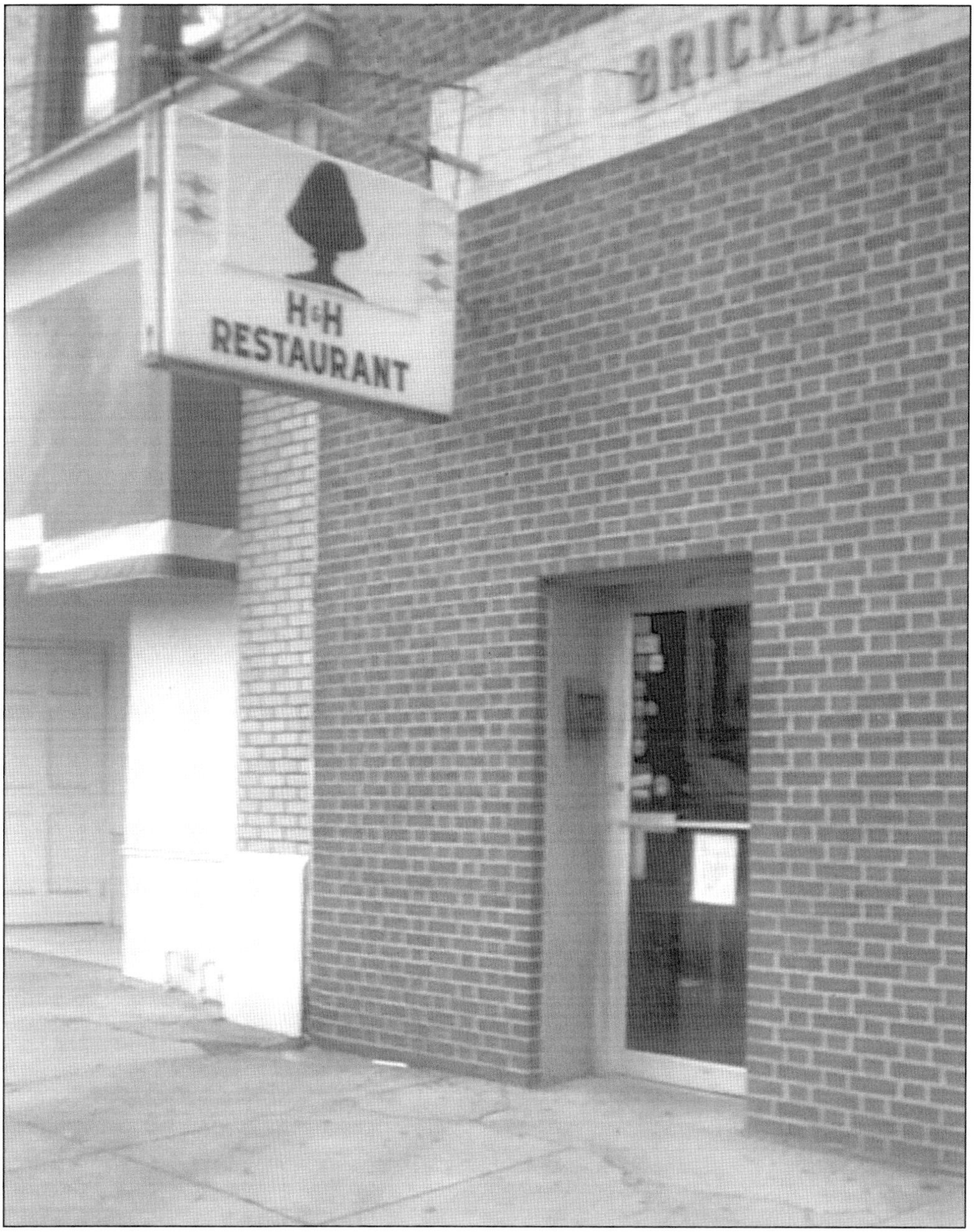

H&H Restaurant. Pictured is one of Macon's enduring establishments. The H&H Restaurant has been in existence since the 1950s (it has not always been in this spot) and has delicious "soul food" served daily. The proprietor is Ms. Louise Hudson. People come from all over Georgia and beyond to taste "Mama Louise's" cooking. The Allman Brothers and other famous celebrities frequent her establishment when they are in the area. It is located on Forsythe Street.

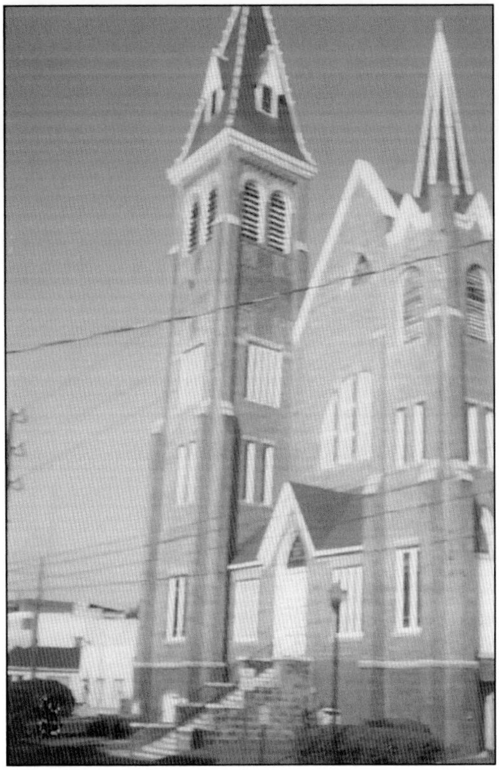

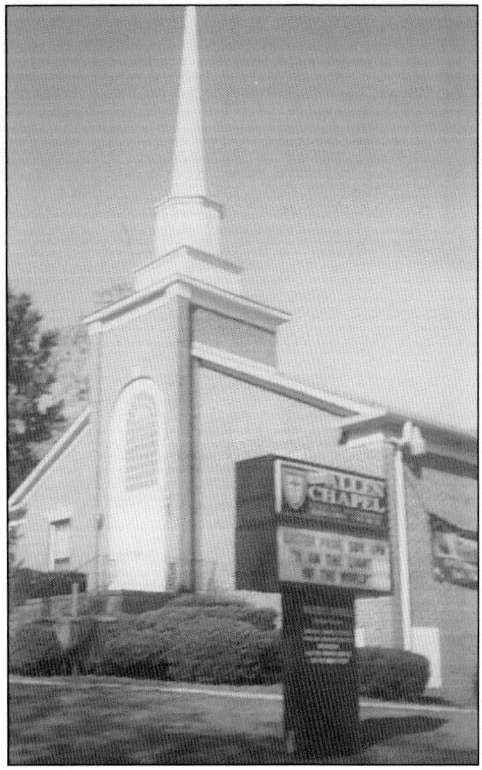

***Left*: The First Baptist Church.** This church was established before 1863, in the early years when blacks and whites worshiped together. For the first few years, 1866–1867, Rev. Milton Tilinghast was the ordained minister. A most elegant edifice, this church is located on Cotton Avenue.

***Right*: Allen Chapel Church.** Located on Pursley Street in Pleasant Hill, this church was established in 1887 by Reverend Stroud. It carries a Methodist congregation.

The Bellvue Baptist Church. Reverend Colts is the current pastor. He has brought many new and exciting plans for the congregation to consider under his tenure.

Five

Religion and Politics:

How They Worked Together

The church is the heart of African-American culture. Whether the individual is a practicing member of a specific denomination or not, if asked most would say that the church and religion is the source of how and why we as a people have been able to survive. Some of the churches that you will see have been a part of the Macon community for over a hundred years. Slaves had to worship in secret—the coming together of black people in a large body was always look upon by whites as a suspicious act and so assembly by blacks was discouraged. Churches were the only place African Americans could freely express themselves and feel a sense of empowerment. Many churches were started in ditches, in caves, or any place out of sight of the oppressors. The early Maconites would sing and call upon the Lord for strength and liberation. After the Civil War and during Reconstruction it was the church that nurtured blacks and was the sustaining force in their lives. In the 1920s and 1930s it was the church that took black Maconites through World War I, the Depression, and into the 1940s and World War II. During these awful times, when America was experiencing problems in the extreme, those problems were doubly worse for blacks.

It would be decades before Macon's African-American community would see some light at the end of the tunnel. The political arena denied blacks' participation. Obstacles like the grandfather clause and the poll tax were put in place to discourage voting by blacks, and much more violent tactics were employed by the Klan. Death could be yours if an attempt was made to vote. The political leadership came from the churches, and the preachers became the spokespersons in black communities all over the South. Religion and politics always worked closely together. Jefferson Long, a Macon politician during Reconstruction, fought many battles for African-American inclusion, and other leaders have followed in his footsteps. Later, in modern times, preachers like Van J. Malone and Julius Hope negotiated, marched, and worked for better treatment of the black community. Henry McNeal Turner was another Macon representative, but was not allowed his seat. Disillusioned and angry, he protested the Georgia General Assembly in a speech entitled "I Will Not Beg For My Rights." When the Civil Rights Act of 1875 did not pass, he lost faith in the liberals.

By the year 1900, Macon's African Americans had lost most of their gains in the area of equal rights. In later years, with the Civil Rights Movement of the 1950s and 1960s, Macon began to struggle again with the equal rights issues. Church leaders and business leaders came together to create a movement of their own. William P. Randall was in the midst of Macon's struggle. Mr. Randall met with Abernathy, King, Jackson, and others on numerous occasions. Working together with Mrs. Ozzie Bell McKay, Rev. G.H. Williams, Rev. Booker Chambers, Reverend Evans, and various concerned white citizens, they helped to create a better Macon.

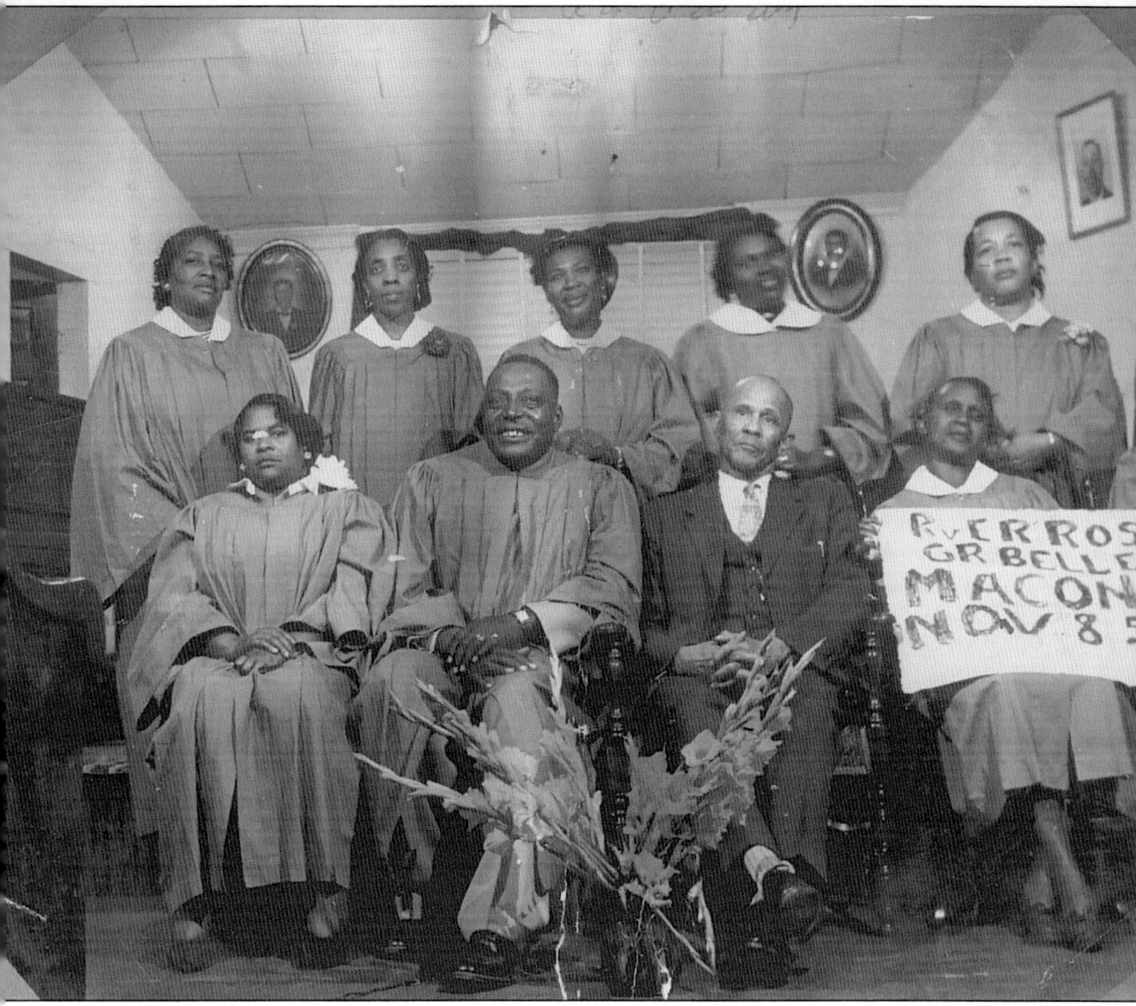

The Bellvue Baptist Senior Choir. Shown here is the senior choir in Bellvue Baptist Church on Montford Road, *c.* 1950s. Seated in the center is the pastor, Rev. E.D. Ross. This picture was taken inside the old church, and there is now a new edifice. This is also the church of the Emanuel Howard family. (Courtesy of Lorena H. Latham.)

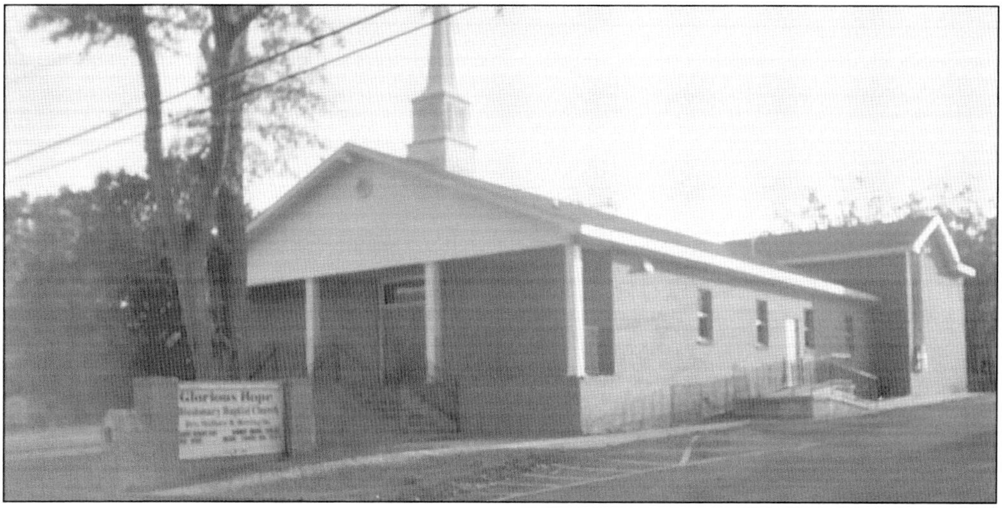

Glorious Hope Baptist Church. This church is located on Scotland Avenue, and Rev. Wallace B. Herring Sr. is the pastor.

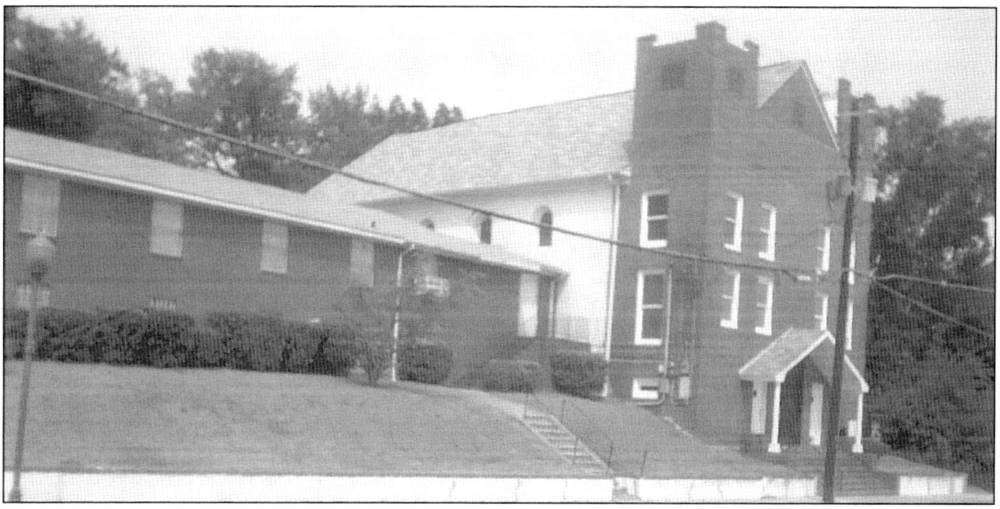

Mount Olive Baptist. This church is located on Oglethorpe Street near downtown Macon.

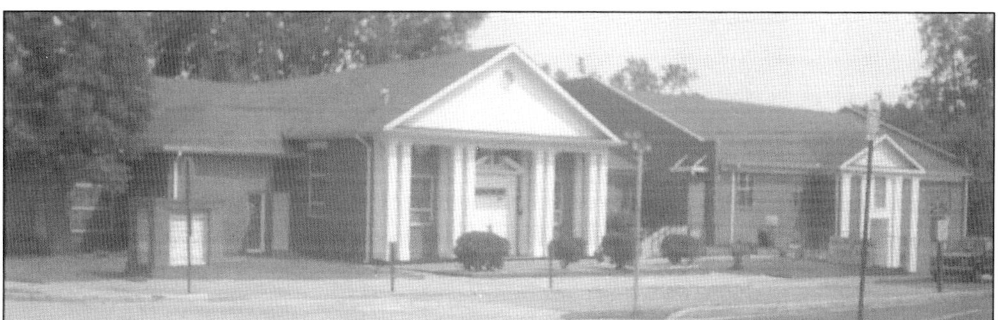

The Community Church of God. This church carries a Pentecostal congregation. It is located on Grant Avenue in the Pleasant Hill community. Rev. James P. Jackson is the pastor.

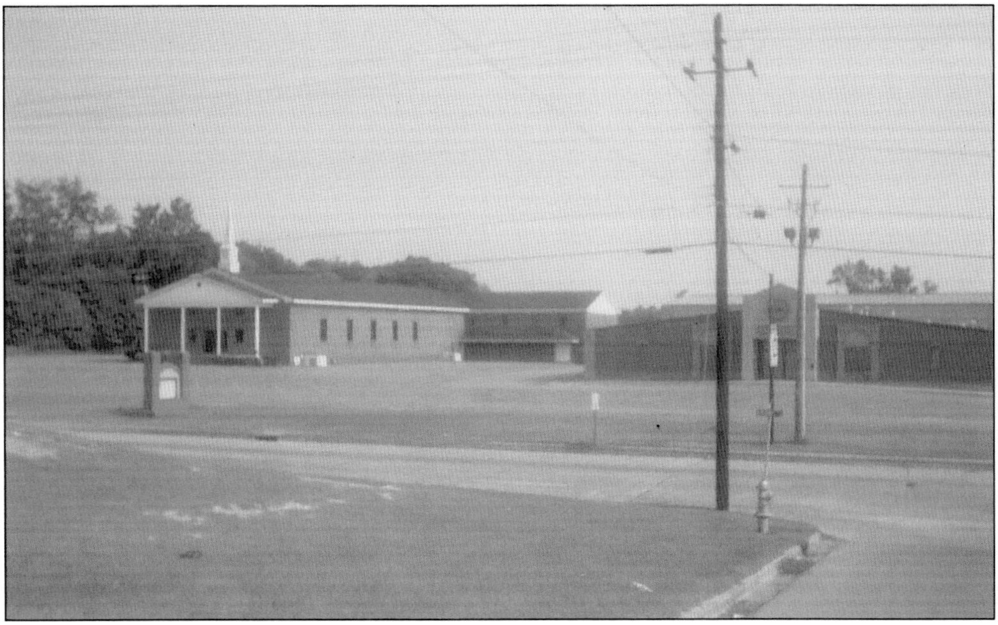

MACEDONIA MISSIONARY BAPTIST. Located on Anthony Road, this church was started by Rev. R. B. Williams in 1893. In its 107-year history there has been many outstanding leaders. Rev. E.D. Smith Sr. is the current pastor.

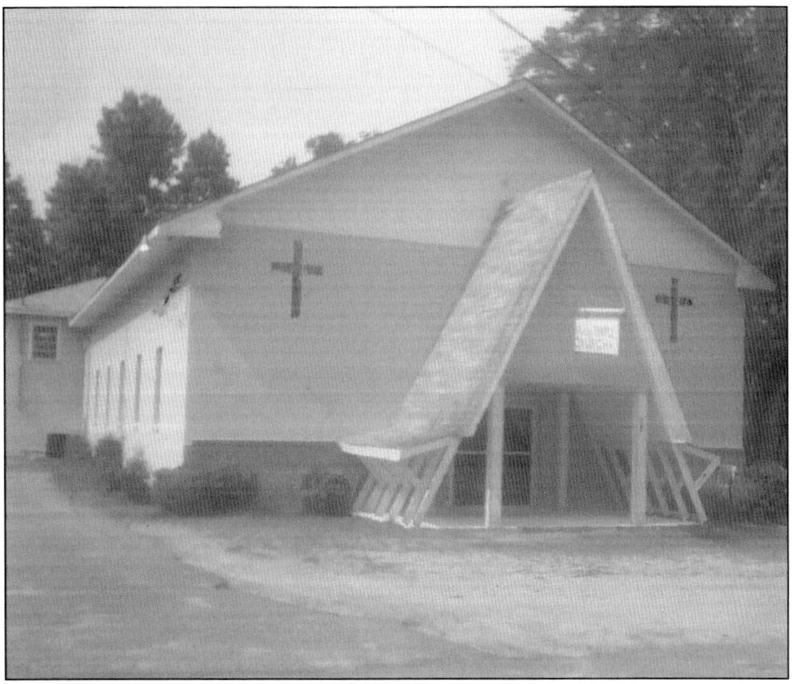

HEALING TEMPLE. This is a church that carries a Pentecostal and Charismatic congregation, revealing divinely inspired gifts of power of miraculous proportions. It is located on Williams Street. Rev. Bishop Percy Welch is the pastor. Evangelist Shirley Caesar, the famous gospel singer, has preached here many times.

WASHINGTON AVENUE PRESBYTERIAN. This church came into being when a slave was designated as a religious leader for blacks in Macon. On May 24, 1839, there was a separation of black and white congregations. Joseph Williams served as the first pastor. It is a beautiful historical structure.

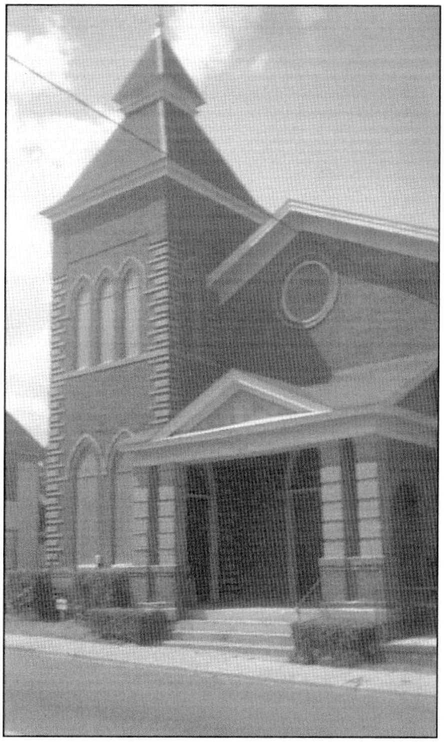

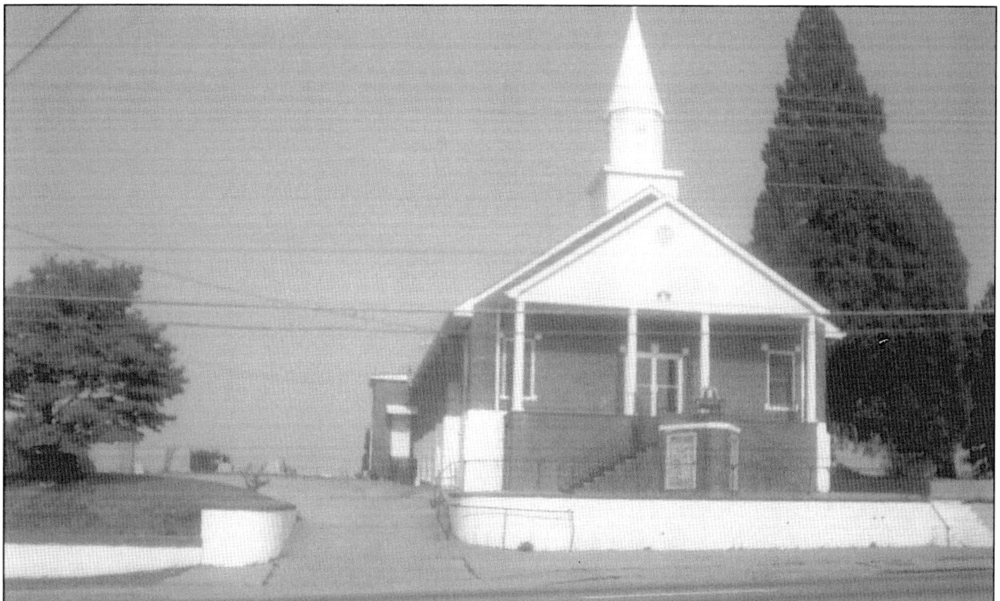

UNIONVILLE MISSIONARY BAPTIST. This church began in 1865 shortly after the Civil War. Some whites were also affiliated with the church in the early years. The church has a long history marked by many accomplishments. Reverend Mack is the current pastor.

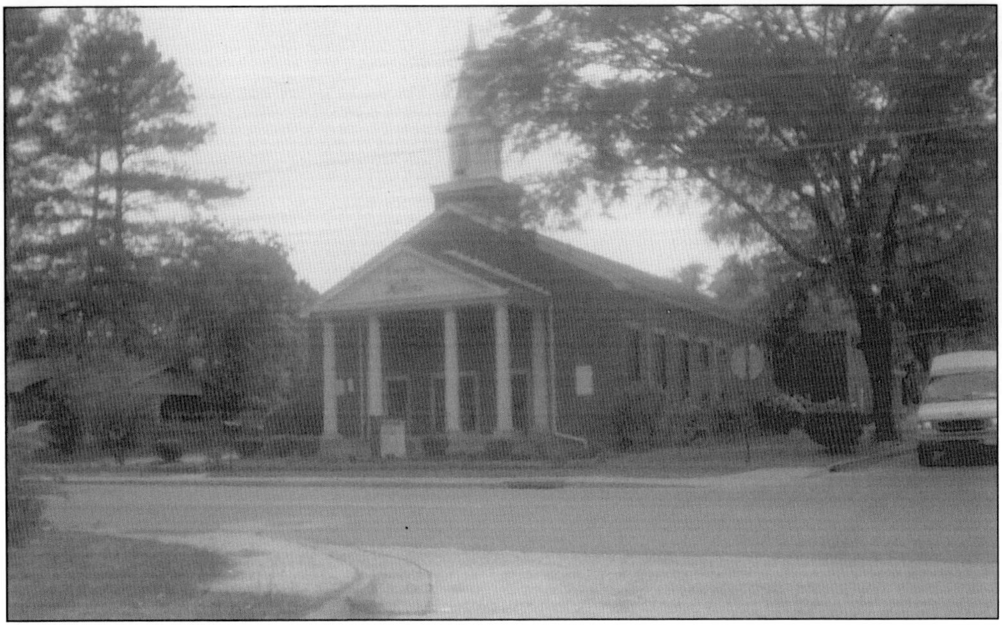

Lizzieboro Baptist. This church is located on Fort Hill Street in East Macon. Rev. Moses Dumas is the pastor.

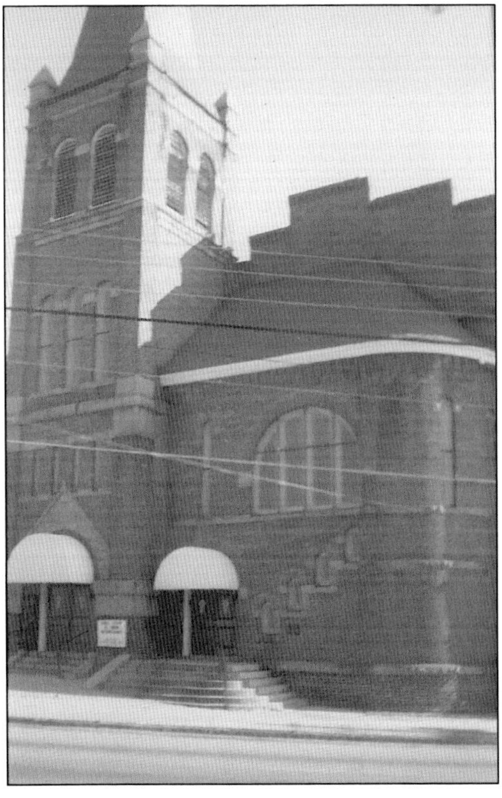

The Steward Chapel AME Church. This photograph shows a place of worship for African Methodist Episcopal followers. The church is well over 100 years old, and is located on Forsythe Street. Many programs benefitting young and elderly members of the community began in the Steward Chapel congregation.

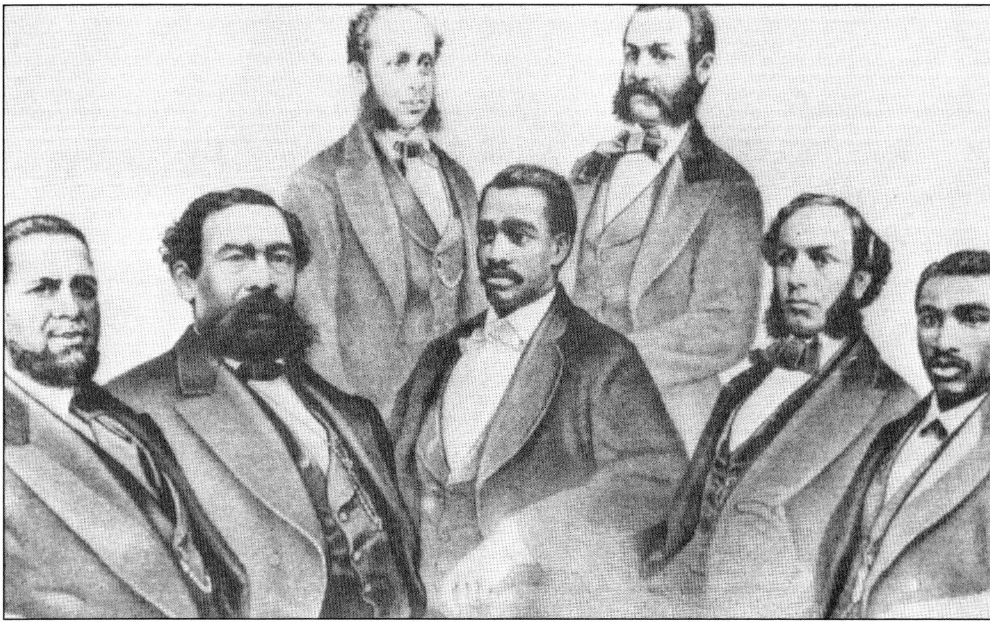

African-American Legislators. This picture shows 7 of the 14 congressmen who served during Reconstruction. Pictured are the following: (front row) Hiram R. Revels, Benjamin S. Turner, Jesiah T. Walls, Joseph H. Rainey, and R. Brown Elliot; (back row) Robert C. DeLarge and Jefferson H. Long, both from Macon, GA.

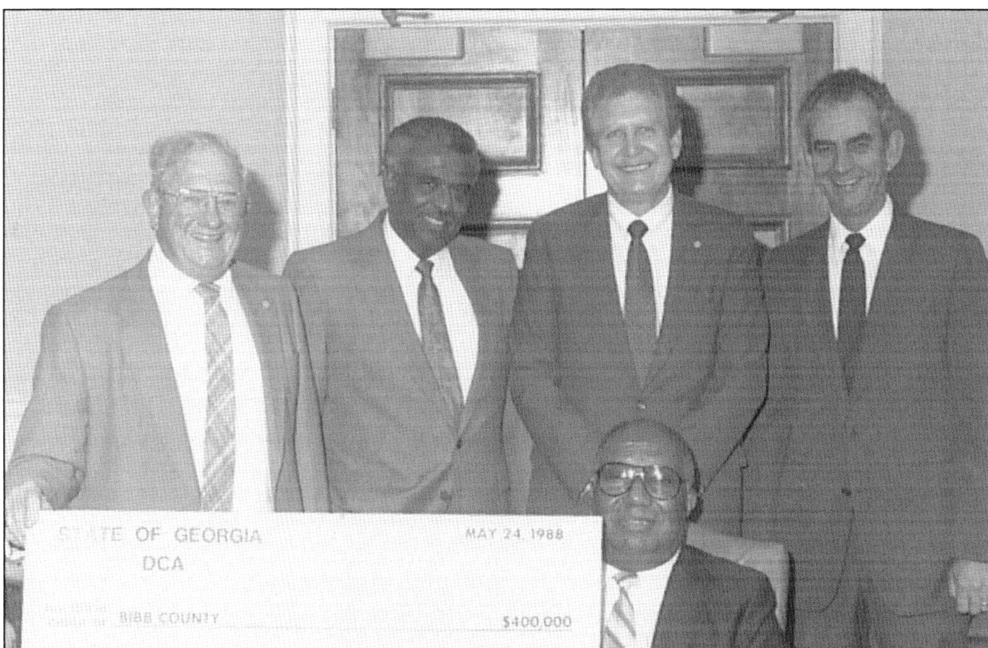

Bibb County (Macon) Government Leaders, *c.* 1988. Pictured from left to right are Earl Zimmerman, Albert Billingslea, Larry Justice, and Emory Greene. William P. Randall is seated. (Courtesy of Judge William and Lauretta Randall.)

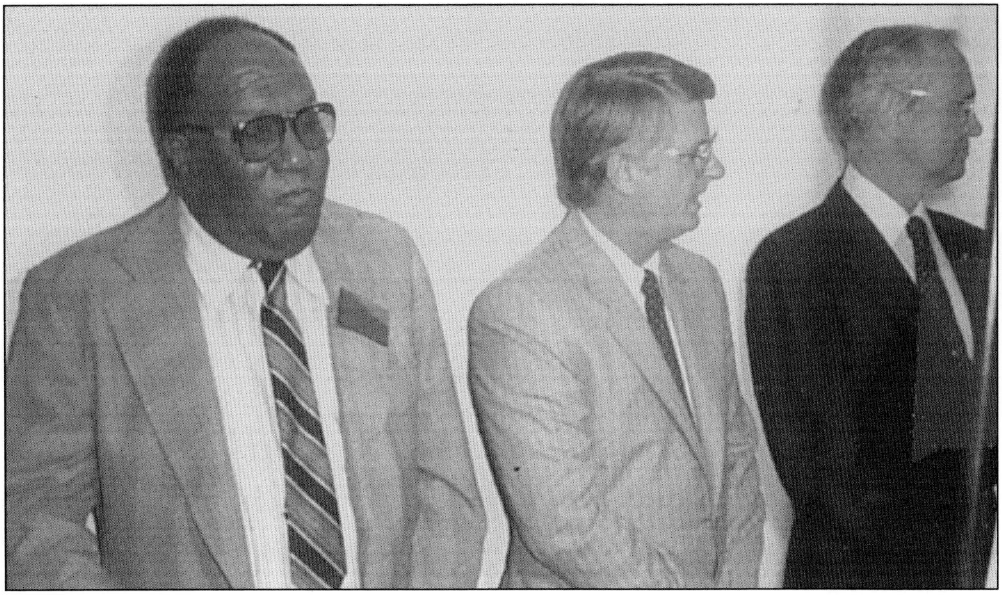

WILLIAM P. RANDALL. Mr. Randall was a kind and generous man who worked diligently to help members of his race. A real fighter for Civil Rights in Macon, he marched with Dr. Martin Luther King Jr. in the 1960s in several of the famous desegregation events. In 1961, in his hometown of Macon, Randall organized a successful "Bus Ride for Freedom" for the youth. He was very active in civic, community, religious, and political affairs all of his life, and served as president of many local, state, and national organizations. Randall was considered a powerful leader by both blacks and whites. The NAACP, SCLC, and the Macon Chamber of Commerce were blessed with his leadership abilities, just to name a few.

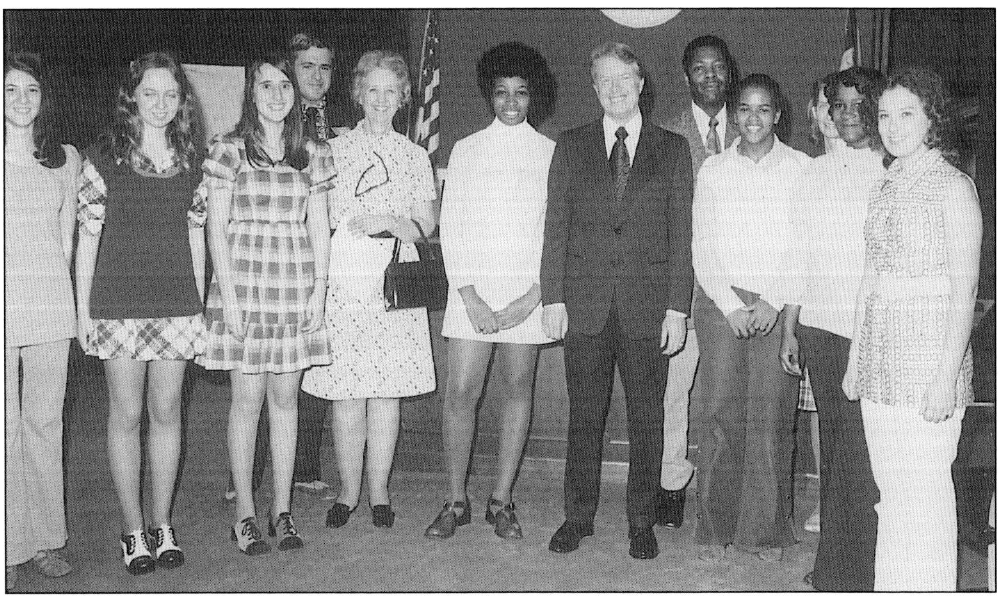

JAMES EARL CARTER. Future president Jimmy Carter and Mr. Washington (behind him), a teacher with the Bibb County Board of Education, are pictured with a group of students honored for good citizenship, *c.* late 1960s.

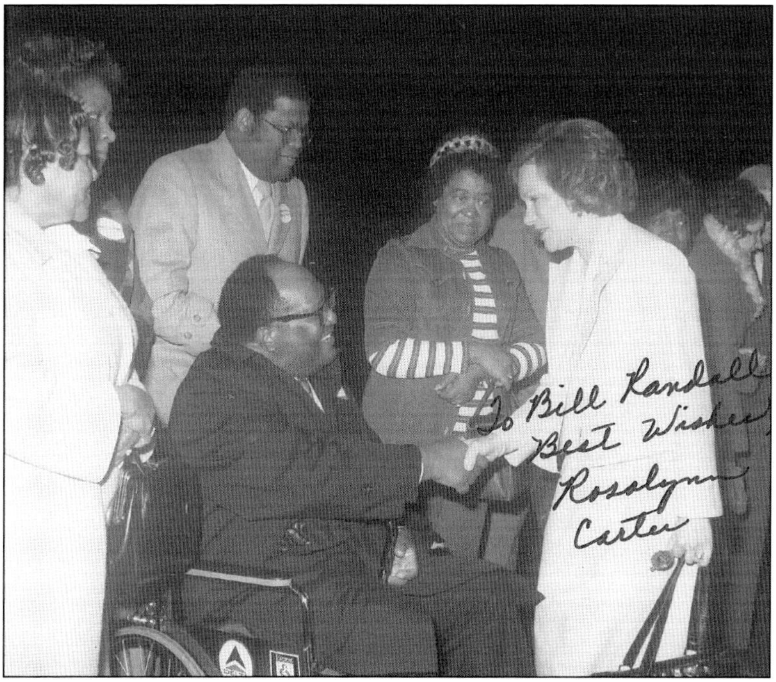

William P. Randall and Mrs. Rosalynn Carter. Mrs. Carter is shaking hands with the senior Mr. Randall., *c.* 1970s (Courtesy of Judge and Mrs. William C. Randall.)

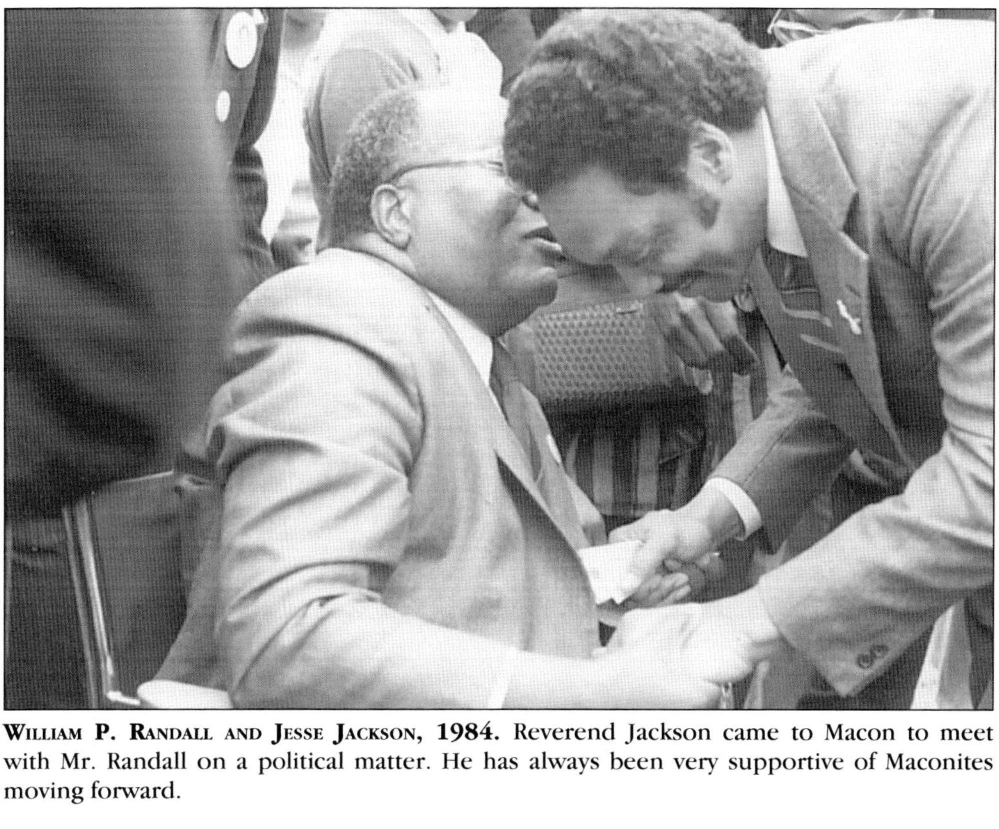

William P. Randall and Jesse Jackson, 1984. Reverend Jackson came to Macon to meet with Mr. Randall on a political matter. He has always been very supportive of Maconites moving forward.

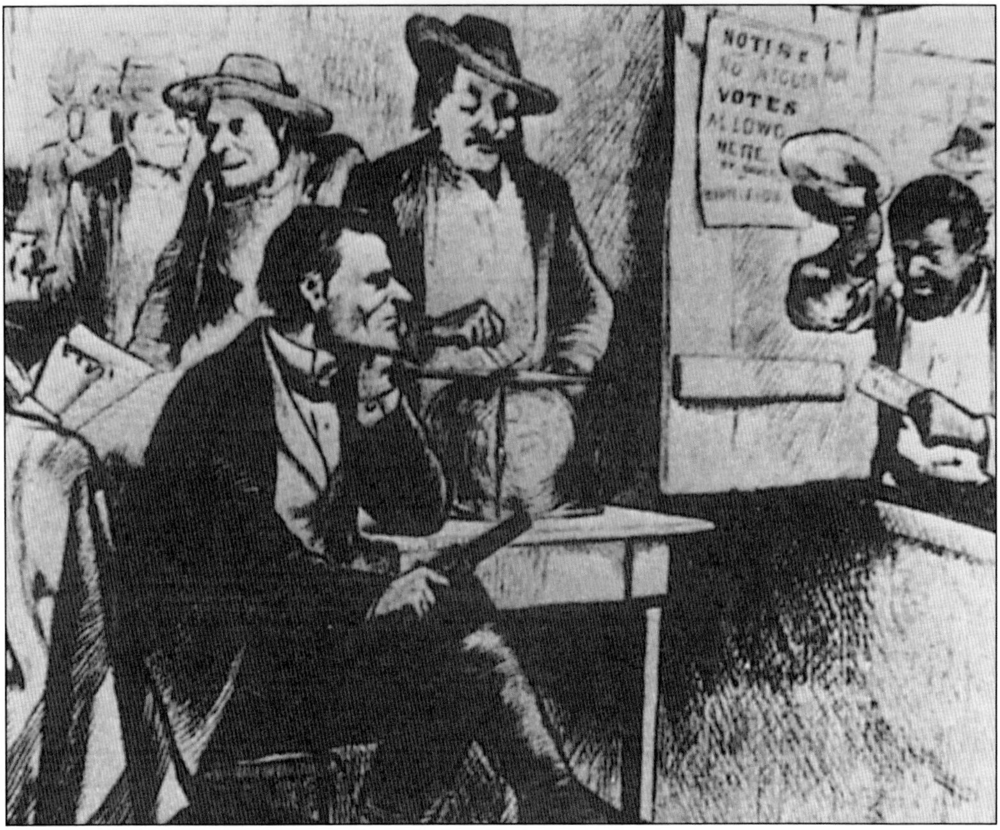

The Right to Vote. This picture shows an African-American male at the polling place wanting to cast his vote, while whites discouraged him. The man sitting at the table is holding a gun—this was an example of the intimidation faced by African Americans in Macon and throughout the country in earlier years.

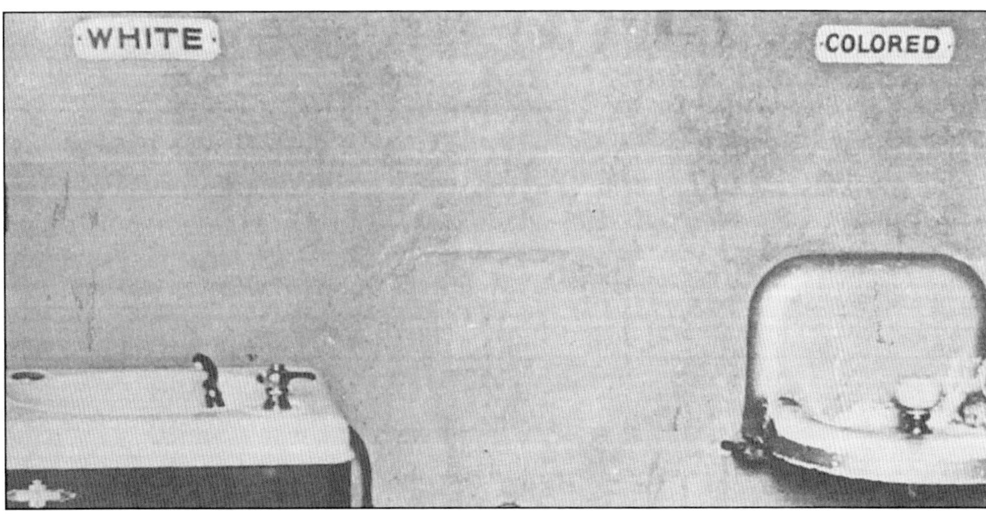

"White and Colored." No words can fully express the depth of humiliation felt by blacks as this picture conveys. It fully illustrates the time of segregation and Jim Crow laws.

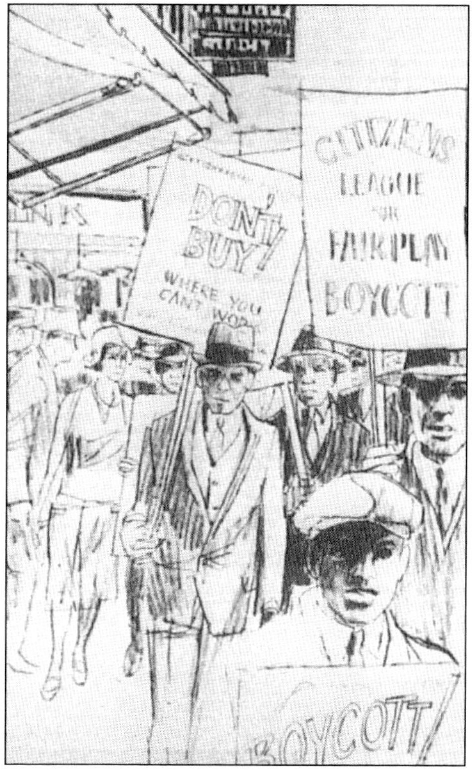

An Act of Protest. Walking the line in order to show discontentment was common in the 1950s and 1960s. Carrying signs and marching were techniques used by Maconites seeking equal rights. Many citizens who marched risked their jobs, safety, and even their lives.

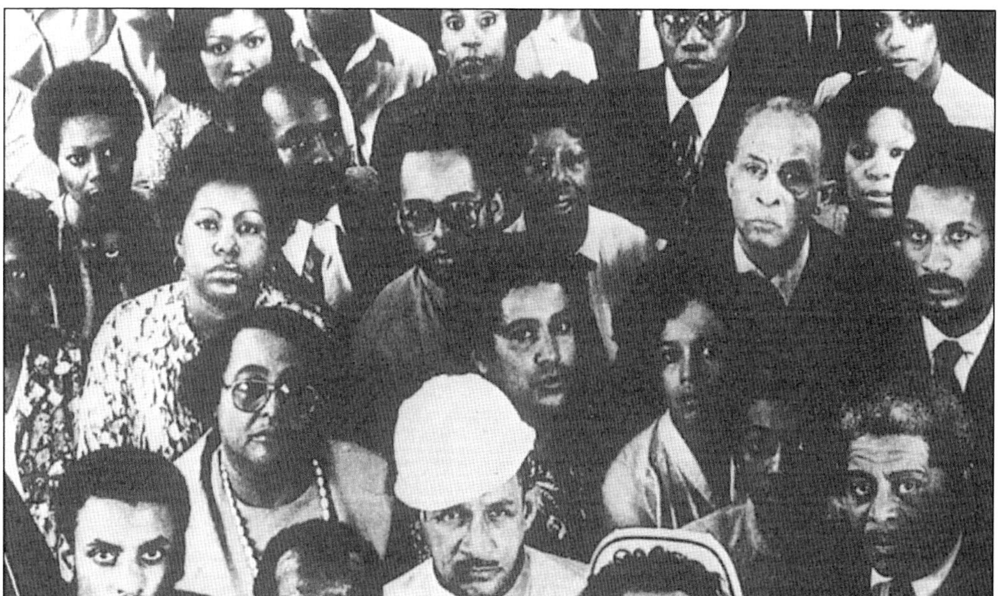

A Group of African-American Citizens. These men and women appear to be seeking their place in America. True identity and ownership are often difficult to find for blacks in this country.

Celebrity and the Arts. This sketch shows African Americans enjoying and participating in music, a medium that allows complete expression.

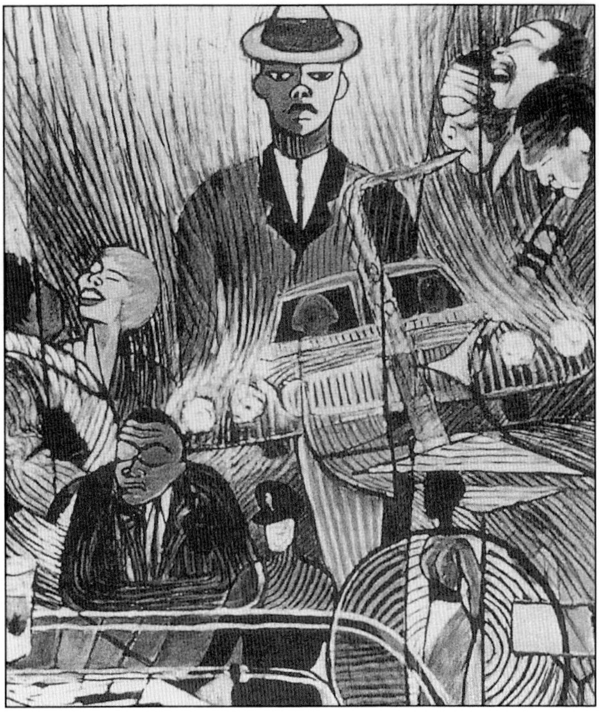

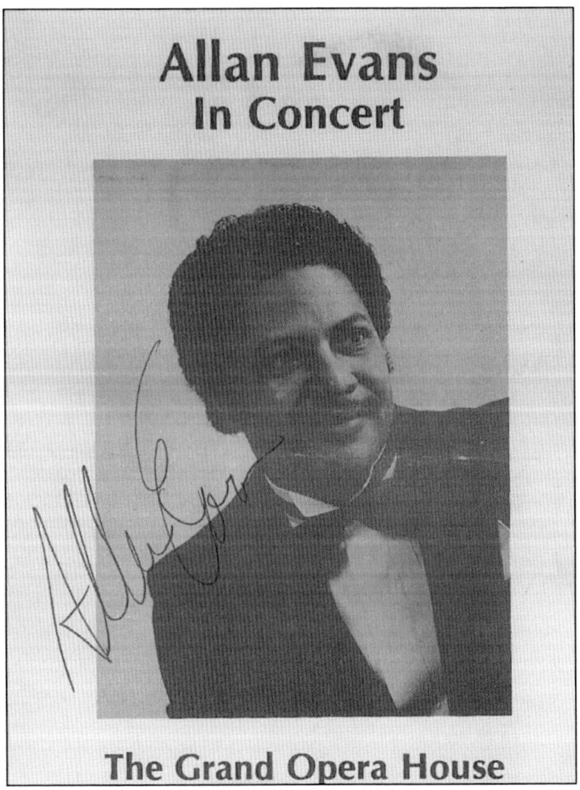

Alan Evans. This picture is on a program that Mr. Evans performed at the Grand Opera House on June 29, 1985. The program was personally autographed by Evans, an international opera star. (Courtesy of Jeanne C. Herring.)

Six

CELEBRITY AND THE ARTS:

OUR STARS

There have been many famous men and women to come out of Macon. These celebrities come from all areas of life—from athletes, opera stars, and writers to R&B pop stars, visual artists, and many more. For many African Americans in Macon, sports was the vehicle that catapulted them into notoriety on the local level; and others were able to conquer state, national, and even international arenas in their sports category. Some used their talents and skills to earn scholarships for college. Others simply wanted a better life than their parents had and chose sports as a way to get ahead in life. These youngsters always had mentors in coaches such as Don Richardson and Robert Slocum. These men were not just coaches, but took on the role of fathers, uncles, and big brothers. Some star athletes to hail from Macon were Miles Patrick, drafted by the L.A. Lakers; Jeff Malone, a first round draft pick of the Washington Bullets; Jim Parker, 1957 first pick by Baltimore Colts and a member of the Professional Football Hall of Fame (1973); Tommy Hart, tenth draft pick by the San Francisco 49ers and who also coached for the Dallas Cowboys; and John "Blue Moon" Odom, an outstanding high school baseball player who signed a $75,000 contract with Kansas City in 1964. The club moved to Oakland, CA, in 1968, and Odom pitched in the 1972, 1973, and 1974 World Series. Other notable athletes include Elmore Smith, drafted by Buffalo as their first draft choice in 1971; Julius Adams, drafted by the New England Patriots; Norm Nixon, who played for the L.A. Lakers; Chris Robinson; and James T. Thomas, first draft pick of the Pittsburg Steelers (cousin of Tommy Hart). Thomas helped the Steelers go to the Super Bowl in 1974 and 1975.

Many of Macon's female athletes also found fame. Alice Coachman was the first African American to win an Olympic gold medal, and Brenda Cliette was selected as an alternate for the U.S. Olympic Track Team.

In the visual arts, none was better than Leo Moss. He was a dollmaker, and his dolls cost from $3,500 to $9,000 today. He was extremely creative, and often traded his dolls for food. His work dates back to the 1830s. Alissi McQueen (a textile artist), Wilfred Stroud, John Oliver Killens, Richard Powell, Tina McElroy Ansa, Little Richard, Otis Redding, and James Brown were writers and musicians whose work is read and heard nationally and internationally. Some outstanding musical groups were the Floats and the Famous Flames. James Duncan and Johnny Jenkins were very talented Macon musicians as well. Johnny Jenkins often stated, "I would have been as famous as Otis Redding, but I didn't like flying." Alan Evans became an international opera star. Charles Welch, Billy Young, and Pearly Brown all contributed to the flavorful musical history of Macon. These artists received their start as hometown talents and blossomed into major stars.

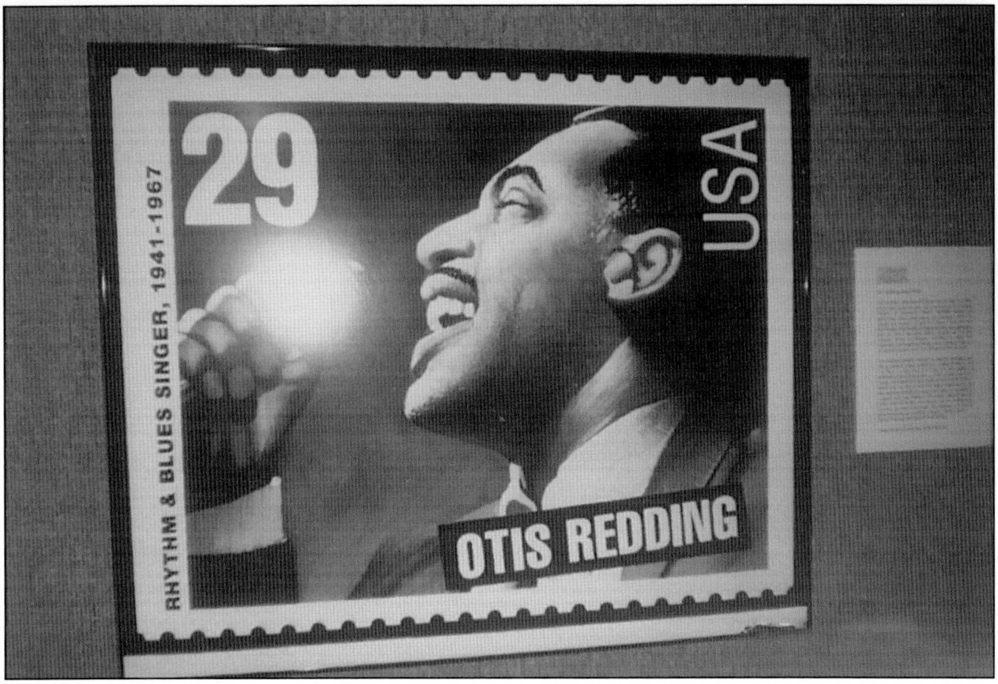

Otis Redding. Mr. Redding's likeness appeared on a U.S. stamp in 1992, and this likeness is hanging in the Tubman Museum. He lost his life in a plane crash in 1967 at the age of 26.

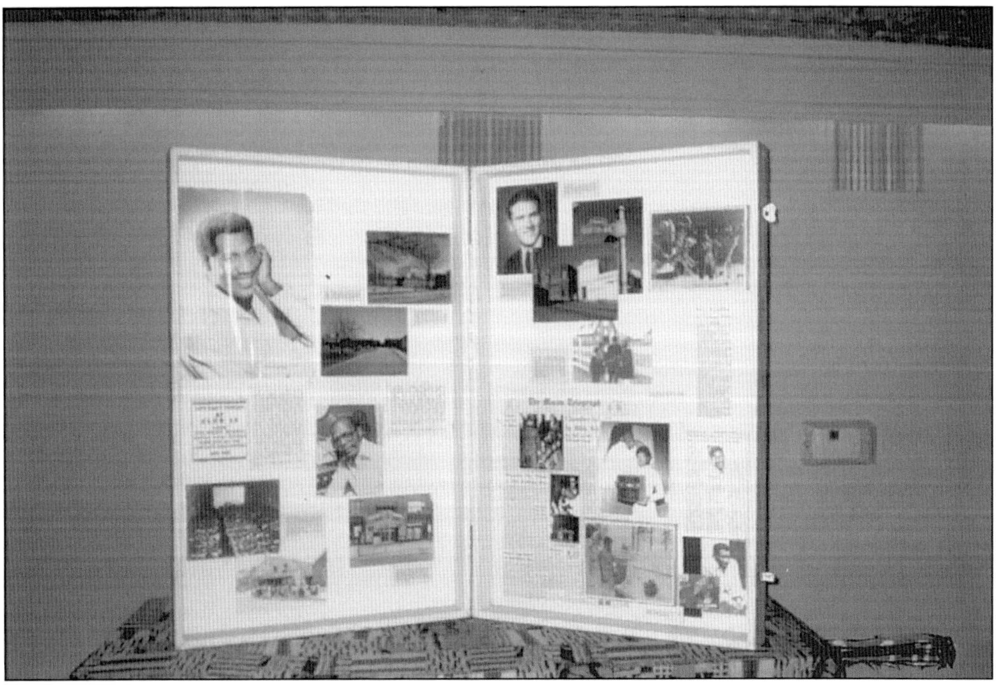

Macon's Own. These pictures illuminate famous personalities from Macon. The display can be seen in the lobby of the Douglass Theatre. There are also other permanent works on display focusing on the history of the Douglass Theatre.

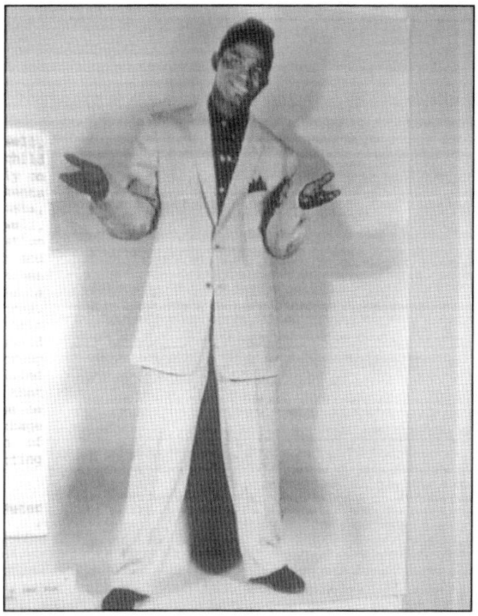

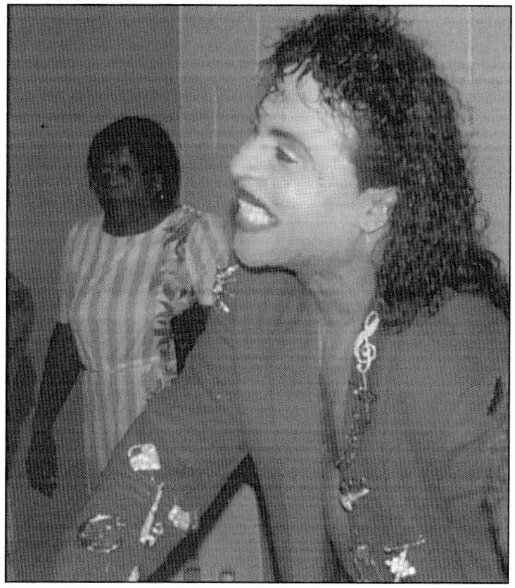

LEFT: **JAMES BROWN.** He was born in Augusta, GA, but spent most of his musical formative years in Macon. He worked with several record promoters—Clint Brantley being one—but he always strove to operate as an independent business enterprise. He is still a major influence to youngsters in Macon who want to be stars; they look to him for inspiration. This photograph was taken from a display inside the Douglass Theatre.

RIGHT: **"LITTLE RICHARD" PENNIMAN.** Once known to Maconites as "Mr. Fourth Avenue," this great star grew up in Pleasant Hill. His special style always appealed to his audiences in Macon and around the world. He often makes the statement, "I am the one that started it all." Here, he is meeting with a group at the Booker T. Washington Center, *c.* 1960s. (Courtesy of Booker T. Washington Center.)

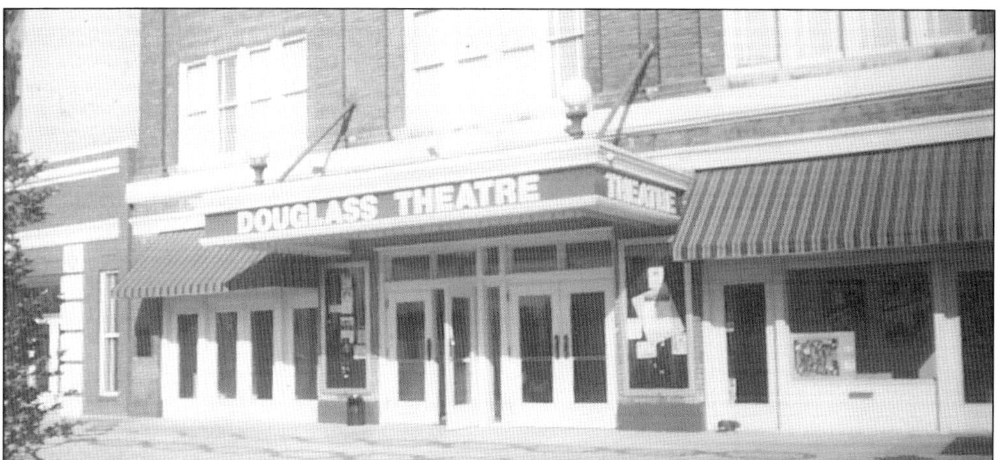

THE DOUGLASS THEATER. Located on Martin Luther King Boulevard, the theatre was built in 1921 and was established by Charles Henry Douglass. It was one of the two movie houses for African Americans in Macon during the years of segregation. It was also a performing arts theater, where stars like Ma Rainey, Otis Redding, James Brown, Little Richard, and many others performed wonderful shows. It has undergone a multi-million dollar renovation in recent years.

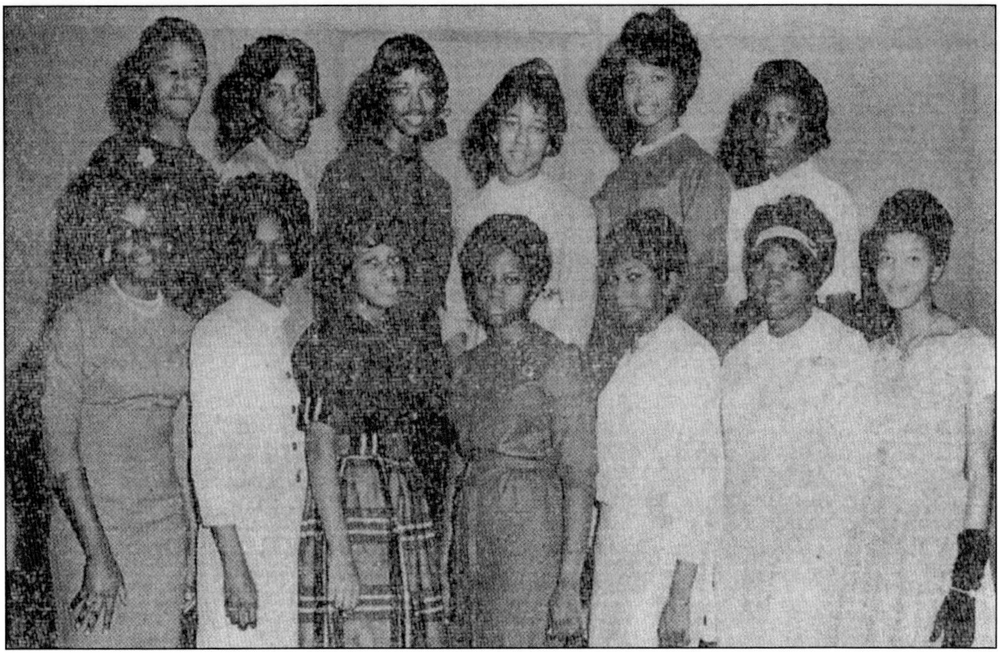

Waiting to Take Their Bows. These young ladies posed for newspapers before a formal presentation to society. They are, from left to right, as follows: (front row) Bernice Johnson, Betty Hamlin, Ann C. Colbert, Essie D. King, Vivian D. Howard, Carolyn S. Davis, and Barbara Ann Colbert; (back row) Delores Gilbert, Jean Clowers, Barbara King, Carol W. Childs, Mary L. Goodrum, and Wynelle Jackson. (Courtesy of Jeanne C. Herring.)

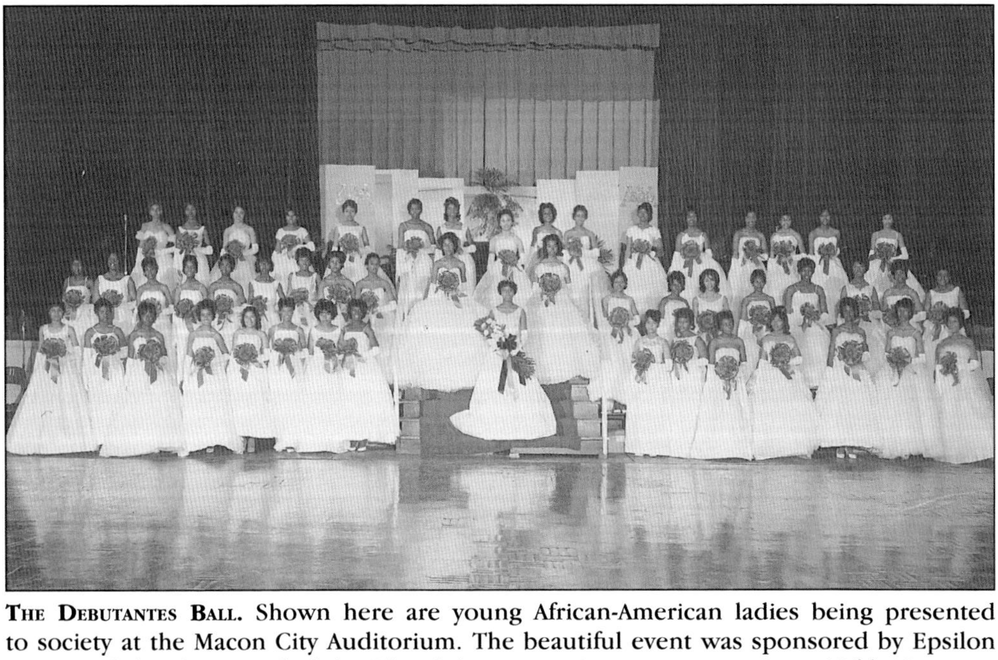

The Debutantes Ball. Shown here are young African-American ladies being presented to society at the Macon City Auditorium. The beautiful event was sponsored by Epsilon Beta Lambda Chapter of Alpha Phi Alpha Fraternity, Incorporated, *c.* 1964 (Courtesy Jeanne C. Herring.)

WILFRED STROUD, *c.* 1970s. Mr. Stroud is a very talented artist. He works in pencil, ink, pastel, acrylic, and oil, and his work has been exhibited in coastal Georgia, Wesleyan College, Mercer University, Fort Valley State, Macon State College, Atlanta galleries, and Atlantic City galleries. His work also hangs in many homes throughout the eastern United States. (Courtesy of Jeanne C. Herring.)

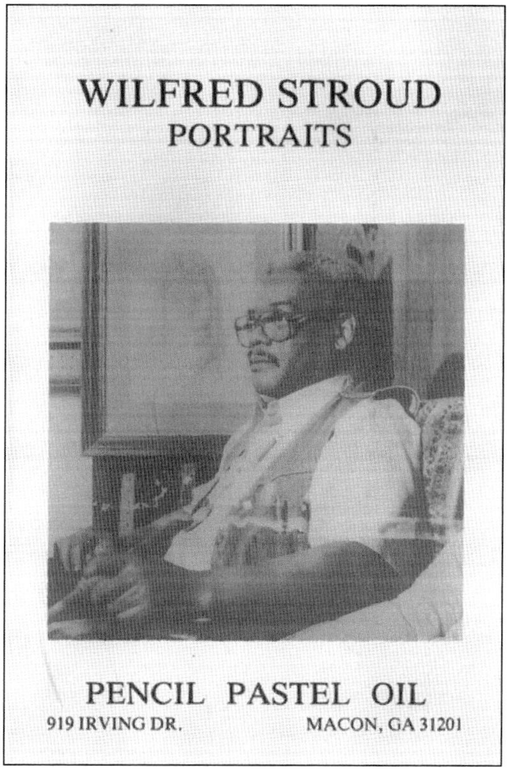

SGT. RODNEY DAVIS. A Macon hero, Sgt. Davis lost his life saving his men in Vietnam in 1967.

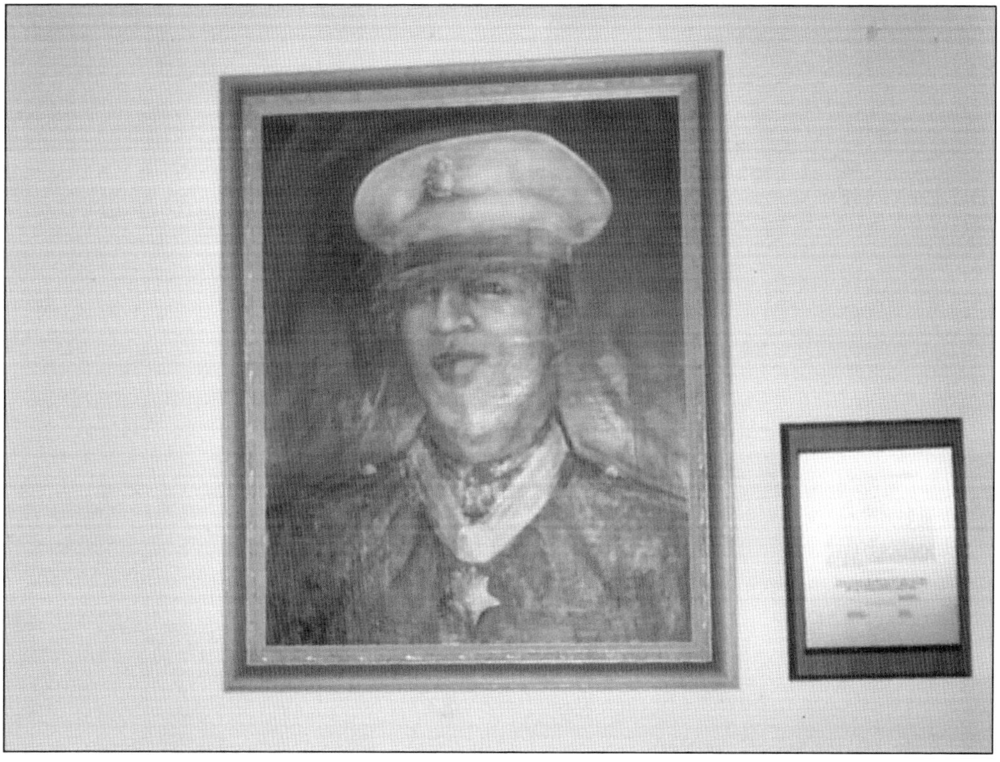

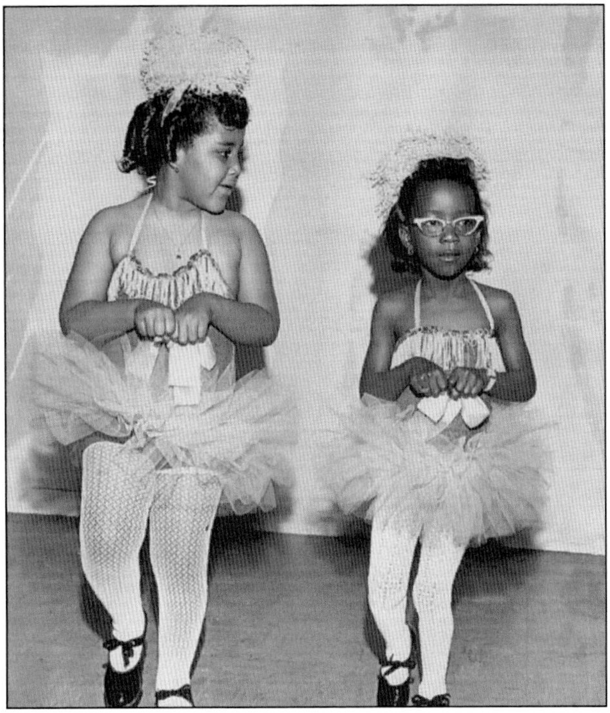

Dancing. Two unidentified young ladies are showing off their dancing talent in a recital sponsored by the Booker T. Washington Center, *c.* 1944 (Courtesy of Booker T. Washington Center.)

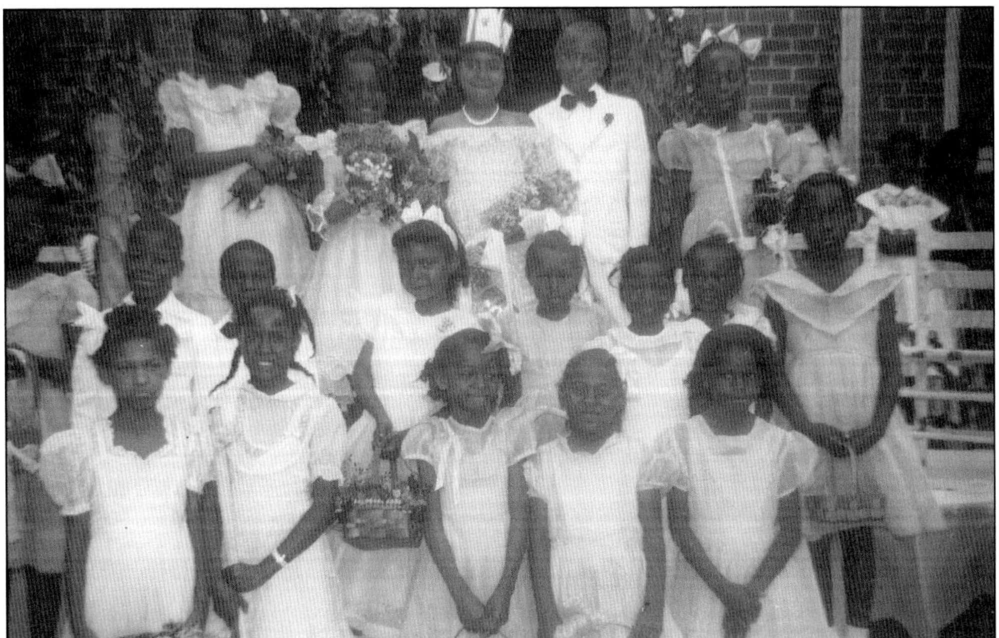

Easter. Easter morning dawns bright and all the church bells ring. These beautifully dressed boys and girls have on their Sunday best. They are pictured here after an Easter program, *c.* 1940s. The eggs have been hidden and all are waiting for the signal. (Courtesy of Booker T. Washington Center.)

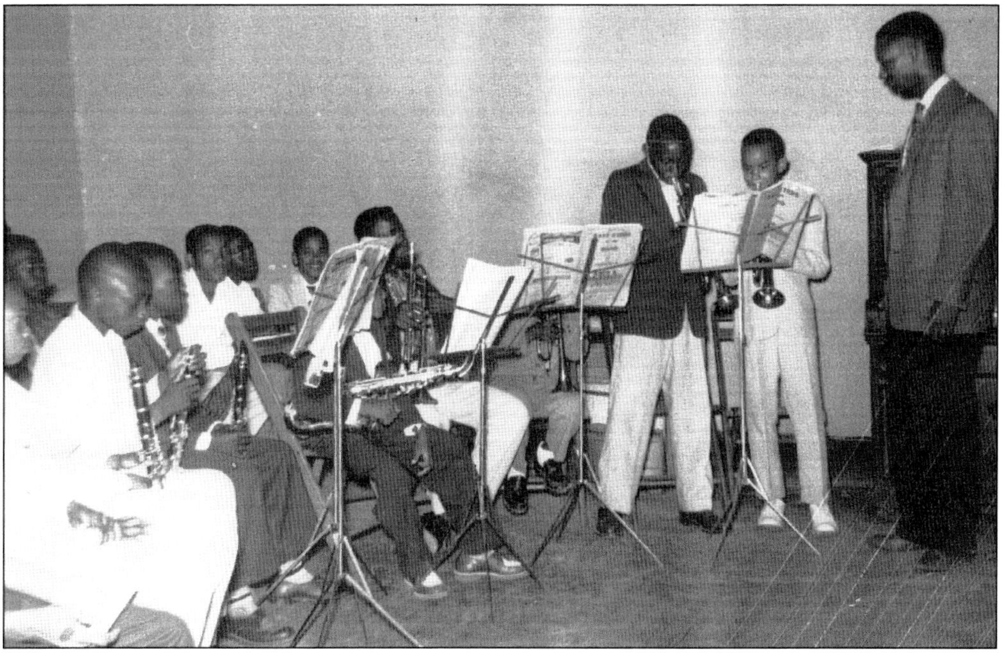

Robert Scott. Band director Robert Scott and a group of young students give a performance, *c.* 1940s (Courtesy of Booker T. Washington Center.)

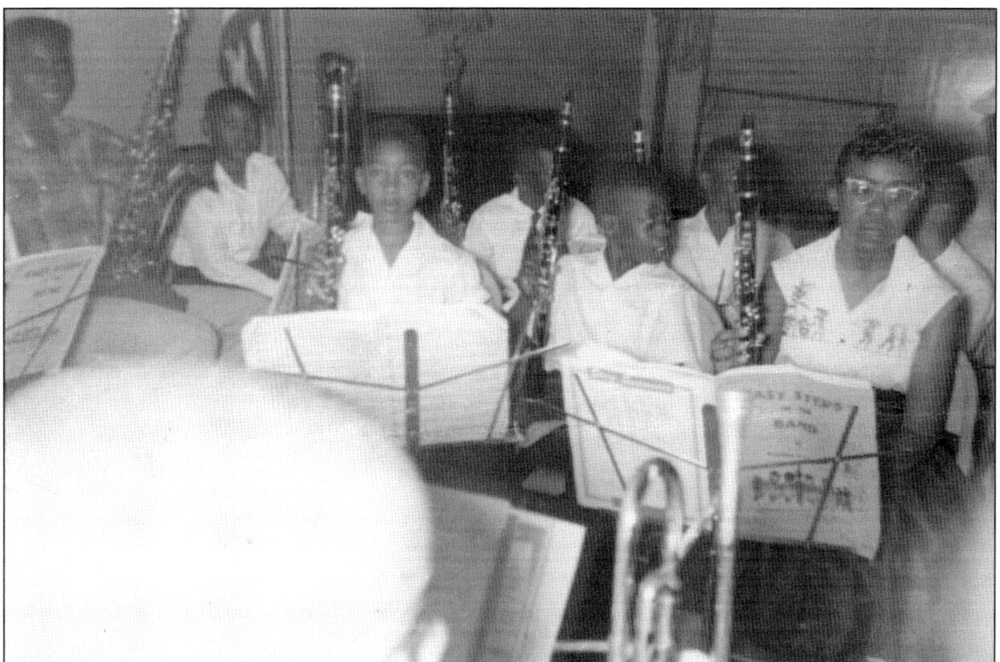

The Band, *c.* 1940s. These young band members are waiting for direction to begin the next musical selection. An unidentified lady sitting in the far right rear of the picture smiles in anticipation. (Courtesy of Booker T. Washington Center.)

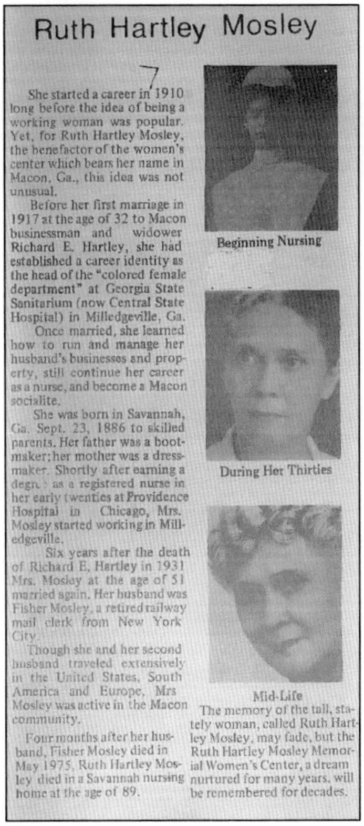

Ruth Hartley Mosley

She started a career in 1910 long before the idea of being a working woman was popular. Yet, for Ruth Hartley Mosley, the benefactor of the women's center which bears her name in Macon, Ga., this idea was not unusual.

Before her first marriage in 1917 at the age of 32 to Macon businessman and widower Richard E. Hartley, she had established a career identity as the head of the "colored female department" at Georgia State Sanitarium (now Central State Hospital) in Milledgeville, Ga.

Once married, she learned how to run and manage her husband's businesses and property, still continue her career as a nurse, and become a Macon socialite.

She was born in Savannah, Ga. Sept. 23, 1886 to skilled parents. Her father was a bootmaker; her mother was a dressmaker. Shortly after earning a degree as a registered nurse in her early twenties at Providence Hospital in Chicago, Mrs. Mosley started working in Milledgeville.

Six years after the death of Richard E. Hartley in 1931 Mrs. Mosley at the age of 51 married again. Her husband was Fisher Mosley, a retired railway mail clerk from New York City.

Though she and her second husband traveled extensively in the United States, South America and Europe, Mrs Mosley was active in the Macon community.

Four months after her husband, Fisher Mosley died in May 1975, Ruth Hartley Mosley died in a Savannah nursing home at the age of 89.

Beginning Nursing

During Her Thirties

Mid-Life

The memory of the tall, stately woman, called Ruth Hartley Mosley, may fade, but the Ruth Hartley Mosley Memorial Women's Center, a dream nurtured for many years, will be remembered for decades.

The Ruth Hartley Mosley Memorial Women's Center: An Institution for Women of Today. A very enterprising woman, Ruth Hartley started this institution. She started a career in 1910, long before the idea of being a "working woman" was popular. This idea was not unusual for Mrs. Hartley. Before her first marriage in 1917 at the age of 32 to Macon businessman and widower Richard E. Hartley, she had established a career identity as the head of the "Colored Female Department" at Georgia State Sanitarium (now Central State Hospital) in Milledgeville, GA. She was born in Savannah, GA, to skilled parents. Her father was a boot maker, her mother a dressmaker. Ruth Hartley Mosley left a legacy to the city of Macon. In her will, written in 1972, she set up two trusts. One was designed to provide loans to individuals seeking to further their education. The other trust called for the establishment of the Ruth Hartley Mosley Memorial Women's Center, which is now housed in Mrs. Mosley's home. The center was designed with a primary concern of the enhancement of women—emotionally, spiritually, and academically.

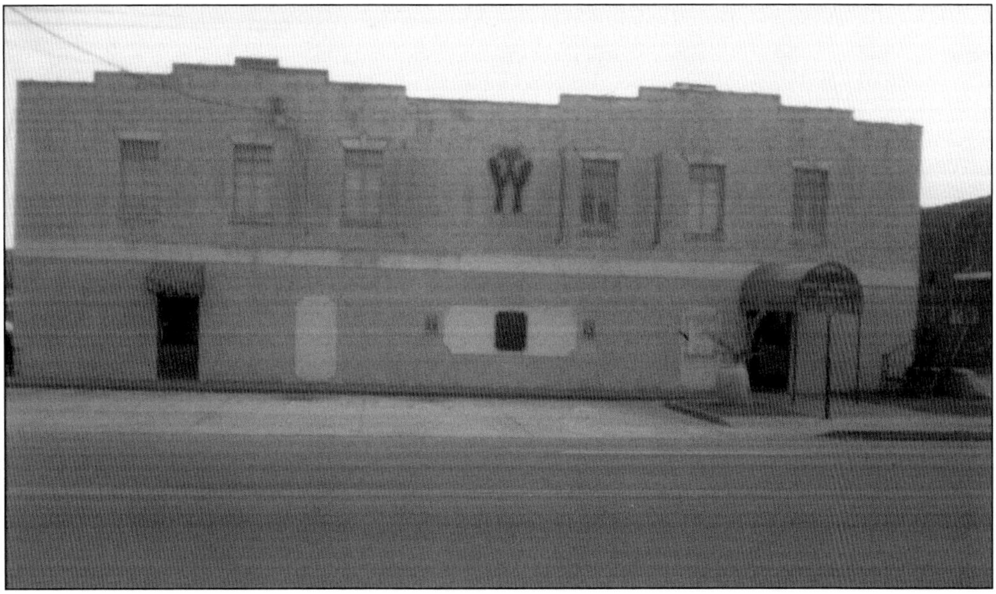

The Harriet Tubman Museum. Pictured is the current home of the Harriet Tubman Museum, located on Walnut Street. This museum highlights the history and accomplishments of African Americans in Macon and surrounding areas. It was established in 1981 by Father Richard Keil, who was the pastor of St. Peter Claver Catholic Church.

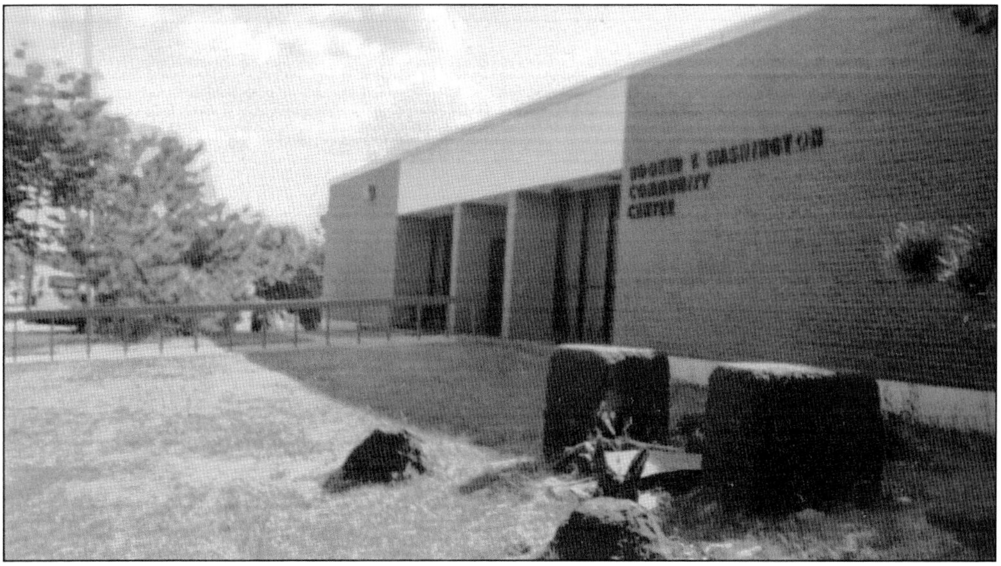

The Booker T. Washington Community Center. This center is a place where African-American children and adults can go to participate in recreational activities. Because of the widespread embrace of Jim Crow laws in the Macon area, blacks and whites were not allowed any integration of social events. Consequently, the establishment of the recreation center was needed. An interracial cooperation was formed, with whites and blacks working together for the benefit of the black community. In 1938, the recreation division of the Works Progress Administration (WPA) proposed the creation of 10 to 12 experimental community centers to provide for the health, educational, and recreational needs of African Americans. The proposal targeted the Southeast, where the inequalities of Jim Crow, coupled with the ravages of the Great Depression, had severely undermined the quality of life for black citizens. For this completed project, Willis B. Sheftall, a social worker with the Bibb County Public Welfare Department, became Booker T. Washington Community Center's first director in 1939. (Courtesy of Booker T. Washington Center.)

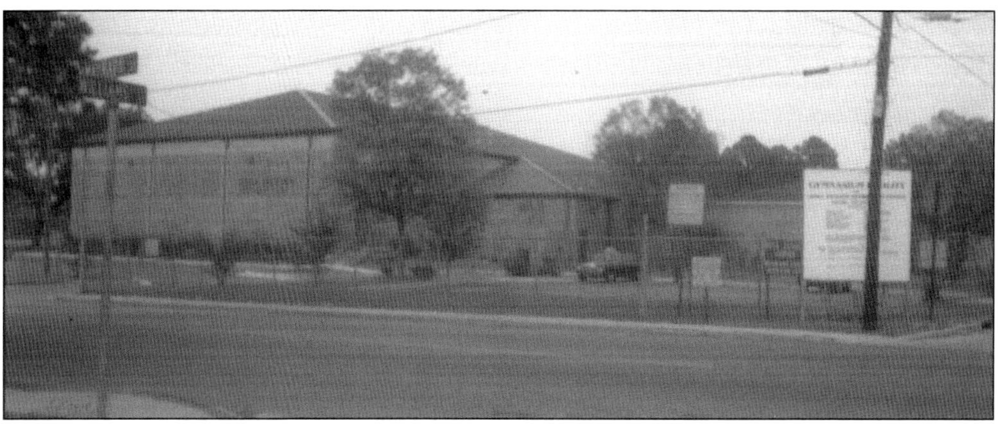

The Rosa Jackson Community Center. This recreation facility is located on Maynard Street in East Macon. It is an establishment that was designed primarily to enhance the social, educational, physical, and spiritual growth of African-American children. The creations of tutorial and summer camp programs continue to be a priority with the directors who lead this center.

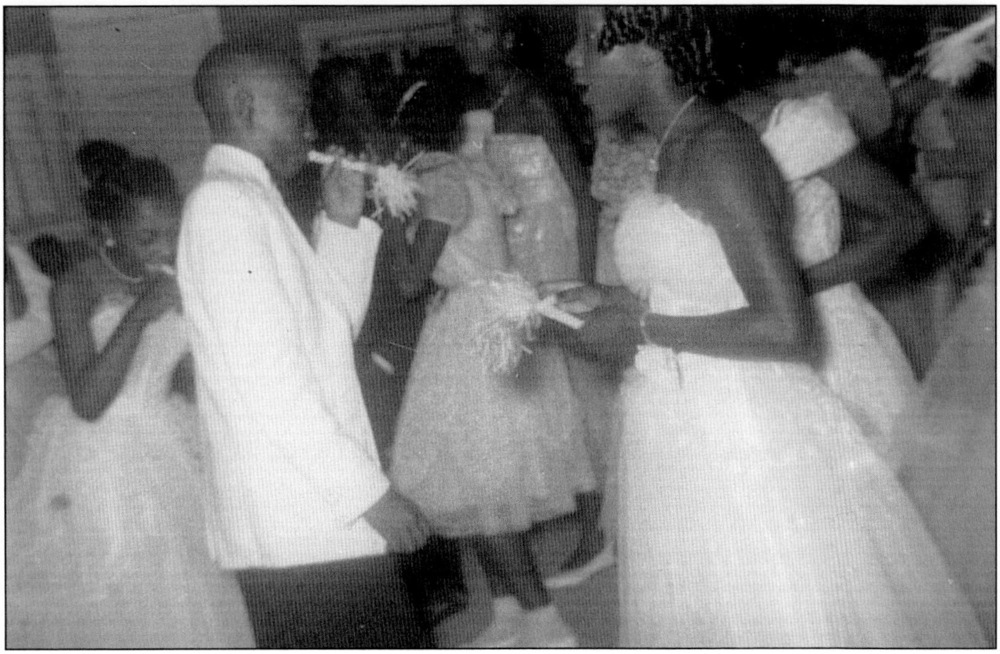

THE PROM. Young couples enjoy the latest steps, *c.* 1954. (Courtesy of Booker T. Washington Center.)

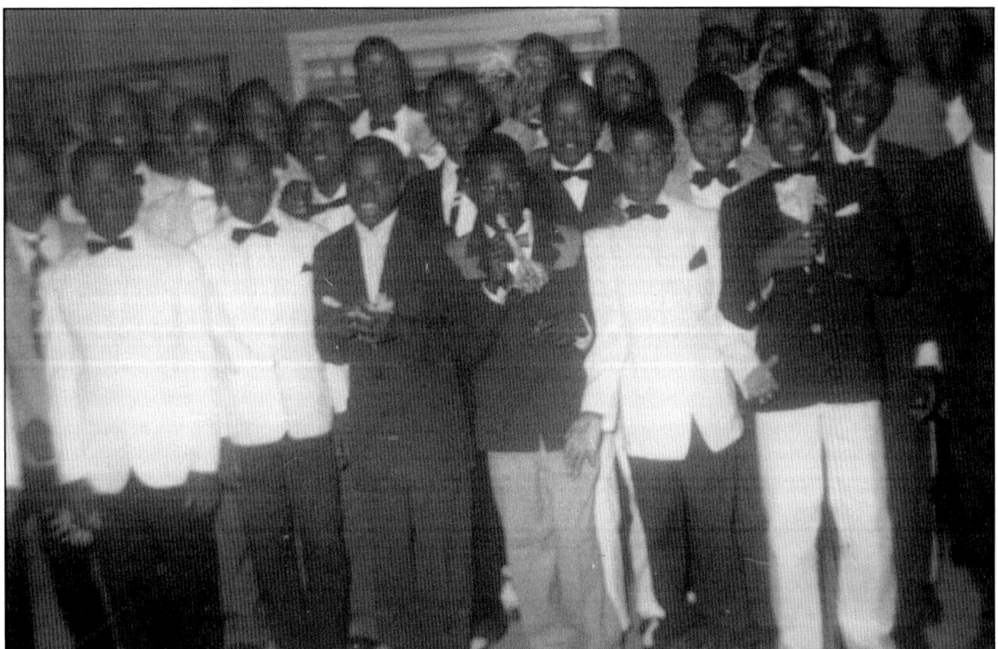

THE PROM. These young men, waiting for the girls, are ready for the fun to begin, *c.* 1954 (Courtesy of Booker T. Washington Center.)

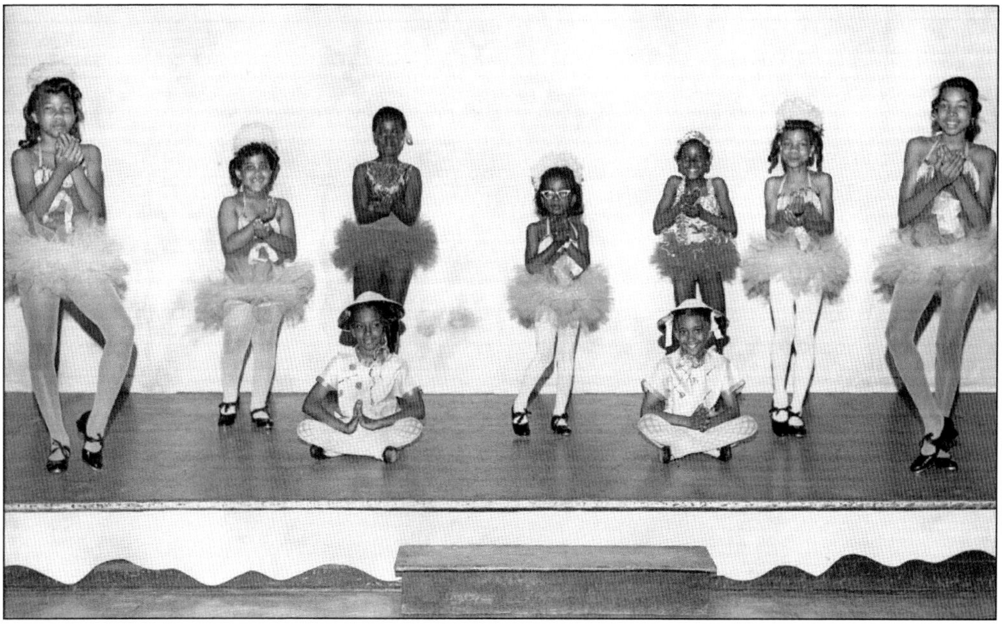

The Dance. A group of young ladies give an enthusiastic tap dance performance at the Booker T. Washington Center. They are all smiles, *c.* 1944 (Courtesy of Booker T. Washington Center.)

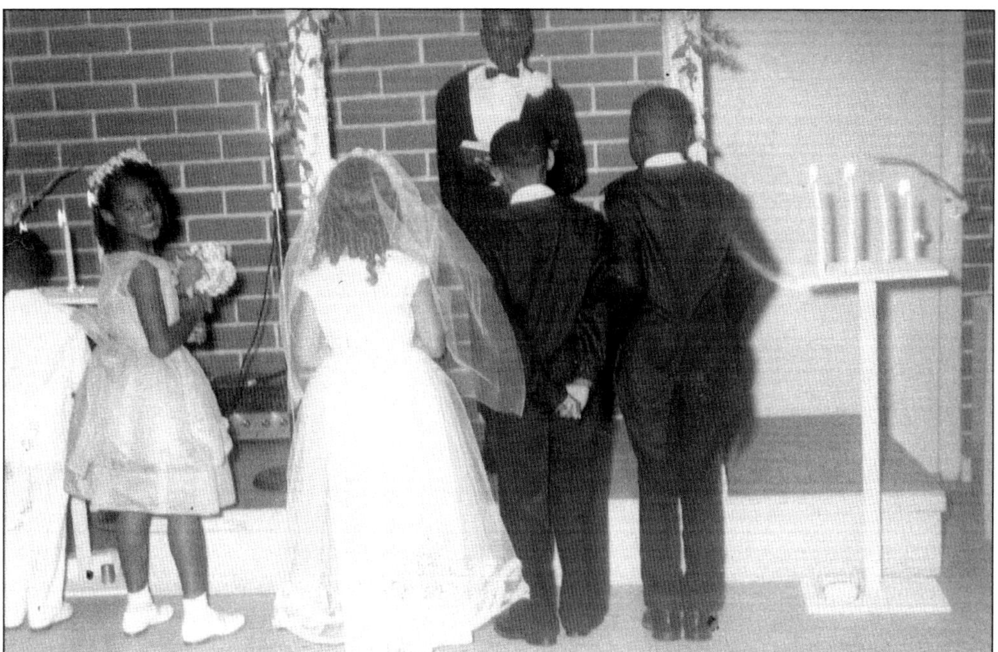

"I Do." These unidentified students are participating in a mock wedding. The maid of honor is smiling for the camera, *c.* 1940s. (Courtesy of Booker T. Washington Center.)

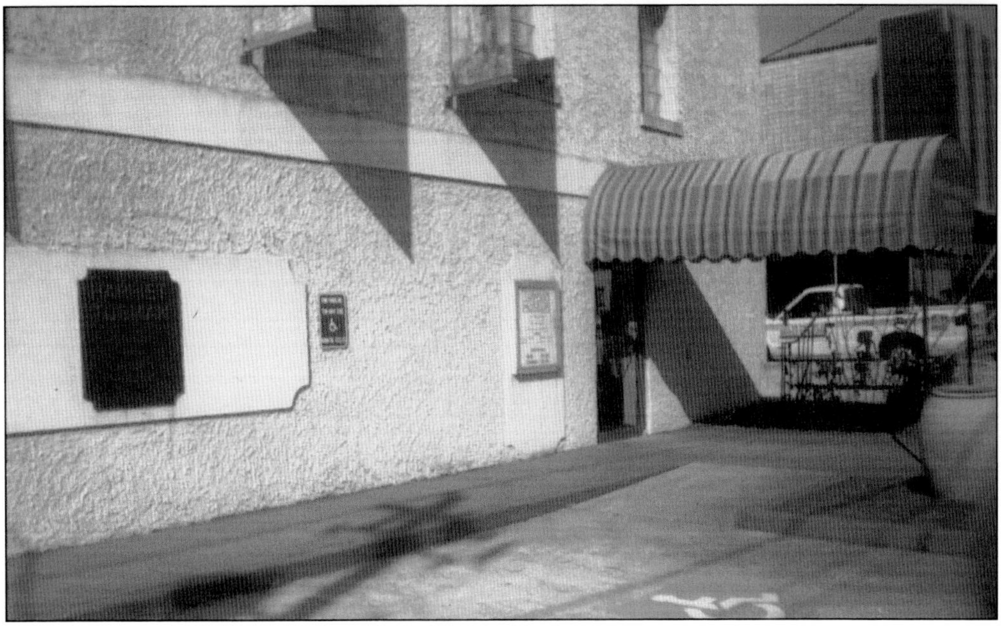

ANOTHER VIEW OF THE HARRIET TUBMAN MUSEUM.

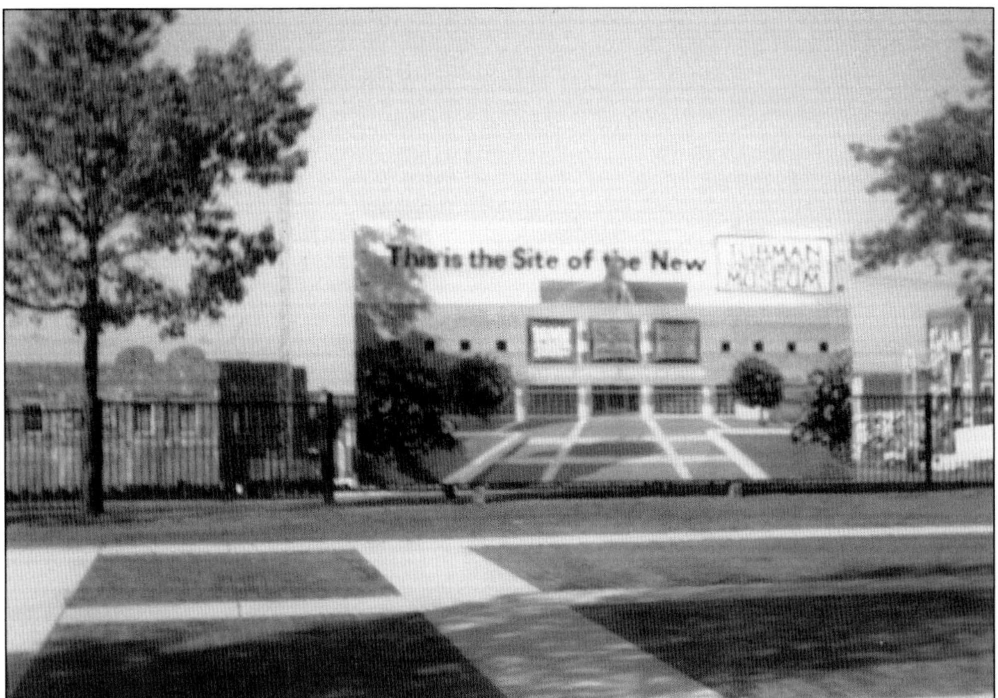

THE FUTURE HOME FOR THE TUBMAN MUSEUM. This picture shows the future location for the Harriet Tubman Museum on Cherry Street. This larger facility will be able to house additional collections of Macon's African-American history.

MACON'S NOTABLE ACCOMPLISHMENTS BY AFRICAN AMERICANS

Adams, Virgil: First assistant district attorney, 1980.

African Americans vote in primaries, 1945.

American Baptist Home Mission Board: Started Central City College, 1889.

American Missionary Association: Built the first high school for African-Americans, 1868.

Amour, Rosetta: First woman colonel; America's first female Air Force ROTC instructor; first military person to receive the Alfred E. Wright award.

Ansa, Tina McElroy: One of Macon's successful modern writers to acquire national acclaim.

Bailey, Sarah: Started the first Girl Scout troop in Macon, 1945; a campground is named for her.

Baker, Buddy: One of the first to hold position in the sheriff's department.

Baker, Martin: One of the first to hold position in the sheriff's department.

Ballard, Stephen H.: Built Ballard Normal School, 1888.

Billingslea, Albert: First to be elected to the position as county commissioner, 1980.

Bivins, Bert: First African-American student to be accepted to Dudley Hughes.

Bivins, Hester: One of the first civil rights activists in Macon.

Brantley, Clint: One of the first successful music and entertainment promoters, 1950s–1960s.

Braswell, Palmira: First Cherry Blossom Queen, 1989.

Brown, Otis: First chairman of the Industrial Authority, 1988.

Brooks, Delores: One of the first to be elected to city council after desegregation, 1975.

Chambers, Rev. Booker W.: First elected to Water and Sewage Authority, 1975.

Clemons, Mamie: Founded Clemons Conservatory of Music and Arts in 1920s.

Clowers, Elsie Mae Gray: One of the first poro trained hair pressers in Pleasant Hill, 1935.

Colbert, Vernon: One of the first to be elected to city council after desegregation, 1975.

Colton Avenue School: First African-American public school, 1872.

Cook, Delores: One of the first to be elected to the school board, 1972.

Davis, Sgt. Rodney M. (d. 9/6/1967): Military hero; lost his life in the Vietnam War by throwing himself on a grenade to save his men.

Dennard, Herbert: First appointed president of Concerned Citizens, 1975.

Dilliard, Thelma: Added to city council, 1980.

Dyer, C.W.E.: Organized and founded St. Luke Hospital, the first incorporated hospital in Macon, 1928.

Ellis, Jack: Macon's first African-American mayor, 1999.

Evans, Alan: First international opera star.

Evans, Rev. E.S.: One of the first civil rights activists in Macon.

Fite, Eve Belle, and Catherine Harris, Irene Madison, Margiee Tomlinson, and Johnnie Lou Tyler: First women recruited for the WAAC, 1943.

Flowers, Tiger: First famous boxer.

Gastin, Joe and Walter Jones: First police officers, 1948.

Harriet Tubman Museum: First African-American museum in Macon; opened in 1985.

Harvey, Gerald: Added to city council, 1980.

Hazel Street, East Macon, Green Street, and Pleasant Hill Schools: Added seventh grade to its curriculum in 1918–1920.

Hicks, Tina: First WMAZ-TV news anchor, 1972.

Hope, Rev. Julius C.: First African-American to run for mayor of Macon, 1975.

Hudson Industrial High: First public high school for African-Americans; established in 1922.

Humpheries, Solomon: First noteworthy "freeblack"; a landowner and a businessman; purchased his wife and father out of slavery.

Hutchings, Bettye: First to hold a position of crime commissioner, 1981.

Irvin, Angel: First WMAZ-TV Special Feature Person, 1972.

Jackson, Thomas: First to serve as a judge in Bibb County.

Jones, Dr. Bobby: First tenured professor at Mercer University; became chairperson of Education Department, 1972; first to receive the Spencer P. King Award; founding president of the HarrietTubman Museum.

Killens, John (b. 1916): First noteworthy author.

Long, Jefferson Franklin (1836–1901): First congressman from Macon in 1871.

Lucas, David: One of the first representatives from Bibb County since Reconstruction, 1974.

Lunch Counters in Macon integrated, 1961.

Lundy, Dr.: Organized and founded the first hospital for African Americans in Macon, 1920s.

Malone, Rev. Van J.: One of the first civil rights activists in Macon.

Marlowe, Herman and Ruby: Started the first African American-owned florist.

Martin, Dr. R.J.: First African-American elected to Bibb County School Board, 1972; first principal of Ballard Hudson Sr. High School.

May, Agnes: First Jeans supervisor for Bibb County, 1942.

McKay, Ossie Belle: One of the first very successful female insurance agents and civil rights activists.

Mercer University: Dropped racial barriers for accepting African-American students.

Miller, Yvette: First African-American Miss Macon, 1977.

Mosley, Ruth Price Hartley: First woman supervisor at Georgia State Sanitarium in Milledgeville, 1916.

Moss, Leo (b. 1860): First noteworthy sculptor and dollmaker.

Parker, Jim: First African American inducted into the Georgia Athletic Hall of Fame.

Paschal, Rev. B.P.: One of the first civil rights activists in Macon.

Penniman, Richard: First R&B superstar.

Public Education for African Americans begins in Macon, 1822.

Rancifer, Rev.: One of the first civil rights activists in Macon.

Randall, William C.: First elected Representative from Macon since Reconstruction, 1974.

Randall, William P.: Elected to county commissioner position and one of the first civil rights activists.

Rayfield, Wallace: Macon's first African-American architect.

Seller, Adriadine: Started the first school for African Americans in her father's home, 1865–1866.

Sheftall, Willis B.: Became the first director of the Booker T. Washington Center, 1939

Singleton, Minnie: Editor of the *Macon Telegraph* (Colored), 1950s.

Smith, Lovia T.: First public health nurse, 1934.

Smith, Minnie L.: Established Beda Etta College, 1921.

Smith, Rev. Eddie: One of the first to be elected to city council after desegregation., 1975.

Stroud, Wilfred: First noteworthy artist.

Swain, Hamp: First radio disc jockey, 1954.

Taylor, LaConstance: First to hold position in the Macon Housing Authority, 1973.

Thomas, Leroy Thomas: First talk show host, 1977.

Tillghast, Rev. Milton: First ordained African-American minister.

Tuggle, Herbert: Became the first to head the reference department at the Washington Memorial Library.

Welch, Charles: First to work with Metropolitan Opera House from Macon.

Walton, Dr. D.T.: First to hold the position in the Macon (Bibb County) Transit Authority, 1981.

Vineville Baptist Church: First church in the Georgia Baptist Convention to integrate.

Vinson, Julius: One of the first to be elected to city council after desegregation, 1975.

Walton, Dr. Dewitt Jr.: Became first African-American appointed to Bibb County Board of Education.

Washington, Gloria: First woman to be selected as supervising principal at Southwest Complex, 1988.

Williams, Robert: First supervising principal of central complex; first assistant superintendent of schools for Bibb County.

Woodliff, Edward: One of Macon's first aldermen during Reconstruction, 1870.

ACKNOWLEDGMENTS

I wish to personally thank everyone who was supportive of this project. The following list of credits includes the names of organizations and individuals who worked very diligently to secure illustrations for this publication: Howard L. Scott III, director of the Booker T. Washington Center; Lois Howard Miller; Lorena Howard Latham; Susie Pope Ussery ; Judge William C. and Mrs. Lauretta Randall; James Ragland; George D. Crawley Jr., director of education, Harriett Tubman Museum; Mayor C. Jack Ellis; Rev. W.B. and Lena Jordan-Herring; Rev. J.R. Herring Sr.; The *Macon Telegraph and News*.

Thanks to the Booker T. Washington Center and Howard L. Scott II and the board of directors for making many historical photographs available to me. Even though the center was preparing for their 60th anniversary, Mr. Scott very generously allowed me the privilege of using several photographs. Thanks to Ms. Jackson in the Genealogy Department at the Washington Memorial Library for her assistance in uncovering facts about Macon's African-American community. Thanks to Julie C. Groce who provided reference material from her publication, *Invisible Hands: The Role of Black Americans in Macon's Architectural Heritage.* It was a great help. Thanks also to my editor, Katie White, who listened patiently to my questions and concerns about this work, and to Arcadia Publishing, for producing the book. Thanks to my typist, Renee Ladner, who took on this task at short notice and made many sacrifices of her time to help me make my deadline. Thanks to my husband and family for their encouraging words. And thanks be to God for his inspiring spirit, for without the strength that I acquired from calling upon his name daily, this work would never have been completed.

BIBLIOGRAPHY

Architectural Historical Guide. "A Brief History of Macon, Georgia." Georgia Historical Society, 1996.

Articles from the *Macon Telegraph and News*.

Bills, Steve. "Another Place and Time: Summerfield reunion aims to Rekindle Community Spirit." *Macon Telegraph and News*, 1997.

Burnham, Robert A. *Interracial Cooperation in the Age of Jim Crow: The Booker T. Washington Community Center of Macon, Georgia.* Macon, GA: Macon State College, 1989.

Coleman, Kenneth. *Georgia History in Outline.* Athens: University of Georgia Press, 1978.

Dates of Historical Note for African-Americans in Macon and Bibb County, Georgia. Washington Memorial Library.

Georgia Sports Museum.

Georgia Music Hall of Fame.

Groce, Julie C. "Invisible Hands: The Role of Black Americans in Macon's Architectural Heritage." Macon Heritage Foundation, Inc. Julie Groce, Curator, 619 Orange Street, Macon, GA, 1990s.

Lawrence R. Hepburn. *The Georgia History Book.* Athens: Institute of Georgia, University of Georgia, 1982.

Long, Susan. "Pleasant Hill's Rich History May Be Recognized." *Macon Telegraph and News*, 1996.

Macon's Black Heritage: The Untold Story. Tubman African-American Museum, Macon, GA, 1997.

People's Publishing Group, Inc. *In Our Own Image: An African-American History.* Rochester, New York: The Peoples Publishing Group, 1983.

Pomerantz, Gary M. *Where Peachtree Meets Sweet Auburn: The sign of two families and the making of Atlanta.* New York: Screbner, 1996

Smith, Jane. *The History of America.* New York: Random House, 1972.

Ussery, Tammy. "Bill Randall to Quit Politics at End of 1995." *Macon Telegraph and News*, 1995.

Vanzant, Iyanla. *Acts of Faith: Daily Meditations for People of Color.* New York: Simon and Schuster, 1993.

Wilder, Larry D. "A New Life: Pleasant Hill's Listing on National Historic Register Hailed as Signal of Rebirth." *Macon Telegraph and News*, 1996.

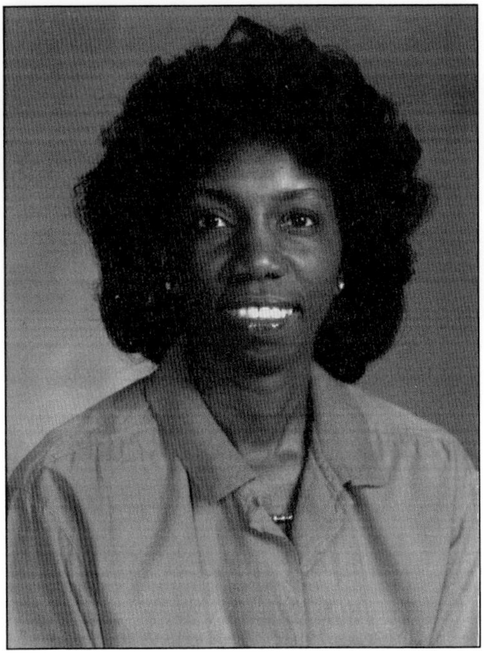

About the Author

Growing up an only child had its advantages and disadvantages. From the time that I was a very young child, it seemed that my family catered to me. This perception caused me to believe that the world revolved around me. I was fortunate in that both sets of grandparents were involved in my upbringing. My bubble soon burst when I entered school and found out I wasn't "the only pebble on the beach." What a reality check I experienced as I took on the challenging task of life.

My love of history probably stemmed from my parents and grandparents. They would talk about what life was like in the 1920s, 1930s, and early 1940s. Some of their conversations would be about what meals they ate, how food was prepared, what their salaries were, what things cost, how they dealt with prejudice and discrimination, the black condition in Macon, and even courting. One funny story I recall my paternal grandmother telling was about the time my grandfather came to call on her before they married. She and her brothers and sisters had been chopping cotton on their parents' small farm in Gray (Jones County), GA, on a Saturday evening, when my grandfather came to visit. Her hair was full of dust and cotton. Her legs were covered with dirt and dust. Not wanting her beau to see her that way, she ran to the back of the house and into the kitchen. She quickly rubbed lard over her legs and arms to take away the ashy look. When she presented herself on the front porch where my grandfather was waiting, cotton was clinging to her arms and legs. Big embarrassment!

When I was growing up in the 1950s and 1960s, I would have appreciated a book like this one. Many other books are being published these days that tell of our African ancestral home and our American experiences. However, when I was a child, there were none. Even though there were no books available, I realize now that my family's stories were the unprinted history books.

Looking back over my elementary, high school, and even college years of study, I realize now that heritage education was not emphasized enough. I feel extremely blessed that I have progressed to this point in my life, where I feel a true commitment to the discipline of history and especially heritage education. I have taught school and worked with young people in several capacities for at least 25 years. I am a graduate of St. Peter Claver Parochial School and Ballard-Hudson Senior High School. My higher educational training was done at Paine College in Augusta, GA, and Ft. Valley State College in Ft. Valley, GA. I earned a Masters Degree at Mercer University in Macon, GA, and an ED.S. (Educational Specialist Degree) from Troy State University in Phenix City, AL. In addition, I am a Sunday school teacher, and I enjoy reading, antiquing, and traveling. I have been married for 31 years to James R. Herring Sr., who is a pastor. Together we have raised three sons.

In this pictorial effort, I have tried to explore a different side of Macon's history, examining the lives of people who once called this area home by way of historical documents and pictures. I hope this book will serve readers in a positive way, igniting an interest in history to anyone who reads it . . . for life is not worth living if one does not know and understand the past.

—Jeanne C. Herring